STRESS IN HEALTH
AND DISEASE

AMERICAN COLLEGE OF PSYCHIATRISTS

Stress in Health and Disease

Edited by
MICHAEL R. ZALES, M.D.

*Associate Clinical Professor of Psychiatry,
Yale University*

BRUNNER/MAZEL, *Publishers* • New York

Library of Congress Cataloging in Publication Data
Main entry under title:

Stress in health and disease.

   Product of the 21st annual meeting of the American
College of Psychiatrists, held in 1984 in Coronado, Calif.
   Includes bibliographies and indexes.
   1. Stress (Psychology)—Congresses.   2. Stress
(Physiology)—Congresses.   3. Medicine, Psychosomatic—
Congresses.   I. Zales, Michael R., 1937-   .
II. American College of Psychiatrists. Meeting
(21st : 1984 : Coronado, Calif.) [DNLM: 1. Stress,
Psychological—congresses. WM 172 S9153 1984]
BF575.S75S7733   1984   616.9′8   84-17026

ISBN 0-87630-376-9

Copyright © 1985 by The American College of Psychiatrists

Published by
Brunner/Mazel, Inc.
19 Union Square West
New York, New York 10003

MANUFACTURED IN THE UNITED STATES OF AMERICA

Contributors

M. HARVEY BRENNER, Ph.D.

Professor, Operations Research and Behavioral Sciences, The Johns Hopkins University School of Hygiene and Public Health, Baltimore, Maryland

MARGARET A. CHESNEY, Ph.D.

Director, Department of Behavioral Medicine, Stanford Research Institute, Menlo Park, California

LEONARD J. DUHL, M.D.

Professor of Public Health and City Planning, University of California at Berkeley; Clinical Professor of Psychiatry, University of California, San Francisco, California

CARL EISDORFER, Ph.D., M.D.

President, Montefiore Medical Center; Professor, Departments of Psychiatry and Neurosciences, Albert Einstein College of Medicine, Bronx, New York

MARDI J. HOROWITZ, M.D.

Professor of Psychiatry and Director, Center for the Study of Neuroses, Langley Porter Institute, University of California, San Francisco, California

JAMES J. HYNES, B.A.

School of Public Health and Department of City Planning, University of California, Berkeley, California

SEYMOUR S. KETY, M.D.

Associate Director for Basic Research, National Institute of Mental Health, Bethesda, Maryland

ALAN A. McLEAN, M.D.

Clinical Associate Professor of Psychiatry, Cornell University Medical College; Area Medical Director, IBM Corporation, New York, New York

ROBERT MICHELS, M.D.

Barklie McKee Henry Professor and Chairman, Department of Psychiatry, Cornell University Medical College; Psychiatrist-in-Chief, The New York Hospital, New York, New York

RAY H. ROSENMAN, M.D.

Senior Research Physician, Department of Behavioral Medicine, Stanford Research Institute, Menlo Park, California

STEVEN J. SCHLEIFER, M.D.

Assistant Professor of Psychiatry, Mount Sinai School of Medicine, New York, New York

MARVIN STEIN, M.D.

Esther and Joseph Klingenstein Professor and Chairman, Department of Psychiatry, Mount Sinai School of Medicine, New York, New York

HERBERT WEINER, M.D.

Professor of Psychiatry and Chief of Behavioral Medicine, Neuropsychiatric Institute; Member, Brain Research Institute, UCLA School of Medicine, Los Angeles, California

Contents

PART IV

STRESS MANAGEMENT AND THE ROLE OF PSYCHIATRY

Preface

The 21st annual meeting represents symbolically a perception of a major problem of our 20th and 21st centuries. Stress seems to be part and parcel of our daily lives and shapes the outcomes of our aspirations, as well as of our disease patterns.

The American College of Psychiatrists, which was founded over 20 years ago, is a highly respected professional organization. It was founded by Dr. Henry Laughlin, who, with the help of others, designed an organization to honor distinguished psychiatrists and to bring younger psychiatrists of promise and potential together in a college. The College meets annually for a four-day symposium presented by its own members and outstanding guest lecturers in pursuit of self-education. Each year the theme of the program provides a coherent thread for the contributors to discuss comprehensively a critical, topical area.

Along with its members, the College invites to this meeting a number of Laughlin Fellows. They are psychiatrists-in-training who benefit from the symposium and the collegiality of the meeting. Because of its emphasis on education, the College also supports the Psychiatry Residents-in-Training Assessment Examination.

This year's theme, "Stress in Health and Disease," is a topic that extends through all branches of medicine and this volume provides a reflection on medicine, the interfaces of psychiatry with genetics, pharmacology, internal medicine, immunology, other branches of medicine, and other facets of our societal life.

Dr. Michael R. Zales, who has served as the editor of three previous publications of our College, ends his term with this book. The College wishes to extend its gratitude for his able and competent editorship.

HAROLD M. VISOTSKY, M.D.
President, 1983–1984
American College of
Psychiatrists

Introduction

Since its inception, the American College of Psychiatrists has sought to provide through its annual meeting a forum for the discussion of new and synthesized material, leading to the best application and utilization of psychiatric knowledge, principles, and therapy. This volume is the product of the 1984 scientific meeting held in Coronado, California, the theme of which was "Stress in Health and Disease." Credit for developing the program and assembling the outstanding experts whose essays follow is due to the Program Committee, whose very able Chairperson and Co-Chairperson were George H. Pollock and George L. Adams, respectively.

Each of us throughout our lives encounters loss, drastic changes of location and responsibilities, the threat of serious illness or lasting disability, and many other emotionally charged events of many kinds and of deep personal significance. It is, therefore, not surprising that "stress" is today the "hot" topic, evoking widespread professional and public interest. But, as Hamburg points out so clearly in *Stress and Human Health* (1), there has been a marked discrepancy between this very high level of interest and the rather low priority of scientific commitment to the subject. A number of theories have been posed to account for this. Is it that the topic is too complex and the problems too difficult? Is it that too few investigators with the appropriate scientific training have addressed themselves to this area? Perhaps — but it is more likely, as one sees from the marvelously varied backgrounds of the contributors to this volume, that the problems inherent in the topic are interdisciplinary by nature, and we have so very much to learn about the conduct of interdisciplinary efforts in most of science.

A continuing inability to define "stress" with any precision has contributed to substantial confusion. The many definitions to be found in the essays that follow are not intended to confuse; rather, they exist in order to meet specific needs for different types of research. They have evolved over the last decades, and their evolution is a story in itself and beyond the scope of this book.

The reader will quickly appreciate how far research has brought us in the area of stress. Yet, as this year's contributors repeatedly remind us, we have only scratched the surface of our knowledge. It is thus the timely significance of the essays that comprises the substance of this work.

The chapters in this book fall rather naturally into an order of presentation. Part I is devoted to Conceptual Approaches to Stress. Eisdorfer's chapter leads the way, and he gracefully completes the Herculean assignment of presenting a conceptual overview of stress in health and disease. He emphasizes the complexity of the construct that we usually call stress and the pitfalls of research in this arena. He points out that the linkage between the occurrence of stress and the development of disease is especially weak, and he suggests that stress is more likely to fit agreeably into a risk factor model of disease than into a single, causal agent model.

Eisdorfer goes on to recommend that the subject of stress can be conceptualized best if it is considered to be made up of four variables: 1) the potential *activator(s)*; 2) the immediate *reaction(s)*; 3) the longer time *consequence(s)*; and 4) the *mediator(s)* which may be physical, psychological, environmental, or behavioral. He warns that to treat the construct of stress in a simplistic manner is to do it a disservice, to destroy its utility, and to delay our understanding of what it does.

Biological research has clarified a good deal about the ways in which our species has adapted, though so much more remains in doubt. One crucial linkage of the biomedical and behavioral sciences occurs in a final common pathway through which the brain controls the endocrine and autonomic nervous systems.

Morton Reiser, who stands at the forefront of a new biology of stress, was in attendance at the meeting in Coronado and was willing to preface the next chapter of this book with some interesting thoughts about biological correlates.

His thesis was that one must regard the brain as central to understanding the individual in illness and health. The brain functions to receive, process, evaluate, regulate, and store information (meaning) and energy as they flow in both directions (and are at points transduced) along the society-mind-brain-body continuum. The brain simultaneously subserves and coordinates mental functions, behavior, and processes that regulate bodily functions — for example, homeostatic and immunologic mechanisms — and these processes in turn influence tissue receptivity or resistance to pathogenic vectors of all types. In so doing, the brain provides a nexus of pathways and circuits that can serve as conduits for connecting both physicochemical and meaningful aspects of the *environment* with the corresponding aspects of the *individual*.

Reiser concluded his remarks by stating that the cerebral hemispheres may function autonomously and with very different operational patterns that generate different modes of cognitive and affective functions of potential clinical interest. The dazzling complex of functions undergoes developmental evolution, initially programmed by genetic instructions and subsequently molded — often in profound ways — by experience (especially early in life), throughout the entire life cycle.

Weiner's contribution to this volume follows, and it is a veritable *tour de force*. He begins with the concept of stress and what Selye *really* said. This leads him to stress in the social and behavioral sciences with a complete discussion of natural and man-made catastrophes, their psychopathological sequelae, as well as the disease consequences of war and danger. He examines the psychobiology of danger, fear, and anxiety, and the vicissitudes of life as stressful events. Turning to economic change as a stressor, he discusses unemployment (a subject to be returned to repeatedly in other chapters) as a stressful event, those changes in psychological and physical health that are carried in the train of unemployment, including physiology, effects on the family, and coping aspects.

Finally, Weiner focuses on loss, separation, and bereavement. After dealing with grief and pathological mourning, he reviews the literature on the psychobiology of loss and separation in young animals and in adults and, in the setting of loss, the onset of illness and disease. Using experimental evidence to support his hypotheses, he then discusses the "choice" of disease following bereavement and carefully considers age as a factor in disease onset. His conclusions regarding the status of the concept of stress and the future of stress research are marvelously supported by the corpus of the essay, and the 185 references are an added bonus to a chapter worth reading more than once.

Part II is devoted to Immunity and Genetics. We know of the extensive literature linking stress and the central nervous system (CNS), endocrine system, health, and illness. Stein and Schleifer turn to the immune system as another major integrative network involved in biological adaptation, and they recall the striking advances in immunology in the past decades and that immunological function plays a major role in both the onset and course of a host of illnesses. Considerable evidence is now accumulating, demonstrating that a range of stressful experiences influences the CNS, which may thereby result in the enhancement or suppression of immune activity. Accordingly, changes in immune function may increase or decrease the risk of onset, as well as the subsequent course, of a wide variety of clinical disorders.

In this fascinating chapter, Stein and Schleifer review the clinical and experimental studies concerned with the influence of stress effects on immunological reactions, in addition to considering some of the psychobiological mechanisms which may be involved. The sections on bereavement and lymphocyte function, and depression and immunity, should prove particularly valuable to the clinician.

Certainly, research has shown that life stressors are associated with a wide array of physical and mental disorders, and almost any organ system may be involved. Impressive evidence suggests that these stressors are significant factors in the development of various mental disorders. This does not mean, of course, that stressful experience is the sole or even the primary cause; both genetic and environmental mediators shape the biological reactions and clinical consequences of stressful experience.

Kety responds to the great need for genetic studies to be integrated with those of environmentally caused variation in response to stress. While stating from the onset that the mode of transmission, loci, and expression of genetic factors are as yet unspecified, Kety provides excellent evidence of their operation. He begins by presenting the interaction of particular stressors with genetic factors in schizophrenia. Following a review of the research to this point (much of it his own), he then turns to his considerable knowledge of depression and suicide. The studies he cites are intriguing, and his conclusion, as expected, is most wise:

> We cannot dismiss the possibility that the genetic factor in suicide is an inability to control impulsive behavior, while depression, other mental illness, as well as overwhelming environmental stressors, serve as potentiating mechanisms. . . . Suicide illustrates . . . the very crucial and important interactions between genetic factors and environmental influences, in which neither may be sufficient and both are necessary.

Thus, Kety reminds the reader again that different individuals may clearly respond to the same environmental stimulus quite differently, and he pleads for further research into the as yet ill-defined interaction between gene and environment.

Part III concerns itself with Sociocultural Aspects. From numerous epidemiological studies there has come considerable convergence of evidence indicating that many disorders are brought on by environmental stressors — moving, unemployment, bereavement, community disintegration, lack of social supports, etc. The number of stressful events in an individual's life, too, has been found to affect illness, productivity, as well as life expectancy itself. It is to these issues that the three chapters are devoted.

Duhl and Hynes suggest that future psychiatrists will have to be schooled in the broadest based system, wherein an understanding of the environment and those socio-ecological stressors likely to support or destroy the mental health of citizens is mandatory. They posit that the traditional, doctor-patient, fee-for-service relationship may soon become a thing of the past. Data are cited from diverse sources which indicate that mental illness is more likely to result from the destruction of community-based support systems than from the abnormal psychodynamics of its members. In rectifying these problems, the psychiatrist must be prepared to work creatively with legislators, community planners, ecologically-trained architects, and others to solve the sociocultural problems of communities, rather than passively waiting in his* office for patients to appear with diagnosable psychiatric illness for which third parties will be willing to reimburse him. Prevention, rather than treatment, will become increasingly appealing both to cost-conscious legislators and humanistic community planners.

The authors suggest that both the crisis and the opportunity for the field of psychiatry over the next generation will be its capacity to train a new cadre of physicians knowledgeable about and sensitive to socio-ecological factors in mental illness. They must be capable of interacting creatively with other experts and with the consumers of their services in order to plan new and viable solutions to problems. Like the ecologically sophisticated farmer, the psychiatrist of the future must be aware of the "climate" and "soil" of a community. Only then will he be able to prevent or diminish the likelihood that disease will occur in the first place. This represents the challenge for psychiatry in the final 15 years of the 20th century, as it prepares for its role in the century that awaits us.

McLean's essay on the corporate environment and stress is an interesting addition to the growing body of theory and research on work organizations, which demonstrates that major stressors in these settings are more often than not associated with adverse physical and mental health consequences. This essay reads so easily that an initial tendency is to perceive McLean's observations as obvious when they are not. He defines stress, stressor, and stress reaction in his own, unique style; presents two anecdotal cases to make his point; discusses the meaning of work and stressors; and then turns to research in this area and makes a short but fascinating exposition of worker compensation. McLean then writes of various "modifiers" and social support as a buffer. Finally, he discusses the psychiatrist's function in an occupational setting from the vantage point of an individual considered by many to be the true expert in this area. The conclusions he reaches are clear and interesting; his "Comment" is fascinating.

Completing this section is Brenner's chapter. As he points out, both the psychoanalytic and sociological literatures identify losses, including economic

---

*Throughout this volume the generic "he" shall be used, unless otherwise indicated.

ones, as important factors in suicide and depressive illness. Epidemiological, sociological, and stressful life event studies tend to support these classic formulations. Brenner tests the hypothesis that economic losses — especially unemployment, business failure, and income decline — are important sources of explanation of trends and fluctuations in the U.S. suicide rate since 1950. In this complete and thoughtful presentation, he takes into account other risk factors of depressive illness and suicide, including interpersonal separation (i.e., living alone or being single, divorced, or widowed), catastrophic physical illness, and alcoholism and alcohol abuse.

The mechanisms through which economic losses and other risk factors to suicide are integrated into a single, explanatory model are via the "economic change model of pathology." This population model allows Brenner to test the explanatory power of each of the principal risk factors, separately and jointly, to suicide rate changes. His results demonstrate the critical influence of economic loss, interpersonal separations, severe physical illness, and heavy alcohol consumption on changes in the suicide rate.

Part IV is devoted to Stress Management and the Role of the Psychiatrist. Horowitz's brief and illuminating essay points out that psychological responses to serious life events consist of at least five components. These are: the universal stress-response tendencies found in most human beings; the typological stress-response tendencies found in those with a given personality type; the habitual but individual stylistic responses to a given stress or event; individual responses because of the nature of the individual's current social and physical environment; and, finally, psychological responses as dictated by current neurobiological capacity.

Through the use of an illustrative case example and fascinating Tables, Horowitz guides the therapist through the patient's denial and intrusive phases, establishes priorities of treatment, and provides the reader with a sample of a 12-session dynamic therapy for stress disorders. He ends with a useful discussion of "defects" of hysterical, obsessional, and narcissistic styles, along with their counteractants in therapy.

Rosenman and Chesney's chapter could well be subtitled, "Everything You Always Wanted to Know about Type A Behavior." Beginning with the association of coronary heart disease (CHD) with psychological and psychosocial factors, they then turn to Type A Behavior (TAB) per se, the background of the concept as well as the relationship between TAB and CHD, coronary artherosclerosis, and the precipitation of coronary events. Demographic and socioeconomic variables are included, along with other risk factors and biochemical findings. The authors also present the hereditary and developmental antecedents of TAB.

Reviewing the literature of the past 25 years, Rosenman and Chesney conclude that modification of coronary-prone TAB, both for primary and secondary prevention of CHD, is absolutely valid. They thus turn their attention to both pharmacological and behavioral interventions. Finally, their extensive references provide a marvelous opportunity for further study for those wishing to pursue this interesting topic.

The final chapter is most timely. Michels reminds us that as medicine in general focuses on health promotion and disease prevention, persons with and without symptoms of physical or mental disorder will be urged to take more individual responsibility for their own health. Epidemiologists, psychologists, and psychiatrists will all contribute useful information in this domain.

In terms of the future, Michels believes that psychiatrists can make significant contributions through the personal psychiatric care system by intervening clinically in situations known to increase the probability of disorder (bereavement, family crisis, and other stressors that exceed a person's coping capacity), and also by participating in the design and evaluation of procedures that could potentially promote health or prevent disease.

As the reader can see, the material contained in this volume is reflective of one of the major concerns in psychiatry today. Although the authors have paid particular attention to the "disease" aspects or deleterious effects of stress, it is becoming increasingly evident that some stress may, under certain circumstances, enhance personal growth and development. Is there any doubt that exposure to stressors at one period fosters the later development of needed competencies, self-esteem, empathy, and even the ability to take advantage of new opportunities? Perhaps a future College publication will address this viewpoint.

Since this is the last of four volumes that I have edited for the American College of Psychiatrists, I would like to express my personal gratitude to the four Presidents at whose discretion I have served. I am most appreciative for the support and encouragement of Drs. Shervert H. Frazier, John C. Nemiah, Robert L. Williams, and Harold M. Visotsky, respectively.

My special thanks are extended to the entire Publications Committee for their diligent efforts over these years, to Susan Barrows and Ann Alhadeff of Brunner/Mazel for sharing their expertise with me, and to Bernie Mazel for cooperation beyond the call of duty. Finally, taking editorial license, I would like my wife, Ruth, to know how indebted I am to her for never questioning the time I have taken to pursue this often trying but always rewarding task.

Michael R. Zales, M.D.
Greenwich, Connecticut

REFERENCE

1. Elliot, G. R., and Eisdorfer, C. (Eds.): *Stress and Human Health*. New York: Springer, 1982.

STRESS IN HEALTH
AND DISEASE

Part I

CONCEPTUAL APPROACHES
TO STRESS

1

The Conceptualization of Stress and a Model for Further Study

Carl Eisdorfer, Ph.D., M.D.

Ernst Mayr, the great zoologist and scientific historian, has pointed out that while *discoveries* are the symbol of science in the mind of the public, "In biological science, most major progress was made by the introduction of new *concepts*, or the improvement of existing concepts" (1).

It has been suggested (2) that "the stress paradigm has emerged as one of the more cogent schemata for understanding psychopathology" (p. 223). Stress has also been described (3) as "dealing with a riddle wrapped in an enigma wrapped in more of the same" (p. 39).

The challenge is to make some progress toward unwrapping the concept of stress and understanding its role in human disease and health, as well as its clinical mediation and prevention.

It is probably only slightly inaccurate to propose that, in order to study and understand the phenomena of nature, we must often undertake unnatural acts in unnatural settings in order to control a series of events. This unnatural activity under appropriate circumstances can be organized around shared — or, more precisely, sharable — measures, and the consequences of the act, taking place in the appropriate setting, can be published as a scientific statement.

The tables and Figure (1) in this chapter are reprinted with permission from Springer Publishing Company, from the book, *Stress and Human Health* (Glenn R. Elliott, Carl Eisdorfer, eds.), 1982.

5

Of course, we assume that the organizer of the setting and action is in a position to share with us a new truth in the form of accurate, replicable data.

Thus, superpowerful magnets, vacuum chambers, chemical isotopes, genetically pure animal strains, and appropriately handled subjects become as intimately woven into the fabric of science as are the threads in a piece of fine silk. Knowledge based on the conceptions and data derived from scientific methods has had, is having, and will hopefully continue to have profound positive effects on our ability to function adaptively in the world. This new knowledge and corresponding technology all carry a risk, but examination of that risk is not appropriately addressed here.

Whatever truth emerges from science, a parallel "truth" also exists, that subjective sense of reality stemming from personal observation, a life of experience, and a sort of "pop" anthropology involving what has come to be called common sense. It is in the coming together of these areas of knowledge—the obvious commonsense approach to life and the science—that we begin to encounter the subject of stress.

A reasonable amount of data and some speculation have gone into the concept that living organisms are in a relatively precarious balance with the external environment to which they must adapt. This balance is successfully accomplished by an internal juggling act of rather incredible dimensions. Through a combination of automatic physiologic measures and learned environmental manipulations, we retain what the French call our "milieu intérieur" at a relatively neat balance—the homeostasis described by Cannon (4). Moderate changes in the environment, internally or externally, lead to changes that are barely discernible, if at all, in somatic, experiential, or behavioral measures.

Theoretically, under highly controlled circumstances it might be possible to protect ourselves from major disruptions in our environments; however, this seems hardly possible over any reasonable life span. We must then face the common sense idea that traumatic events in our lives have effects, and that these effects are likely to be undesirable. This latter assumption, namely that of undesirability, stems from the notion that initial traumatic stimuli are usually unpleasant experiences, and it seems reasonable to expect that undesirable experiences lead to undesirable consequences (a note about this qualitative issue later).

This straightforward observation is probably the basis for much of the strong belief of the lay public that stress is an important cause of problems. It may also account for the public's extraordinary interest and expenditure of resources for stress mediation, which far outstrips the scientific or clinical state of the field.

TABLE 1
Typical Stressors Used in Animal Research

Cardiac catheterization	Immobilization
Cold exposure	Maternal deprivation
Competitive social interaction	Novel environments
Electric shock	Prolonged forced swimming
Food deprivation	Sensory deprivation
Handling	Sleep deprivation
Heat exposure	Social crowding
Immersion in ice water	Social isolation

As these examples of stressors show, we have used venipuncture, noise, mental arithmetic, heat exposure, the placement of limbs in buckets of ice water, electric shock, (and even what, for some, is the most unnatural stressor of all, physical exercise) as part of a wide array of stressors to study changes in the body as the result of such stimulation. The findings have been remarkable and have demonstrated elevations in free fatty acids, epinephrine and norepinephrine, as well as the urinary byproducts of catecholamines, adrenocorticosteroids, and other chemicals reflecting a humoral response to disruptive stimulations. In addition, such other measures as blood pressure, heart rate, and skin conductance have also been shown to reflect significant changes under such situations (5).

Encouraged by such data, but historically in advance of much of it, we

TABLE 2
Typical Stressors Used in Human Research

Experimental Stimuli	
Acute Stressors	*Chronic Stressors*
Threatening, unpleasant films	Sleep deprivation
Understimulation/Demand underload	
Overstimulation/Demand overload	
Noise, unexpected or uncontrollable	
Prestige or status loss	
Electric shock	
Approach-avoidance conflicts	
Uncontrollable situations	

TABLE 3
Typical Stressors Used in Human Research

Natural Events

Acute stressors
Physical illness (including surgery, hospitalization)
Threats to self-esteem
Traumatic experiences

Stress-event sequences
Bereavement
Losses of any type (physical, psychological, or social)
Migration
Retirement
Status change (e.g., job change, salary change, marriage)

Chronic and chronic intermittent stressors
Daily "hassles"
Demand overload or underload
Role strains
Social isolation

examined students taking tests, people in highly demanding occupations, or those who had to cope with multiple intense stimuli: driving in heavily trafficked streets, going into surgery, or undergoing changes in roles and status. We usually reached the conclusion that bad things externally lead to bad things internally (5, 6, 15).

Much of the data we collected demonstrated short-term disruption of the somatic state. It became reasonable, of course, to assume that if stress, as described in the classic work of Selye (7), resulted in dramatic changes in body chemistry, such changes would have a significant role to play in the etiology of disease. This is a particularly appealing hypothesis, since the nature of the short-term reaction to powerful stimulation could be characterized physiologically as an emergency response and catabolic, rather than anabolic, in nature.

Unfortunately, the data do not always support what seems obvious. Peptic ulcers were at one time used as a model for stress-caused disease, yet the data simply do not confirm that assumption, common sense and short-term studies on gastric secretion notwithstanding. In his superb treatise on psychobiology and human disease, Weiner (8) states, "At the present time we know somewhat more about the factors that predispose to this disease than about the factors that cause or sustain it" (p. 82). As he points out, not all persons with hypersecretion of acid and pepsin have ulcers, and not all patients with duodenal ulcers are hypersecreters.

Just to complicate matters, Cobb and Rose (9) did find an increased occurrence of peptic ulcers among air traffic controllers, particularly those in so-called high stress centers.

Putting together earlier work by a number of authors (10) indicates that more than 20 individual factors may be involved in altering the risk for peptic ulcers, ranging from genetic to behavioral to the nature of unresolved conflicts over dependency. Thus, stress per se must be seen as a highly general concept—albeit not without merit—perhaps like illness or disease in its heuristic value.

Engel's report (11) that people do, on occasion, appear to become "scared to death" seems to be an example of science following common wisdom—in this case institutionalized in the form of an American idiom. The evidence for stress as an effective agent in cardiovascular disease is intriguing. Without going into great detail, recall the work on the Type A personality by Friedman and Rosenman (12), showing that those unusually aggressive, time-bound, and work-oriented persons do have a higher risk for heart attacks than do Type B, their more relaxed, age-matched controls.

A range of biochemical changes which might contribute to cardiovascular disease has been related to stress, but detailed studies of the process have not been convincing, however intriguing. This is, perhaps, because the etiology of atherosclerosis is itself still obscure. Animal experiments involving noise (13), avoidance learning (14), and social crowding (15) suggest that some environmental disruptions produce transient but not persistent elevations in blood pressure, while others produce a sustained response. Still unclear, however, are the mechanisms by which disruptive psychosocial events can cause or contribute to sustained hypertension.

Changes in the immune mechanisms of the body are a most recent and particularly exciting research arena. Since the immune system is so crucial a substrate in the development of a broad spectrum of medical and surgical disease, the works of Ader (16), Stein (17), and others which suggest that it, too, is not immune to the effects of brain-mediated psychosocial factors have substantial importance for health.

Endocrine disorders and psychiatric illness—particularly depression, sleep disturbances, alcoholism, drug abuse, and even cancer—have been related to psychosocial events, especially losses, or to personality factors such as isolation from parents and peers, or to chronic cumulative disruptions (10). In each instance, the evidence is stimulating and convincing, but largely to those already convinced.

While the credibility of the stress construct is high among laymen and many professionals, the concept of stress as a major theme is still a "problem" among a considerable number of nonpsychiatric clinicians and the scientific community. There is merit, then, in examining the conceptualization of stress and its strengths and weaknesses as a construct on which to build a base of scientific and clinically useful knowledge.

Miller (18) has suggested that stress has become a surrogate for behavioral medicine, and that that emergent field undertakes to integrate behavioral and biomedical knowledge relevant to health and disease. Stress in that context is perceived to be an alteration in the state of the organism which makes the individual more likely to experience unpleasant states, to suffer from somatic and psychological pathology, or to adversely influence the course of a disease.

This logically leads to the acceptance of stress itself as a disease state, as described by DSM-III (19), i.e., the post-traumatic stress syndrome. Indeed, this syndrome was only recently the basis of a lead article in the *American Journal of Psychiatry* (20). The *post-traumatic stress syndrome* is defined as a clinical state relatable to "a recognizable stressor that would evoke significant symptoms of distress in almost anyone" (19, p. 137). This disorder is specifically differentiated from other disorders involving adjustment or anxiety.

However, it is clear that the term "stress" has come to signify more things than a psychiatric state or a synonym for behavioral medicine. Before we understand the concept of stress, we are well advised to examine the various definitions of the term and only then to pursue its scientific substrate.

This author is not given to the notion that scientific data have to pass a popularity contest and objects to the misguided concept that puts certain forms of research on a "basic science" pedestal, ranking prestige and quality according to the nature of what is being studied. We ought not to accept that there is anything more basic or inherently scientific about studying physical phenomena as in physics, or star systems as in astronomy, or biochemical reactions than there is about investigating individual or group behavior. However, there are challenges to stress as an identifiable construct, and it is helpful to study any valid criticism and, to the extent possible, learn from our errors. This is both an opportunity and a responsibility.

The first criticism in dealing with stress is a semantic one. The term "stress" is used in the research literature to define independent, dependent, and intervening variables indiscriminately. When we do studies clinically, we observe that stress is a cause of a problem, an explanation for a range of disorders, or a disorder itself. We are consequently at high risk for tautologic thinking—that is, stressors cause stress, and stress, in turn, is caused by stressors.

This is not merely a semantic problem; it has practical implications as well. It has already been observed (5) that biologic scientists tend to use an independent variable approach, applying stressors to study the response, while social and psychological scientists tend to evoke stress as an intervening or explanatory construct. Clinicians appear to use it as an end-state or dependent variable as well.

The second difficulty we face is in identifying the precise nature of a stimulus purported to induce stress. There are certainly some stimuli — extremes of temperature and acutely imposed pain, for example — which persistently cause a physiologic response, although many of the more moderate environmental or psychological variables may act as stressors on some occasions and not on others. However, the physiological effects of even significant physical change are altered by changing the psychological perception of the event to make it less threatening (21).

For example, the age or sex of the subjects can significantly alter the psychological (22) or physiologic reaction to an event (23, 24). The classic adrenocorticosteroid response to a rapid increase in temperature does not occur in primates if the temperature increase is gradual, even to the same high levels. A stimulus that is perceived to be stressful on one occasion is likely, on repetition, to be less disruptive in its measurable consequences. Boredom — itself a series of sub-acts each of which is likely to be nonevocative — as a cumulative event is reportedly so disruptive as to be definable as a stressor.

The subjectivity of a stress stimulus is a facet of this problem — what is sauce for the goose is quite clearly not necessarily so for the gander. Even the pressures characterizing most Type A individuals are of small moment to many successful individuals.

Response specificity to stressor stimulation is also well documented, and Mason (25), Dimsdale and Moss (26), and Ward, Mefford, Parker, Chesney, Taylor, Keegan, and Barchas (27) have reported catecholamine response to specific stimuli. For example, epinephrine — but not norepinephrine — elevations were reported in response to a cognitive task, while norepinephrine was elevated in response to physical challenge (27). The conclusion one can draw is that the concept of stress as a universal, generalized, physiologic reaction must be questioned.

Examining a different aspect of the problem, it is worth noting that stressors have traditionally been perceived to be negative. There is ample evidence, however, that environmental events which can be socially identified as positive by a culture, such as job promotion, increased income, moving to a more desirable location, birth of a child, and even humorous or sexually arousing movies can have a physiological consequence not distinguishable from stimuli which would be characteristically perceived as negative in quality.

Furthermore, the reaction to highly traumatic, negatively charged events may have positive, longer-term consequences, and, indeed, successful mediation of quite unpleasant psychosocial events doubtless has a positive value for growth. This is the basis for crisis therapy.

Apart from problems of definition and stimulus variability, stress as a causal agent reflects upon a major conceptual issue in all of biomedicine. Perhaps initially in medicine we had our successes in diagnosing and treating trauma at the hunt or battlefield. It was easy to identify the cause of problems inflicted by horns, hooves, and rocks. We conjectured about other unknown airborne problems, and we postulated spirits and miasmas, with a consequent alteration in the balance of such internal humors such as yellow or black bile (the famous melan-cholie), and so on.

We improved on that data base and discovered microbes to which we again attributed causal roles; that is to say, we learned that microbes *caused* disease. Of course, there was, and probably still is, a small group that feels that microbes really do not exist, while another group recognizes that it is not the organism that causes the disease, but rather that disease is the end-product of an organism-host interaction. Sadly, however, I believe it is hardly overstated to argue that a simplistic approach to causality dominated and continues to dominate much of clinical and even scientific thinking.

In 1965, Dubos (28) contended that endogenous infections had replaced exogenous ones as a major cause of human illness. Regarding the endogenous infection, the question is, "How has the environment altered the host-agent balance?" Dubos suggested that old methods are not sufficient to deal with agents which are ubiquitous in the community and dormant in most of its members. I believe that we will see a rebirth of stress as an important factor when we have gotten away from the simplistic notion that stress *causes* disease.

With the increased recognition given the Framingham longitudinal study of cardiovascular disease has come a rebirth of the concept of risk factors. The recent ads of the tobacco industry notwithstanding, we now appreciate that it is not necessary to have a meticulous understanding of the process by which tobacco smoke affects the body in order to make statistically significant predictions about its undesirable disease consequences.

Hypertension is a significant risk factor for strokes. Each day we are improving our understanding of why and how, but we have known about the relationship and the need to manage hypertension even before we fully understood the cardiovascular dynamics involved. We know, too, that certain gene pools result in a heightened probability for certain types of illness, but in most instances we have not the faintest idea of exactly how that works. As risk factor models approach more widespread credibility, they may prove to be among the most important approaches to mediating diseases since the development of the microscope.

It seems clear that the role of stress is, in the main, more likely to fit into a risk factor model than a single agent causal model, and as risk factor models become more acceptable, they will carry stress in tandem.

I do not doubt that there are more complex hypothetical structures in science than stress — I simply do not know any. Stress is complex for a variety of reasons. It is, of course, complex in its hierarchical interaction; that is to say, stimuli of one sort, such as social or behavioral variables, may have their maximum measurable effect at another level, such as enzymatic or physiologic. The same stimuli do not necessarily cause the same response over time. The role of unidentified mediators may cause variations in stimulus effect, not only as a function of the quality of the stimulus, but also in relation to its sequence in the life span of the individual, and so on.

The subject of stress is extraordinarily complex, and its co-variations with age, sex, genetic pool, personality structure, and physiologic variation within the individual constitute a long and as yet incomplete list.

It is much simpler to do other kinds of research. The interdisciplinary requirement for stress research puts a particular burden on scientists. First of all, not all scientists are well socialized, and interdisciplinary research usually implies that the scientist be capable of working with other people. Second, one must develop a sensitivity to the need for interdisciplinary research. Interdisciplinary and multidisciplinary research are, of course, among the most complex to do and hardest to fund. The strategies of prospective versus retrospective research make the interpretive difficulties of long-term studies even more complicated.

No less an authority than Lazarus (29) has suggested that we need a different model for stress research. He proposes that we ought to limit the number of human subjects to a very few whom we study intensively, rather than take on projects that yield statistically significant data based upon large subject pools. His argument is that normative psychology seeks principles that apply to all persons but fails to account for the unique circumstances under which single individuals develop or function. As a consequence, he proposes that we need a different design, decreasing the number of persons observed in favor of more observations per person. We would, of course, need a new type of journal to publish such studies.

The inertia of the scientific community is an important factor that limits knowledge. Here the fuel in the form of outside support for stress research has not developed the sort of energy needed to promote this field of endeavor. Unless we put incremental energy into the system, we are unlikely to get much change. Scientific inertia may, on the other hand, be more related to a derivation of "Sutton's Law" — namely, that people, researchers included, tend to go where the money is.

The concept of stress crosses another set of conceptual boundaries. It has been suggested elsewhere (30) that medicine has traditionally developed along three general lines. One of these is the structural, that is to say, a focus on anatomy, stemming, perhaps, from the initial development of surgeons who removed arrows and spearheads, performed amputations, and ventilated the brains of Pharaohs. This structural-organ oriented approach, with its substrate of anatomy, has been the precursor of such contemporary miracles as vascular microsurgery and organ transplantation.

A second approach was rooted in an understanding of the four basic humors, and transformed eventually into physiology, biochemistry, and now molecular biology, as well as the practice of internal medicine, pediatrics, and their various subspecialties. This humoral group is not as well regarded by the public as the organist group; it is clear that organists are paid more by society for their operations than are humorists for their labors. Indeed, the humorist cardiologist acting like an organist in using a cardiac catheter, for example, gets paid several times more per moment than he does when working with the patient around life-style issues and other risk factors which may substantially curtail the patient's life. Third-party payers in our society are obviously much more organ- and operation- than humorally-oriented.

Most of us have evolved, I believe, from another conceptual tradition in medicine, that of the spiritual. The early history of behavioral disruptions was traceable to infusions of the wrong sorts of spirits. However, interestingly enough, from the turn of this century, psychiatry seems to have split into two branches: one, an organ-oriented branch, the other organ-irrelevant. In this latter case, while we paid lip service to the concepts of instincts and genetics, we postulated a set of principles which had only a tangential relationship to the physical organism per se.

The balance of ego, id, and superego with the social and psychological forces at work were in some theories relatable to the body in the loosest possible way. A group of non-medically trained spiritualists took very much the same approach. I am referring here to the psychologists and other applied behavioral scientists, with their interest in conditioning and learning theory and a stimulus-response paradigm of behavior. Here, too, the organism is viewed as a "black box," playing only a modest mediating role in the sequence of stimuli responses and reinforcers. The brain and its anatomy or chemistry are not subjects for the concern of the organ-irrelevant branch of medicine.

Thus, psychoanalysis and behavior therapy have considerably more in common than might be superficially apparent.

There is, of course, the other main branch of psychiatry which is purely organ-oriented. The brain is the target organ, though historically we took an excursion into the pineal. For the organist-psychiatrist, psychosocial mediators are of little moment compared with the problem of having insufficient serum levels of one or another medication. The picture has been painted in extremes to make a point. The main themes in medicine have not been interactive as much as they have focused on organ, humoral, or spiritual directions, with occasional outbursts of hostility among the practitioners of those three orientations.

It is very clear, therefore, that a concept like stress, which cuts across biologic, psychologic, and social dimensions, and involves an integrated view of the individual, is atypical in the subspecialization orientation of medicine. One is tempted to invoke an integrating theme like holistic medicine, except for the fact that that term has come to be synonymous with so many different fringe issues as to become more confusing than helpful.

Following much initial enthusiasm for stress as a key causal factor in disease, there emerged a recognition that it is difficult in many instances to support its specific etiologic role. The work cited earlier on ulcers, emerging data on schizophrenia, and claims that stress causes diseases ranging from hypertension to herpes and asthma to angina may be accurate, but they lack the necessary supportive data. There simply is not the empirical base necessary to make such outcome statements with a sufficient degree of validity at this time, even in instances where stress is, in all likelihood, a major contributory factor to illness.

The lay perception of stress as a purely negative influence and its consequent qualitative loading is not accurate. Coming to grips with stress is an important part of the maturational process of personality. Erikson's (31) writings in this regard are only exemplary of those which should remind us that challenging experiences can be growth experiences.

I alluded to this earlier in relation to grief. We all know now that if grief is appropriately expressed and handled, it can lead to a greater degree of maturation, while if denied and suppressed, with its subjective experience actually minimized, it can lead to longer-term maladaptive consequences. It seems important, therefore, that we not put a qualitative evaluation on the stimulus event, but that we be quite guarded and look to the long-term consequences before we come to any conclusion concerning the desirability of an event or type of event per se.

CONCEPTUALIZATION OF STRESS

In addressing stress, I have outlined its parameters. Stress is a process that is multilevel, interactive, and dynamic, with input and output variables which may array in organizational hierarchy from the molecular to the behavioral-social.

Based on the recent work of the panel studying stress and human health at the Institute of Medicine/National Academy of Sciences (5), I will present here a simple framework for dealing with stress variables and offer a semantics for that framework so that the five essential elements of the dynamic may be explicated.

Figure 1 shows the interactive nature of the model. There are four sets of variables to consider, as well as a Descriptor component. x is identified as the Potential *Activator,* y as the immediate *Reaction,* and z as the longer-

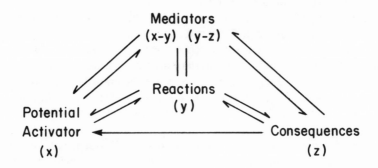

FIGURE 1. A framework for interactions between the individual and the environment.

term *Consequence*. The bidirectional arrows reflect the reciprocal nature of the elements of this paradigm. Of particular importance is the mediator component of that diagram. Mediators may be physical or psychological, environmental or behavioral. Coping strategies, prior experience, and stage of life are all variables that, based on existing data, will affect the x-y and y-z sequence.

Activators are endogenous or exogenous events which change an individual's present state. Activators may be more broadly defined than stimuli, since even the absence of an event can be a potential activator — e.g., an unmet desire.

A falling tree is not an activator unless you see and hear it. If it falls near someone, it produces fear, a potent activator. If it hits someone, pain and injury become activators, and there may be a memory of this event which has potential activating properties in future walks in the forest — or safely at home in bed.

A subset of activators is sufficiently intense to produce significant physical or psychosocial reactions. For this category, I use the term "stressor." Potential stressors may be identified and described by investigating activators in the context of the other elements of the model and the population being studied. Such an approach has considerable merit, since it lends itself readily to a probability statement.

Reactions are the biological or psychological responses of an individual to the activator. Like the activator, the reaction can occur at many different levels, from the molecular to the cognitive or social-interactive. Descriptors for the elements of the construct include not only hierarchical levels of complexity, but also intensity, quantity, and temporal pattern — a few of the ways to describe activators, reactions, consequences, and mediators.

Over time, or with experience, or by some other mediational process, reactions may change in relation to objectively similar activators. This is clearly identifiable qualitatively and quantitatively. Most reactions are transient; these include changes in serum chemistry, blood pressure, withdrawal behavior, and the like, some resulting in important consequences to the individual.

Consequences are prolonged effects of reactions. For most psychiatrists, the consequences of greatest professional interest are those affecting health and behavior. Consequences can be biological, as in renal or hepatic damage or some persistent alteration in brain chemistry, or psychological, as in an anxiety disorder or depression, or related to other psychosocial maladies such as marital discord or job-related difficulties. Consequences may be desirable, as well. Greater independence, maturity, or athletic prowess may be longer-term changes resulting from an unpleasant x-y sequence. In the case of sports, for example, trainers often maintain "no pain, no gain."

Again, the descriptors of level, intensity, temporality and quantity should be applied to the consequence. Consequences are also the only elements to which we should assign any qualitative loading. Activators and reactions are neither good nor bad.

Mediators may be the most intriguing of the elements. They filter and modify all of the other variables in the x-y-z sequence. Tables 4, 5, and 6 show three classes of mediator. In employing descriptors to the mediators, one fact is clear — mediation at one hierarchical level is able to affect change at another. Style of coping can modify the physiologic reaction to prior activators (29, 32). Genetic mediation will clearly affect the unique consequences to an individual of the activation-reaction sequence, and so on.

The importance of mediation is reflected even in such broad conceptions of disease as that of the sociologist Antonovsky (33), who postulates that a feeling of confidence that environments are predictable and that things will work out is the individual's and society's best defense against disease. "Salu-dogenesis," a term he coined, indicates that, in our terminology here, there is a mediator, namely, some cognitive explanation for a stressor-activator sequence which profoundly reduces its undesirable consequence. To put it more simply, cognitive appraisal and explanation is an important mediator which has positive health consequences.

The model can also be used for clinical and research purposes alike. In a recent study (34), investigators examined the highly stressful experience of caring for a relative with Alzheimer's disease. That situation had as potential activators those included in Table 7.

As reactions, we could have measured fear, anger, grief, denial, and muscle tension or cardiovascular dynamics in relation to a sequence of patient-initiated activators. Although a number of the subjective states and behaviors were studied, I would like to go on to the consequences of the x-y-z sequence and the mediators.

TABLE 4

Process Factors

Cognitive appraisal (meaning of an event, significance for well-being)

Coping (strategies used to react to or negate the effects of an event)

TABLE 5

Environmental Factors

Interpersonal factors (social networks, social supports)

Other external factors

Physical setting (geographic and architectural characteristics)

Organizational factors (institution size and structure)

Human aggregate (characteristics of the persons inhabiting a particular environment)

Social climate (social prejudice, social expectation)

Cultural factors (cultural belief systems, institutionalized means for dealing with change)

Other environmental stressors (war, economic upheaval)

TABLE 6

Person Factors

Personality (personality traits, coping dispositions)

Personal resources (intelligence, special skills, motivation; some personality variables)

Temperament (beliefs, attitudes)

Past history (past experiences, repertoire of skills, previous psychiatric history)

Sociodemographic variables (age, sex, race, socioeconomic status)

Genetic variables (biological predispositions to illness)

Biological variables not genetically transmitted (physical condition, diseased organs)

TABLE 7

Potential Activators (X)

Severity of dementia

Duration of illness

Burden on caregiver

Life change events not related to care of patient

TABLE 8

Reaction (Y) to Caring for Alzheimer Patient-Relative

Affect: grief, sadness, anger
Cognitive: denial, ongoing concern, attribution
Psychophysiologic: automatic nervous system reaction, sleep deprivation
Behavioral: hostility, irritability, withdrawal

The results of the study (34) were that all family members reported stress. There were long-term negative consequences in about half of the primary care-givers who lived with their Alzheimer-patient relatives. In support of Anton-ovsky's thesis, the reactions of helplessness acted as mediators in contribut-ing to this outcome. Thus, it is possible to state that primary caregiver relatives living with a patient and manifesting a cognitive outlook of hopelessness are at significant risk for a clinically diagnosable depression. This analysis de-parts from a global notion of stress, points up areas of intervention – and pre-vention – and identifies variables for further study.

Stress, then, is like a pathogen which is omnipresent in human life. Holmes, Masuda, and Rahe (35, 36) have demonstrated that it is possible for the de-fense system to be overwhelmed by the bunching up of life events over brief periods of time. For the most part, however, potential activators and reac-

TABLE 9

Mediators

Family dynamics
Psychosocial networks
Attributional style
Physical proximity
Cognitive appraisal
Age
Health
Availability of professional resources

---

tions do not yield widespread disease as a consequence. Perhaps because of mediation, the stress paradigm can become a model, therefore, not just for the understanding of activators-reactions and untoward consequences, but for all of psychosocial adaptation and psychiatric disruption.

Finally, let me cite Goldstein, the neurologist, whose classic monograph, *The Organism* (37), was subtitled, "A Holistic Approach to Biology Derived from Pathologic Data in Man." Goldstein stated that our first task is to describe carefully all living beings as they actually are. Mindful of the problems of scientific investigation which takes things apart in order to study them, Goldstein states, "the riddle of biology is the riddle of the systems themselves" (p. 6). This extraordinary clinician-scholar notes further, "A definition of life cannot be other than a concept derived from a study of . . . behavior. . . . Such a definition would, of necessity, be obliged to follow, rather than precede our observations" (p. 5).

In summary, we must redefine our terminology and constructs, and we must integrate elements at various levels of analysis and establish a pattern of integrated hypotheses and data. We must recognize the need to disprove our simple assumptions, because if everything is possible, nothing is absolute. One can feel stress but not show it and can display major somatic change without any experience of disruption. While the world is falling apart, some will wonder what the fuss is all about.

The salutory effects of x's, y's, and mediators need to be understood and a developmental orientation incorporated into the model. In the last analysis, the constellation of responses based upon systematic observation in the laboratory, community, and clinic holds the promise for improving the accuracy and value of stress as a concept.

In looking at all of this, I am reminded of a simple rule: Behind every complex issue there is a simple explanation — and that explanation is invariably wrong. Stress is a powerful, explanatory construct which is hierarchical, complex, and interactive. To treat it in a simplistic manner would be to do it a disservice, to destroy its utility, and to delay our understanding of what it does.

REFERENCES

1. Mayr, E.: *The Growth of Biologic Thought*. Cambridge, MA: Harvard University Press, 1982.
2. Eisdorfer, C.: Critique of the stress and coping paradigm. In: C. Eisdorfer, D. Cohen, A. Kleinman, and P. Maxim (Eds.), *Models for Clinical Psychopathology*. New York: Spectrum Publishers, 1981.
3. Eisdorfer, C.: Stress, disease and cognitive change in the aged. In: C. Eisdorfer, and R. O.

Friedel (Eds.), *Cognitive and Emotional Disturbance in the Elderly: Clinical Issues.* Chicago: Year Book Medical Publishers, 1977.

4. Cannon, W. B.: *The Wisdom of the Body.* New York: Morton, 1939.

5. Elliott, G. R., and Eisdorfer, C. (Eds.): *Stress and Human Health: A Study by the Institute of Medicine/National Academy of Sciences.* New York: Springer, 1982.

6. Linn, B. S., Linn, M. W., and Jensen, J.: Surgical stress in the healthy elderly. *J. Amer. Geriat. Soc.,* 31:544–548, 1983.

7. Selye, H.: *The Stress of Life.* New York: McGraw-Hill, 1956.

8. Weiner, H. *Psychobiology and Human Disease.* New York: Elsevier, 1977.

9. Cobb, L. A., and Rose, R. M.: Hypertension, peptic ulcer and diabetes in air traffic controllers. *J.A.M.A.,* 224:489–492, 1973.

10. Bunney, W., Jr., Shapiro, A., Ader, R., Davis, J., et al.: Panel report on stress and illness. In: G. R. Elliott, and C. Eisdorfer (Eds.), *Stress and Human Health.* New York: Springer, 1982.

11. Engel, G. L.: Sudden and rapid death during psychological stress: Folk lore or folk wisdom? *Ann. Intern. Med.,* 74:771–782, 1971.

12. Friedman, M., and Rosenman, R. H.: Association of specific overt behavior pattern with blood and cardiovascular findings. *J.A.M.A.,* 169:1286–1296, 1959.

13. Farris, E. J., Yeakel, E. H., and Medaff, H. S.: Development of hypertension in emotional gray Norway rats after air blasting. *Amer. J. Physiol.,* 144:331–333, 1945.

14. Benson, H., Herd, J. A., Morse, W. H., and Kelleher, R. T.: Behavioral induction of arterial hypertension and its reversal. *Am. J. Physiol.,* 217:30–34, 1969.

15. Henry, J. P., Stephens, P. M., and Santisteban, G. A.: A model of psychosocial hypertension showing reversibility and progression of cardiovascular complications. *Circ. Res.,* 36: 156–164, 1975.

16. Ader, R. (Ed.): *Psychoneuroimmunology.* New York: Academic Press, 1981.

17. Stein, M., Keller, S. E., and Schleifer, S. J. The hypothalamus and the immunoresponse. *Brain Behav. Bodily Dis.,* 59:45–64, 1980.

18. Miller, N. E.: Behavioral medicine: Symbiosis between laboratory and clinic. *Ann. Rev. Psych.,* 34:1–31, 1983.

19. American Psychiatric Association. Quick reference to the diagnostic criteria DSM III. Washington, DC: American Psychiatric Association, 1980.

20. Terr, L. C.: Chowchilla revisited: The effects of psychic trauma four years after a school-bus kidnapping. *Amer. J. Psychiat.,* 140:1543–1550, 1983.

21. Mason, J. W.: A reevaluation of the concept of non-specificity in stress theory. *J. Psychiat. Res.,* 8:323–333, 1971.

22. Neugarten, B. L.: Personality change in late life: A developmental perspective. In: C. Eisdorfer, and M. P. Lawton (Eds.), *The Psychology of Adult Development and Aging.* Washington, DC: American Psychological Association, 1973.

23. Eisdorfer, C., Powell, A. H., Silverman, G., and Bogdonoff, M. D.: The characteristics of lipid mobilization and peripheral disposition in aged individuals. *J. Gerontol.,* 20:511–514, 1965.

24. Eisdorfer, C., and Raskind, M.: Aging, hormones and human behavior. In: B. Eleftheriou, and R. Sprott (Eds.), *Hormonal Correlates of Behavior, Vol. I: A Lifespan View.* New York: Plenum Press, 1975.

25. Mason, J. W.: Specificity in the organization of neuroendocrine response profiles. In: P. Seeman, and G. Brown (Eds.), *Frontiers in Neurology and Neuroscience Research.* Toronto: University of Toronto, 1974.

26. Dimsdale, J. E., and Moss, J.: Plasma catecholamines in stress and exercise. *J.A.M.A.,* 243: 340–342, 1980.
27. Ward, M. M., Mefford, I. N., Parker, S. D., Chesney, M. A., Taylor, B., Keegan, D. L., and Barchas, J.: Epinephrine and norepinephrine responses in continuously collected human plasma to a series of stressors. *Psychosom. Med.,* 45:471–485, 1983.
28. Dubos, R. J.: The evaluation of microbial diseases. In: R. J. Dubos, and J. G. Hirsch (Eds.), *Bacterial and Mycotic Infections of Man.* Philadelphia, PA: Lippincott, 1965.
29. Lazarus, R. S.: The stress and coping paradigm. In: C. Eisdorfer, D. Cohen, A. Kleinman, and P. Maxim (Eds.), *Models for Clinical Psychopathology.* New York: Spectrum Publishers, 1981.
30. Eisdorfer, C.: Care of the aged: The barriers of traditions. *Ann. Int. Med.,* 94:256–260, 1981.
31. Erikson, E. H.: *Childhood and Society, 2nd Ed.* New York: W. W. Norton, 1963.
32. Rivenson, T. A., Wallmon, C. A., and Filton, B. J. Social supports as stress buffers for adult cancer patients. *Psychosom. Med.,* 45:323–331, 1983.
33. Antonovsky, A.: *Health, Stress, and Coping.* San Francisco, CA: Jossey-Bass, 1979.
34. Eisdorfer, C., Cohen, D., Kennedy, G., and Wisnieski, W.: Depression and attributional style in families coping with Alzheimer's disease. Presented at the 36th Annual Meeting of the Gerontological Society of America. San Francisco, CA, 1983.
35. Holmes, T. H., and Masuda, M.: Life change and illness susceptibility. In: J. P. Scott, and E. C. Senay (Eds.), *Symposium on Separation and Depression* (Publication No. 94). Washington, DC: American Association for the Advancement of Science, 1973.
36. Holmes, T. H., and Rahe, R. H.: The social readjustment rating scale. *J. Psychosom. Res.,* 11:213–218, 1967.
37. Goldstein, K. *The Organism.* New York: American Book Co., 1939.

2

The Concept of Stress in the Light of Studies on Disasters, Unemployment, and Loss: A Critical Analysis

Herbert Weiner, M.D.

INTRODUCTION

The use of the term "stress" has been expanded to include any threatening, "overloading," painful, distressing, or depriving physical or social stimulus. It is also employed to refer to mental states produced by events or experiences, or to abiding characteristics ("traits") of certain persons. Building on Selye's investigations, a third group of experts has unsuccessfully tried to define "stress" in terms of specific physiological responses, hormonal or otherwise.

It will be argued that stimuli and situations such as loud noises, a broken leg, or a cold climate can hardly be deemed the equivalent of a profound human experience such as the death of a child. (Human beings are not billiard balls or metal bars to which the laws of Newton or Hooke apply.) Following such experiences people do not of necessity fall ill, nor do they return to their previous state, as the principles laid down by Bernard and Cannon would predict: The experience is stored, and a reorganization of the person occurs — a principle that also applies to complex, albeit, physical objects.

In contrast to the stimuli that Selye called "nonspecific," and the physiological responses and counter-responses to them which he also believed were

24

general (i.e., nonspecific), human beings respond psychobiologically in a specific and individual manner, even to the most dire and overwhelming experiences. Although commonalities exist, variations in their responses are the rule, not the exception.

Furthermore, most of the events and experiences that have been called stressful are not physical in nature but are the result of changes in human relationships. They result either from man's unlimited capacity for inhuman cruelty or from the disruption of human relationships by partings. Conversely, human fellowships buffer the effects of the breaking of the bonds that bind human beings. The study of stress has now become the study of the panoply of human relationships. In the course of this endeavor, the word "stress" has lost its meaning; it cannot conceivably describe the specific subtleties and individual meanings of human relationships. Stress theory cannot predict that human relationships seem crucial to the maintenance or the restoration of the health of many persons. The following account will present arguments supporting these contentions.

THE CONCEPT OF STRESS—WHAT SELYE REALLY SAID

Historians teach us to return to the source of an idea so that we may fully grasp it. Students of stress have frequently paid no attention to this injunction. For that reason alone they have so widened and deepened the concept as to render it virtually meaningless. The term remains undefined; it has come to be used for any stimulus or task, for the organism's response to it, and as an explanation for an almost limitless series of phenomena that have resisted further understanding.

Therefore, some virtue might be found in going back to Selye's (1) original intent: It was to study the organism's bodily but nonspecific responses to a wide variety of contingencies of having "had it"—hard work, prolonged exposure to heat or cold, loss of blood, disease, and agonizing fear, which all produced the *same* response, consisting of feelings of exhaustion. In the face of such very strenuous or damaging situations, most living beings go through three stages: They first experience them as a hardship; then they become used to them; and, finally, they cannot stand them and give up.

Selye relates that while studying medicine he made the observation that many acute and chronic diseases were all accompanied by the same symptoms. At that time physicians sought the diagnosis of disease in specific symptoms and tried to correlate them with a specific pathogen or anatomical lesion. Selye wanted to understand why patients with many different diseases shared common symptoms—loss of appetite, physical strength and weight, sleeplessness, disturbances in temperature regulation, and lethargy. The diseases could be of infectious or neoplastic nature, accompanied by blood loss, follow burns, and/or surgery. What was this general "state of being sick," he asked?

Beginning in 1936 (2), Selye found that restraining rats, the injection of impure glandular extracts or croton oil, burns, infection, fractures, ionizing radiation, anoxia, hemorrhage, heat, and cold all produced adrenocortical hypertrophy, atrophy of, and hemorrhage into the thymus gland and lymph nodes, and gastric erosions. Even local injury produced such a general response mediated by the brain and its two main output channels.

Somewhat later Selye (3, 4) formally divided this general reaction to various noxious agents into the three stages of the General Adaptation Syndrome (G.A.S.):

1) *The alarm reaction.* The organism is restless and tense if the stress is mild; but if it is severe, "depression" and shock occur. In both cases it loses appetite and libido. Heat, severe burns, and trauma may produce morphologic changes in the brain at this stage of the reaction. Catecholamine and adrenocortical steroid production and secretion occur in association with the release of vasopressin and increased autonomic neural discharge. The effects of the stressor in producing "shock," hyperkalemia, hypothermia, hypotension, hemo-concentration and increased membrane permeability, and gastric erosions are counteracted (Figure 1) by this neural and hormonal activation.

The mobilization of hormones and the autonomic nervous system lead to the:

2) *Stage of resistance,* during which appetite is restored to normal but libido is not.

3) *Stage of exhaustion.* The manifestations of the alarm reaction recur, and changes in arterial blood vessels manifest themselves. On reexposure to stress, the defensive measures are no longer instituted.

In Selye's subsequent writings the line between the beneficial ("defense") and the pathogenic effects of the corticosteroid hormones becomes blurred. He wrote extensively about the pathogenic effects on brain, electrolyte metabolism, muscle function, and blood pressure of desoxycorticosterone (DOCA) and of other mineralocorticosteroids. This muddle continues in the literature: Selye's original thought was that bodily damage was produced by the systemic effects of the stressor, while the defensive ("counter-shock") reactions attempted to redress the balance. His later work, however, is concerned with the harmful effects of these very defensive reactions.

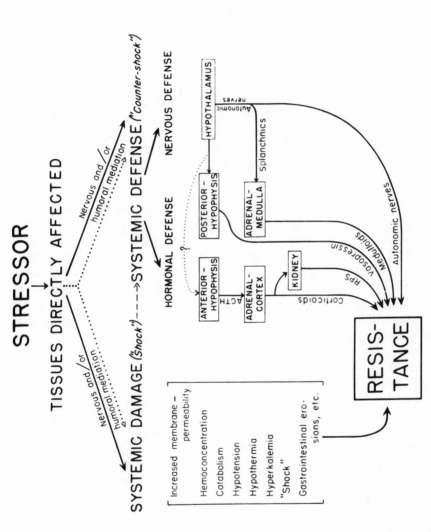

FIGURE 1. A model of the General Adaptation Syndrome: Pathways through which stress elicits systemic reactions. (From Selye, H., and Fortier, C., *Res. Publ. Ass. Nerv. Ment. Dis.*, 29:4, 1950.)

Selye's Definition of Stress

The main outlines of Selye's observations have been presented in order to highlight the possibilities of a conceptual muddle that were later realized. Note that Selye was interested mainly in the effects of noxious agents — infection, radiation, heat or cold, wounds, fractures, and even danger (to cause fear), etc.:

1) The effect of some of these could be on a local part of the body but the reaction was still general and the same regardless of the nature of the agent.
2) The agents are non-specific; they do not determine the generalized response.
3) The response is also nonspecific and stereotyped.
4) The inciting agent — the stressor — is external to the organism.
5) The model proposed is linear.

Yet from Selye's account it is not clear whether stress is defined in terms of the stressor (in his words, "topical" or general stress), or in terms of the response — the G.A.S. — which he called the "biological stress syndrome." Lost in this account was the fact that in addition to these generalized responses, specific bodily responses also occur to noxious agents: cold produces shivering; heat produces sweating and loss of electrolytes and body water; blood loss causes hypovolemia and a fall in blood pressure; and infection causes inflammation and an antibody response. Admittedly, all of them may at times produce a state of shock described in some detail in Stage I of the G.A.S.

After that time, stress — or rather the "state of stress" — was defined by Selye in terms of an "objective" but nonspecific syndrome of bodily changes. It did not just exist as any syndrome, but that concatenation of changes by which the G.A.S. was circumscribed.

It is no wonder that many of those who followed Selye defined stress as an internal state. Wolff (5), for example, wrote that it is a "dynamic state within the organism . . . not a stimulus, assault, load, symbol, burden, or any aspect of the environment, internal, external, social or otherwise" (p. 14). Others have called it a "trait" (6) and still others a "physiological state that prepares the organism for action" (7).

I have traced out some of the history of the stress concept in order to highlight the fact that there is no agreed-upon definition of stress. Nevertheless, Selye (1) was aware that the G.A.S. was not always uniform. Individual response occurred because:

1) Different agents of equal toxicity do not exactly produce the same syndrome; and

2) Individual animals respond to the same agent ("stressor") with different lesions.

Selye accounted for these individual differences in terms of the genetic predisposition, sex, age, diet, and prior exposure to drugs and hormones. Prior social experience as a source of variation does not appear in this account. Selye (1) went on to show that aldosterone (but not cortisol and cortisone) secretion raises the resistance of the organism but may, in conjunction with other experimental procedures (nephrectomy, salt administration), produce hypertension and myocardial necrosis, whereas corticosterone is anti-inflammatory.

Several additional aspects of Selye's account are worth highlighting:

1) Selye did not systematically study the behavior of his animals. As noted, he mentioned that the mildly stressed animal, in the stage of alarm, was aroused behaviorally. Actually, restrained animals lose sleep but remain quietly awake (8) and are not restless or aroused.
2) Selye studied physical and pharmacological stressors, not psychological ones. Although he believed that fear could produce the G.A.S., he never systematically studied its effects.
3) Selye never implied that the catecholamines, adrenal gluco- and mineralo-corticosteroids and vasopression were the only "stress" hormones, as others have designated them.
4) Selye also stated that the stage of resistance of the G.A.S. was an attempt of the organism to restore homeostasis. Ever since that time this *incorrect* concept has pervaded the field: Investigators have attempted to explain some psychobiological responses to stress in this manner. In actuality, only Tyhurst (9) and Rioch (10) have ever conceptualized the fact that dire stresses lead to a reorganization of the organism — a concept (to be discussed later) that is much more in line with modern concepts in physics and one that accords more closely with observation.

The Concept of Stress in the Social and Behavioral Sciences

The concept of stress began to creep into the social and behavioral sciences during and after World War II (11, 12, 13). At the same time it was used to explain the pathogenesis of a variety of diseases — called diseases of adaptation, not of stress (3, 4, 5); the stresses were of both a physical and psychological nature. Today, there is once again a tendency to revert to this way of thinking. The word "stress" has become synonymous with any event, experience, change, or task likely to be encountered in everyday life, and as an explanation of disease.

Therefore, the purpose of this essay is:

1) To argue that the concept of stress should only be used in the sense that Selye first meant it — as a noxious agent productive of fear but most often of unavoidable bodily injury, accompanied by wide-ranging psychobiological effects which are not necessarily uniform. The term should be limited to clearly specified, natural, and man-made catastrophes and disasters, which are known to have different short-term and long-range consequences, implying a total reorganization of the person.
2) To specify the reasons for individual differences in the responses to these events.
3) To suggest that to subsume the events of daily life — separation, bereavement, migration, relocation, working and raising a family, examinations, indebtedness, leadership, retirement, forced unemployment, jet travel, marriage, widowhood, parenthood, and poverty — under the rubric of stress has retarded progress in understanding.

Each of these events requires that it be separately analyzed in terms of its impact on different persons and their families — an impact that is age-specific yet individual. In turn, the meaning of each event is coped with in a different manner. (Parenthetically, the concept of coping also requires rethinking.)

To complete such a program of investigation will require much more data. Despite extensive research on the physiological responses to various psychological and social stressors, our ignorance of the manner in which they are mediated by the brain is profound, because we have so far failed to follow Beach's (14) injunction "to describe accurately the external events responsible for . . . internal changes" (p. 674). Once such a precise analysis is carried out, we may be able to identify the neural circuitry which connects the receptor with the brain's output channels regulating bodily function and action. In that way, we shall also be able to understand how the output is modified, and how, under other circumstances, physiological changes may produce disease.

NATURAL AND MAN-MADE CATASTROPHES AND THEIR CONSEQUENCES

Selye studied the humoral response to injury, infection, and temperature changes in the bodies of rats. He did mention fear as an inciter or "stress," fear being the usual response to danger. (This extensive literature of the psychological responses and adaptations to burns, injury, surgery, etc., will not be reviewed.)

Fear and the related emotions of panic, horror, and terror are the immediate emotional responses to various dangers during which the very life of a person may be threatened. The threat may be anticipated or not; escape may be possible or not. The danger may soon be over; it may mount or be prolonged; it may be predictable or unpredictable. In fact, many natural catastrophes are anticipated, but very often man-made disasters are not.

Natural and man-made catastrophes may, of course, lead to physical injury, death, and disability, but often they do not. The sources of catastrophe are:

Natural catastrophes:
  Hurricanes and tornadoes

  Floods

  Earthquakes

  Fires

  Droughts

  Snowstorms

Man-made catastrophes:
  Aircraft, ship, train, car, and bus accidents

  Industrial accidents and explosions

  Mining accidents

  Collapse of buildings

  Fires

  Nuclear accidents

  War

  Incarceration in P.O.W. and concentration camps

  Toxic air and water pollution

  Acts of terrorism

  Torture

  Rape

  Muggings

  Battery

The purpose of listing these two main classes of catastrophes separately is that the immediate and long-term psychological and behavioral consequences on populations and individuals differ. Each has its own time course, but usually both are beyond the subject's control. The behavioral and psychological responses to natural disasters are for heuristic purposes divided into a sequence of phases (15):

1) *Phase of impact*:
   Fear grading into panic and terror; horror; disbelief; feelings of numbness and paralysis and unreality

   Attempts to cope — flee, rescue, or total helplessness

2) *Phase of heroism*:
   Intense efforts to save lives and property of others and own

   Effort expended on survival and recovery

   Sense of personal strength, worth, altruism

   Overwork: Eating and sleeping omitted

   Heightened irritability, exhaustion, let-down

3) *Phase of honeymoon*:
   Onset from one week to several months after

   Experiences shared with other participants

   External support from various agencies promised

   Help and good outcome anticipated

   Hope and elation; difficulties denied

4) *Phase of disillusionment*:
   Duration two to 12 months

   Disappointment, anger, resentment at agencies for providing no or insufficient promised help

   Victims compare themselves to other victims

   Envy, hostility to those more fortunate

   Spirit of sharing and cooperation fails

   Depressive mood frequent

5) *Phase of reorganization*:
   Victims realize that recovery depends on selves

   As community recovers, individuals rebuild their lives

   If this does not occur, animosity and bitterness pervade and major "stress syndromes" become more prevalent

In situations of man-made violence and disasters, the victims of another's violence frequently experience responses that both differ and are similar to those experienced in the initial phases of natural disasters (15, 16). They may be divided into:

1) *Phase of impact*:
   Fear, terror, disbelief, and a sense of numbness and paralysis.

2) *Phase of interaction*:
A conflict over being victimized develops if some interaction between victim and perpetrator occurs.

3) *Phase of acceptance*:
Expediency may necessitate that the victim betrays his friends and jettisons his own opinions and beliefs. He may be persuaded by the perpetrator's political beliefs and personal attitudes. In this phase, yielding to and imitation of the perpetrator occurs, motivated by the desire to survive and to avoid pain and injury. The perpetrator then becomes the victim's protector.

4) *Phase of acquiescence*:
Surrender, including sexual submission, may occur in the hope of survival and avoidance of injury. The outcome may be increasingly ambiguous. Guilt and a sense of personal worthlessness increase, mixed with feelings of impotence, rage, and humiliation.

The immediate and long-range consequences of acts of terrorism and personal assault are listed in Table 1, while Table 2 lists the various psychiatric conditions that may follow natural disasters. They vary from person to person.

Differences between the responses of those subjected to the will of terrorists and of prisoners of war (P.O.W.) occur. Identification with and servile submission to the perpetrator do not usually occur in P.O.W.'s, despite brainwashing. On the other hand, P.O.W.'s and concentration camp victims who "give up" rapidly die.

TABLE 1
Symptoms Found in Victims of Terrorism

Immediate Symptoms	Long Range Symptoms
Intense apprehension	Depression
Shock (psychic numbing, disbelief)	Paranoid reactions
Anxiety (poor concentration; poor memory; drifting, tangential talk)	Withdrawal, isolation
Insomnia (nightmares)	Psychophysiological reactions
Anorexia	Phobias
Phobias	Alcoholism
Stockholm syndrome	Drug abuse
	Marital discord

TABLE 2
Most Common Psychological Reactions Found in Major
Disasters & Catastrophes

DSM III No.	Name of Disorder
308.30	Post Traumatic Stress Disorder, Acute
309.81	Post Traumatic Stress Disorder, Chronic
300.29	Simple Phobia
300.01	Panic Disorder
300.11	Conversion Disorder
296.2	Major Depression (Unipolar)
301.00	Paranoid Personality Disorder
300.81	Somatization Disorder
300.12	Psychogenic Amnesia
300.13	Psychogenic Fugue
305.0	Alcohol Abuse
305.40	Barbiturate or Sedative Intoxication
305.70	Amphetamine or Similar Sympathomimetic Intoxication

Differences in the response of the victims of natural and man-made disasters and violence are also seen. The victims of natural disasters usually feel no guilt about their failure to prevent the event. They may feel guilty about being more fortunate or not helping others more, but they do not seem humiliated.

Victims of human violence blame themselves for not having avoided it. They feel humiliated, used, and weak. If the outcome is more fortunate for them than for other victims, their guilt is intense. Another difference emerges during and after natural disasters in that laws are broken, and looting and pilfering may occur. The victims of human violence do not usually commit illegal acts, unless caught up in and swept along by a rioting mob.

The Psychopathology and Consequences of
Natural and Man-made Disasters

The a priori prediction from stress theory would be that every major and severe catastrophe, without regard to its source, would spare none of its victims. The fact is that as much as 25% of a population seems untouched by civilian disasters (17) or earthquakes of major proportions (18) and continues to function thereafter without any discernible impairment.

Another 25% of adults will immediately succumb to acute post-traumatic stress disorders (which will be discussed further) and the rest to phobic fears of objects, panic disorders, major depressions, suspicion, bodily symptoms, amnesias or fugues, substance abuse, and chronic post-traumatic stress syndromes (Table 2).

Such individual differences are not only a function of the type and severity of the catastrophe, but also of the kind of person experiencing it. Not all disasters are the same: An impending one, such as the Three Mile Island nuclear power plant accident, demonstrates how an ambiguous, intangible, potentially fatal situation may affect a population (19). For at least one year after this incident, anxiety, worry, and depression overcame the employees of the plant, mothers of young children, and patients attending mental health clinics (20, 21).

The age of the subject is another source of individual difference in the general, psychobiological consequences of natural catastrophes. Our present nomenclature fails to do full justice to the range of effects. Children manifest a series of disturbances of the major psychobiological functions — food intake, sleep, elimination, movement, speech, vision, and hearing; social behavior and the parent-child relationship are altered; early fears are reinstituted; physical complaints are expressed; and school performance deteriorates (Table 3).

Adolescents manifest a series of retrogressive behaviors in speech, social relationships, and performance. Psychobiological functions (activity level, digestion, and sexual interests), concentration, and self-confidence decline (Table 4).

Adults mainly show an increase in a variety of diseases and vital biological systems (food intake and sleep). They withdraw, lose interest in their surroundings, become easily angered, apathetic, or suspicious of others (Table 5). Elderly persons, following natural catastrophes, show many of the same symptoms as adults do, but, in addition, their mental and physical infirmities are exacerbated and accelerated (Table 6).

The two post-traumatic stress disorders differ only in their time course (Table 7). In the acute form, the onset need not immediately follow the catastrophe but begins within six months and is said not to last more than six months. The onset of the chronic form is characterized by a latent period of six months, or its duration is greater than six months. Any of the natural or man-made disasters and catastrophes may precipitate these two syndromes. They occur (and frequently remain undiagnosed) in rape victims, prisoners of war, victims of torture and concentration camps, after military combat,

TABLE 3
Behavior and Symptoms After Major Natural Disasters

AGES	FEELING AND BEHAVIOR SYMPTOMS
CHILDHOOD	RESUMPTION OF BEDWETTING, THUMBSUCKING, FEAR OF DARKNESS
	LOSS OF APPETITE
	BOWEL OR MICTURITION DISORDERS
	SLEEP DISORDERS
	HEADACHES
	COMPLAINTS OF VISUAL OR HEARING PROBLEMS
	DISOBEDIENCE
	INTRACTIBILITY
	TICS (MUSCLE SPASMS)
	SPEECH DIFFICULTIES, E.G. APPEARANCE OF STUTTERING
	REFUSAL TO LEAVE PROXIMITY OF PARENTS
	SCHOOL PHOBIAS
	WITHDRAWAL FROM PLAY GROUP AND FRIENDS
	FIGHTING WITH CLOSE FRIENDS OR SIBLINGS
	LOSS OF INTEREST IN PREVIOUSLY PREFERRED ACTIVITIES
	INABILITY TO CONCENTRATE, DROP IN LEVEL OF SCHOOL ACHIEVEMENT

TABLE 4
Behavior and Symptoms After Major Natural Disasters

AGES	FEELING AND BEHAVIOR SYMPTOMS
ADOLESCENCE	COMPETING WITH YOUNGER SIBLINGS FOR PARENTAL ATTENTION
	FAILURE TO CARRY OUT CHORES PREVIOUSLY COMPLETED
	REAPPEARANCE OF EARLIER SPEECH AND BEHAVIOR HABITS
	DECLINE IN EMANCIPATORY STRUGGLES OVER PARENTAL CONTROL
	DECLINE IN HETEROSEXUAL INTERESTS AND ACTIVITIES
	SKIN RASH
	DISORDERS OF DIGESTION
	LOSS OF INTEREST IN PEER SOCIAL ACTIVITIES
	LOSS OF INTEREST IN HOBBIES AND RECREATIONS
	SHARP INCREASE IN RESISTING PARENTAL OR SCHOOL AUTHORITY
	MARKED INCREASE OR DECLINE IN PHYSICAL ACTIVITY LEVEL
	FREQUENT EXPRESSION OF FEELINGS OF INADEQUACY AND HELPLESSNESS
	INCREASED DIFFICULTIES IN CONCENTRATION ON PLANNED ACTIVITIES

TABLE 5
Behavior and Symptoms After Major Natural Disasters

AGES	FEELING AND BEHAVIOR SYMPTOMS
MIDDLE AGE	PEPTIC ULCERS, DIABETES, HEART DISEASE
	WITHDRAWAL, ANGER, SUSPICION, IRRITABILITY, APATHY
	LOSS OF APPETITE, SLEEP PROBLEMS, LOSS OF INTEREST IN EVERYDAY ACTIVITIES

TABLE 6
Behavior and Symptoms After Major Natural Disasters

AGES	FEELINGS AND BEHAVIOR SYMPTOMS
ELDERLY	DEPRESSION WITHDRAWAL
	APATHY
	AGITATION, ANGER
	IRRITABILITY, SUSPICION
	DISORIENTATION
	CONFUSION
	MEMORY LOSS
	ACCELERATED PHYSICAL DECLINE
	INCREASE IN NUMBER OF SOMATIC COMPLAINTS

TABLE 7

Diagnostic Criteria for Post-traumatic Stress Disorder*

A. Existence of a recognizable stressor that would evoke significant symptoms of distress in almost everyone.

B. Reexperiencing of the trauma as evidenced by at least one of the following:

    (1) recurrent and intrusive recollections of the event
    (2) recurrent dreams of the event
    (3) sudden acting or feeling as if the traumatic event were reoccurring, because of an association with an environmental or ideational stimulus

C. Numbing of responsiveness to or reduced involvement with the external world, beginning some time after the trauma, as shown by at least one of the following:

    (1) markedly diminished interest in one or more significant activities
    (2) feeling of detachment or estrangement from others
    (3) constricted affect

D. At least two of the following symptoms that were not present before the trauma:

    (1) hyperalertness or exaggerated startle response
    (2) sleep disturbance
    (3) guilt about surviving when others have not, or about behavior required for survival
    (4) memory impairment or trouble concentrating
    (5) avoidance of activities that arouse recollection of the traumatic event
    (6) intensification of symptoms by exposure to events that symbolize or resemble the traumatic event

*Reprinted with permission from American Psychiatric Association, Diagnostic and Statistical Manual of Mental Disorders, Third Edition, Washington, D.C., APA, 1980, p. 238.

and in some victims of automobile accidents and robberies. It is not yet clear whether the incidence of these syndromes is greater if malnutrition and bodily (especially head) injury occur during such catastrophes.

The central feature of the syndrome is a flashback to the traumatic experience occurring during the waking and/or sleep state. Any other current experience or event, even faintly reminiscent of the original, may invoke its memory. Such patients seem to be constantly on guard (hypervigilant). They show major memory disturbances to the point of amnesic and dissociative states. Personal relationships are altered: The world and its inhabitants appear hostile, uninteresting, remote, or strange to the point of derealization. The capacities for intimacy, tenderness, and passion are lost. Irritation and anger are poorly controlled. These altered behaviors may or may not be combined with guilt over survival, chronic anxiety, depression, suspiciousness, and alterations in the basic life functions. The victims of these syndromes are at high risk for substance abuse and suicide.

In the literature on the psychobiological consequences of military combat, the argument appears that trauma, weight loss, and malnutrition are the main causes of the cognitive disturbances of veterans. However, the data do not support this conclusion. Askevold (22), in studies on the sequelae of World War II, followed a series of Norwegian merchant mariners for 20 years. They had manned cargo ships which were constantly threatened by German war planes and torpedoes. Some ships were sunk, and some of the sailors were immersed in icy water or injured. But many were not. Within 20 years after the war they became disabled with major cognitive disturbances reminiscent of a presenile dementia. Although presenile dementia of the Alzheimer type may occur following head injury, it is also possible that the chronic exposure to danger and uncertainty may produce similar or the same neuropathological changes.

Cognitive disturbances occurred in 87% of 227 Norwegian survivors of Nazi concentration camps, 57% of whom had suffered severe injury (including head injury), to which Eitinger (23) ascribed these cognitive disturbances; later (24), he changed his opinion, believing that the appalling experiences of the camp survivors were mainly responsible.

Because the victims of the Nazis' unspeakable brutality were also subjected to various combinations of torture, starvation, crowding, cold, frostbite, sleep deprivation, long hours of work, exhaustion, horror, unpredictability, the loss of relatives and friends, and diseases (typhus, intractable diarrhea, pneumonia, encephalitis, tuberculosis), it is impossible to decide the proximal causes of their cognitive disturbances.

The immediate consequences of incarceration consisted of a particularly profound form of the syndrome seen in the other man-made disasters with terror, grading into apathy, mourning, docility, profound denial ("negative hallucinations"), a loss of the capacity to feel, concern about the self in many, and heroism in others (25).

The long-term effects of the Holocaust on its survivors and their children through the second and third generation are permanent. They consist of an abiding post-traumatic stress syndrome on which are engrafted additional features. For the survivors, life is meaningless or empty, never again to be enjoyed. Fatigue is permanent. Despair, feelings of inadequacy, hopelessness, guilt of an especially malignant sort, eternal sorrow, bitterness, and recurrent depressions sweep over the survivor. Other people are not to be trusted. The survivor is cynical and touchy. His sleep is interrupted. His work suffers. Three out of four change occupations, often more than once. Marriages decline. Aging and death are premature (Table 8).

In some, survivors' symptoms appeared after a latency period of several months or years after they were liberated in 1945. However, as time passed, the cognitive disturbances became more prevalent in this group of camp survivors, and included concrete thinking and short-term memory disturbances. In 28% the electroencephalogram was abnormal. By 1964, 70% suffered back pain. Unpleasant experiences and large meals produced diarrhea in 33%; coronary and cerebral atherosclerosis occurred in 30%; asthma, chronic bronchitis, tuberculosis and chronic obstructive pulmonary disease were present in another 30% (23).

One-and-a-half million children died in concentration camps. Those who survived were irreparably damaged as human beings. Their psychosocial development had been permanently arrested. They were hypersensitive, restless, aggressive, volatile in their emotional behavior, bitter, cynical, and pessimistic. New experiences caused anxiety. They clung to their peers, while mistrusting all adults (25).

The Disease Consequences of War and Danger

Natural and man-made disasters exact a fearful toll on mankind. Automobile accidents and violence are the leading causes of death in adolescents in the U.S. (Fig. 2). Fifty million human beings lost their lives in World War II, and one million died in the Vietnam war.

Eitinger's reports demonstrate that cardiovascular (and other) diseases were more prevalent in Norwegian concentration camp survivors (24). Evidence also exists that dangerous events or situations are associated with essential hypertension. Following the explosion of a munitions ship in Texas City, a predominance of the population examined had elevated blood pressure levels maintained for a period of about two months (26). Sustained military combat — in the North African desert and at Stalingrad — were associated with a disproportionate prevalence of high blood pressure (27, 28, 29). Many factors must have played a role in this phenomenon — danger, malnutrition, cold (in Russia), heat (in North Africa), exertion, etc.

TABLE 8

Symptoms Demonstrated at Two Points in Time in Norwegian
Victims Released from Concentration Camps in 1945

SYMPTOMS	1960 $N=$ PER- CENTAGES	1964 %	NO.
Increased fatigability	85	83.7	190
'Nervousness', irritability	78	85.5	194
Disturbances of memory and difficulties of concentration	78	87.2	198
Dysphoria, bitterness	72	55.9	127
Emotional instability	70	56.8	129
Disturbances of sleep	60	65.6	149
Feeling of insufficiency	54	36.1	82
Reduced initiative	54	43.2	98
Headaches	53	60.4	137
Vegetative lability	48	37.9	86
Vertigo	38	53.7	122
Anxiety	55	57.7	131
Nightmares	36	52.0	118
Depression	36	31.7	72
Abuse of alcohol	19	21.6	49
Reduced tolerance	14	13.2	30

From Eitinger, L.: Acute and chronic psychiatric and psychosomatic reactions in concentration camp survivors. In: Levi, L. (Ed.), *Society, Stress and Disease, Vol. 1*, London, Oxford University Press, 1971, p.
233, by permission.

But the matter is even more complex. Although piloting a Naval combat
airplane is conducive to marked changes in cortisol levels, studies of U.S.
naval aviators over a 25-year period show that their blood pressure levels do
not increase with age—a most unusual circumstance in any population. Henry
and Cassel (30) ascribe this phenomenon to the fact that the subculture in
which the pilots live is highly structured and stable with established rules and
traditions, despite the danger of their occupation. Conversely, black persons

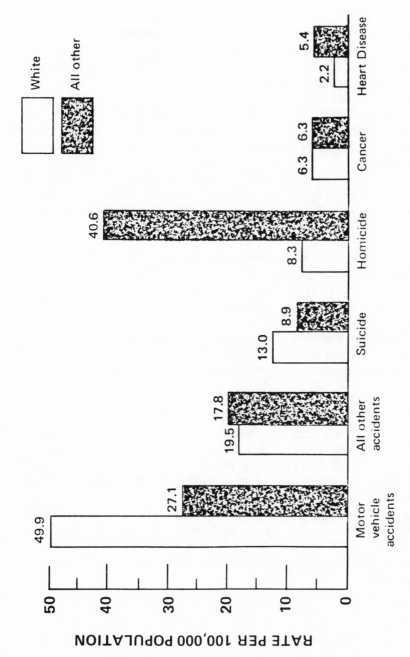

FIGURE 2. Major causes of death for ages 15–24 years: United States, 1978. (Based on data from National Center for Health Statistics Division of Vital Statistics.)

in the U.S. who are exposed to violence and police brutality, who live in crowded conditions in areas of social disorganization and economic deprivation, and whose personal and marital lives are disrupted have higher levels of blood pressure than their black peers living in middle-class neighborhoods in which these conditions do not prevail (31).

Thus, wartime experiences, civilian disasters, and strife promote high blood pressure. English civilians exposed to German aerial bombing attacks suffered an increase in perforations of peptic ulcer (32). Fear and anxiety may precipitate asthmatic attacks, the hyperventilation syndrome, and the irritable bowel syndrome (33).

Danger and fear may be associated with the onset of Graves' disease, especially in its acute form. Many of such patients are already programmed to respond to danger because they have a fear of dying. In the largest series of thyrotoxic patients ever published, 13% of 3,343 patients with Graves' disease had been involved in accidents, were otherwise injured, or had found themselves in a situation of imminent danger, and an additional 7% developed the disease following surgery (34).

Thyrotoxicosis—a generic name for a hypermetabolic state, of which Graves' disease is one example—often increases in incidence during wartime, as long as nutrition is adequate. Major increases in its incidence and prevalence occurred in Denmark and Norway during the German occupation during World War II (35). In countries not invaded, or in those in whom the German invaders starved the population, no such increases occurred.

The Psychobiology of Danger, Fear, and Anxiety

No one to my knowledge has studied the psychobiological correlates of the stress syndromes in man. But a literature is emerging on the psychobiological correlates of exposing human beings to situations that are objectively dangerous and, therefore, elicit fear, or have profound meanings and consequences and generate anxiety.

Stress theory does not predict the individual nature of these responses, nor the anticipatory nature of changes in heart rate (H.R.), blood pressure (B.P.), and free fatty acid (F.F.A.) levels. The sources of these individual differences in physiological responses have partly been identified.

They are:

1) The stereotyped individual nature of physiological responses: Lacey (36) has pointed out that different stimuli and contingencies produce similar responses in the same—but not in another—person. Hence, one source of differences between persons is the relatively character-

istic pattern of physiological responses of individuals, without regard to the manner in which they are incited. Conversely, the same frightening context produces highly individual behavioral and physiological responses across groups of subjects. Individual differences of this kind also characterize the responses of groups of animals to danger; species' differences are also seen.

2) The novelty, or the unpredictability of the situation.

3) The previous experiences the individual has had with the danger.

4) The role assigned to and carried out by the person in the situation of danger — whether, for instance, he is the leader or the follower.

5) The demand characteristics of the situation. For example, Miller and Bernstein (37) showed that under situations of low demand, the intercorrelation between the length of time claustrophobic patients remained in a small chamber, subjective anxiety, and heart and respiratory rate was -0.42, -0.56, and -0.51, respectively. Whereas, under conditions of high demand, there were no intercorrelations. Yet, in other situations, high demand characteristics produce positive correlations with hormonal measures, and low demand ones produce negative ones.

6) The quality of the performance: Does the person succeed or fail at it?

7) The manner in which the person copes with fear or defends himself against anxiety.

These statements are based on the following data obtained while studying certain groups of men carrying out tasks specific to their professions.

1) Examinations

A number of reports have appeared in the literature on the physiological changes accompanying the taking of important tests — such as final, oral, medical-licensure examinations. These habitually caused anxiety and raised B.P. levels to clinically hypertensive levels (above 140/90 mm Hg) in young physicians. The B.P. levels began to rise even before the examination began. Blood pressure levels in some candidates continued to remain elevated when the interrogation was over, but would rise again on requestioning. Individual patterns were seen, but every student showed B.P. increases. Von Uexküll and Wick (38) call this phenomenon "stress-hypertension." They believe that this form of high blood pressure may presage essential hypertension.

Free fatty acid levels increased significantly but only in the most anxious students taking examinations (39). Serum cholesterol levels increased in medical students taking a written examination by 10% to 25%, especially in those who performed poorly (40). Oral examinations seemed to mobilize some hormone levels and not others more than written examinations did. In 131 medical students (compared with 83 controls) a written exam raised human growth hormone (hGH) levels in 33%, and an oral examination raised them 49%. (The highest mean levels of hGH occurred in women students.) Serum insulin levels rose 45% and 43% respectively without changing blood glucose levels. Plasma renin levels rose by 44% after a written examination and 27% following an oral examination. Significant increases in heart rate (44%) occurred during the oral examination (41).

2) Public Presentations

Any young physician knows that one of the most fearsome experiences he must undergo in his early career is to present at Grand Rounds. With the development of reliable techniques for the estimation of epinephrine and norepinephrine in serum, these catecholamines have been measured in physicians making presentations which demand peak performance (42, 43).

Epinephrine levels rose sharply before and at the onset of the talk and then subsided during its course. Norepinephrine levels gradually increased and remained elevated throughout the entire period. Marked individual differences in levels attained and in individual patterns were observed. In some speakers the levels remained unchanged from the beginning to the end of the talk. The changes in catecholamine levels during the presentation differed from those seen during exercise when norepinephrine levels alone increase.

3) Dangerous Sports: The Effects of Driving a Racing Car

Racing a car is generally acknowledged to be one of the most dangerous sports ever invented by man, yet it entails minimal physical effort. Taggart and Carruthers (44) studied 16 drivers just before, during a three-hour period of driving, and immediately following a race. Total catecholamine levels were raised at the time the race began and in the period immediately after it. Most of the increase (86%) was due to elevations of norepinephrine levels. Levels of F.F.A. rose 125% before the race, peaked at its start, remained high after the race, and returned to resting levels after one hour. Triglyceride levels began to increase when the starter dropped his flag and continued to rise after the race was over. One hour later they were 111% above baseline levels. Cholesterol levels remained unchanged throughout the race. A strong positive correlation ($r = 0.81$) was present between total catecholamine levels below 2 μg/1 and F.F.A. levels. When the catecholamine levels were greater than 2 μg/1, the correlation was a mere $r = 0.31$.

This study confirms that F.F.A.s, which are readily measured in serum, are exquisitely sensitive to a wide variety of contingencies including dangerous and anxiety-provoking ones (45). They seem to increase in anticipation of these situations.

4) Parachute Jumping

Cardiorespiratory changes. Training in the use of a parachute is a reliable way of inducing fear even in experienced jumpers. Fenz and Epstein (46) compared 10 novice and 10 experienced jumpers while rating fear, heart (H.R.) and respiratory (R.R.) rates, and skin conductance before, during, and after a jump from 5,000 feet. The novices were frightened to the point of being disorganized in thought and behavior; most of them found the first jumps terrifying while some others found it thrilling.

In both experienced and novice jumpers, anticipatory fear manifested itself in the bus on the way to the airfield. But, in the experienced jumpers, fear declined at the point of maximum danger — when jumping out of the aircraft. During the actual fall, they were relatively relaxed. The novices, on the other hand, continued to experience mounting fear until they had landed. The R.R. was the first to increase; then the H.R. rose; and finally skin conductance fell in both groups. In experienced jumpers, the physiological changes peaked and then fell after they entered the aircraft, but, in the inexperienced ones, they continued to increase in the expected manner with the actual jump. Precise correlations between the fear self-ratings and the physiological changes occurred in the novices. In the experienced jumpers a dissociation between fear and the physiological changes took place while preparing for and engaging in the jump.

Even experienced jumpers perform differently when rated by two jumpmasters. Those who performed poorly had the greatest physiological changes. Their R.R.s rose sharply until the point that the engines of the aircraft were warming up and then plateaued, but their H.R.s continued to increase until the jump was completed. By contrast, in the good performers, the R.R.s first increased, then fell, and the H.R.s leveled off.

The experienced men who performed poorly showed physiological patterns reminiscent of novice jumpers. It follows that the individual manner in which persons respond psychophysiologically to a frightening situation depends on both their experience and their performance during it (47).

Hormonal responses. Fourteen young soldiers had blood drawn for prolactin (PRL), thyrotropin (TSH), and hGH before and after their first military parachute jump. Baseline values for all three hormones were measured at 6 A.M. and also 13 and three days before the jump. On the day of the jump samples were obtained at 6 A.M. and 1 P.M. The jump was made from 366 m altitude. A final blood sample was obtained on landing. There were significant increases in the mean levels of all three hormones as follows:

PRL: From 10.4 ng/ml to 19.3 ± 3.1 ng/ml (Range: 6.5 to 40 ng/ml)
TSH: 2.9 ± 0.6 μU/ml to 4.1 ± 0.6 μU/ml (Range: 1.8 – 9 mU/ml)
hGH: 4.2 ± 1.2 ng/ml to 13.6 ± 3.5 ng/ml (Range: 1 to 42 ng/ml)

The authors of this report discounted the effects of cold, exertion, and altitude on the changes in hormone levels. This was a "one-trial" study. It did not attempt to examine the effects of repeated exposure to jumping nor to account for the individual differences in hormonal responses in the 14 recruits (48). Ursin and his colleagues (49) carried out such a study on 44 young, novice soldiers undergoing parachute training. The patterns of fear displayed were similar to those seen in Fenz and his colleagues' studies (46, 47), previously reviewed.

But Ursin et al. reported that 13 of the 44 soldiers quit training after the first jump, during which they had experienced great fear, very high levels of epinephrine and norepinephrine, and elevated blood glucose, F.F.A.s, and testosterone levels. The remaining 31 soldiers performed variably. The good performers were relatively unafraid. They were impatient to try the jump, which they found thrilling, again. They had the highest F.F.A.s and moderate epinephrine and norepinephrine increases during the jump. As they became increasingly adept, the acute increases in these measures became less with each successive jump. Throughout the series their cortisol levels were low. Those who performed poorly throughout and claimed to be unafraid had the largest rises in serum cortisol and hGH levels. Only minor increases in epinephrine, norepinephrine, and PRL levels occurred. Those soldiers who ultimately failed the course had a rise in PRL and a fall in testosterone levels.

These studies document that the novelty of a dangerous situation, the manner in which persons react psychologically to it, and the manner in which they perform in it determine the nature and the extent of the physiological responses.

Until Ursin and his colleagues reported their work, most studies were devoted to the examination of a single, isolated variable — cortisol, a catecholamine, or hGH. This strategy has limited our understanding of the manner in which cardiovascular or hormonal patterns are generated during danger, fear, or anxiety. Only recently has it become apparent that different physiological patterns are developed in several different bodily systems depending upon the specific type of frightening situation, the attitude with which it is faced, and the performance and experience of the participants. Each of these modifies an integrated pattern of hormonal response: "Any. variable which can be described or measured independently is actually a component of several such patterns" (50, p. 218).

5) Training for or Actual Military Combat

Underwater demolition training is one of the most dangerous military procedures known: It consistently raised serum cortisol levels in men to three times normal levels (22 μg/dl). With the introduction of novel procedures or unfamiliar equipment—for example, scuba tanks and new masks—during such training, further increases of serum cortisol levels occurred. As soon as the new equipment was mastered, these additional levels returned to steady, high basal levels (51).

The landing of jet-fighter planes on aircraft carriers produces a high death or accident rate in pilots and their crews. The successful completion of any landing is always in doubt. Even experienced pilots were fearful; they rated themselves as *less* frightened than the crewmen who operated the plane's radar equipment. Yet the pilots showed a threefold increase in serum cortisol levels (from 4 to 13 μg/dl). The greatest increments occurred in the pilots during day landings despite the fact that landing at night is even more perilous. Even simulated landings in a laboratory were associated with a rise in cortisol levels in pilots (52).

3-Methoxy, 4-hydroxy phenylglycol (MHPG)—but not urine volume—rose significantly in the pilots and radar officers of U.S. Navy jet fighters making aircraft landings. The highest levels were obtained in pilots during actual night landings. Lesser increases in levels occurred during day landings. Simulated landings in a laboratory produced no changes in MHPG levels (53). (Norepinephrine is metabolized to MHPG. Twenty-five percent of all MHPG in urine is believed to derive from brain norepinephrine stores.)

The conclusion that the responsible person is more likely to secrete more corticosteroid than the subordinate one is substantiated by the observations made by Bourne and his co-workers (54, 55). They studied the experienced officers and men of a Green Beret combat unit in Vietnam, who were anticipating and experienced a pre-announced Viet Cong attack. The highest increases in levels of 17-hydroxycorticosteroid (17-OHCS) excretion occurred in the two officers and in the radio operator. In the enlisted men, the levels fell during the attack and then returned to baseline levels.

When other soldiers under fire are carrying out their customary duties and rituals with hope, or when resorting to prayer, seemingly oblivious to the threat of injury or death, they have lower urinary 17-OHCS levels than predicted by their body weight (54).

The acute psychobiological effects of dangerous situations have been described; the consequences of persistent or intermittent but long-term exposure to danger are largely unknown. By contrast, we are gradually learning about the long-term psychological, physiological, and health consequences of forced unemployment (56), and of separation or bereavement (57, 58), both of which rank high in any list of the stresses of everyday life.

Studies of the physiological responses of acutely dangerous situations in man do not confirm Selye's observations of a "nonspecific," ubiquitous adaptation syndrome. Because of a paucity of available biochemical techniques in his day, he emphasized the role of the adrenal corticosteroids in response to stress. Studies in man suggest that cortisol is produced and secreted in anticipation of a task, to novel and unpredictable situations, acutely painful stimuli, malnutrition, melancholic depression, and sustained danger, but not in everyone. The studies of cortisol responses in real-life dangerous situations and occupations begin to reveal the nature of the individual differences in hormone responses, including cortisol. What is dangerous to one person is a thrill to another. Novelty, ambiguity, and inexperience are more likely to mobilize physiological responses, especially heart rate, catecholamine, free fatty acids, and cortisol responses. Oral examinations are more likely to raise blood pressure levels than written ones. Good rather than poor performance is more habitually associated with a decline in physiological responses during the task. The demand characteristics of a situation in part determine physiological responses. Leaders are more responsive physiologically than followers in situations of danger. Note, however, that almost all the data on the physiological responses to danger are obtained in acute situations and with *male* subjects. The long-term physiological effects of danger, fear, and anxiety are unknown, and the empirical link of fear and anxiety to bodily disease states is at best tenuous.

An attempt has been made to underline the fact that fear and anxiety are truly biological — not only clinical — phenomena. They play a central role in alerting the organism to danger. Without it, men and animals would not survive predation and bodily harm; they would be selected out. The organism's performance in such situations, including its physiological responses, will determine whether it survives or not.

The Vicissitudes of Life as Stressful Events

The term "stress," with its implications of physical injury, catastrophe, disaster, horror, and inhumanity, has also been applied to the vicissitudes of daily life. Any demand on, change, or event in the lives of human beings is deemed to be potentially "stressful" because it is the setting in which illnesses and diseases of a variety of kinds may begin. Yet the same event or change is of no consequence to others.

From this perspective, human beings are repeatedly being buffeted by a sequence of storms, which submerge many, and from which others are saved by virtue of their own endeavors or the help of others. On the other hand, other authors give the reader the impression that the sea of life is constantly rough and that a new but relatively minor wave upsets the boat. Reading the literature on stress research inclines one to a tragic view of life.

What is remarkable in this view is that anyone at all is saved. The fact remains that most human beings survive the vicissitudes of daily life, much to the surprise of those who investigate stressful life events. On the other hand, most physicians who are interested in disease are dubious that the experiences of daily living could have anything to do with the onset of disease. Despite their reservations, some will still tell their patients to reduce stress, without specifying why such a reduction should be preventive or therapeutic.

Quantifying Life "Stress"

In the past 15 years, in an attempt to document the role of "stressful" life events in illness and disease, a major effort has been made to quantitate them with the aid of the Schedule of Recent Experience (S.R.E.) (Table 9) (59). The quantification of life changes and events allowed the investigator to predict that high S.R.E. scores—either due to a large number of changes or a few of the most profound sort—would be associated with the onset of illness and disease within a year.

An inspection of the individual items on the S.R.E. reveals that those with the highest loadings pertain to separation or disruption and loss of key personal relationships (a topic to which some of the rest of this chapter will be devoted). These disruptions by implication are not desirable in a variety of predictive and retrospective sudies of many different populations, where confirmation of the role of antecedent changes in the lives of patients and the onset of disease and illness have been obtained. Accidents, illness, and disease of a variety of kinds—myocardial infarction, mental illness, infections, the complications of pregnancy, gastric and duodenal ulcer, etc.—are more likely

TABLE 9

Results of Social Readjustment Rating Questionnaire

Life Event	Mean Value	Life Event	Mean Value
1. Death of spouse	100	24. Trouble with in-laws	29
2. Divorce	73	25. Outstanding personal achievement	28
3. Marital separation	65	26. Wife begins or stops work	26
4. Jail term	63	27. Begin or end school	26
5. Death of close family member	63	28. Change in living conditions	25
6. Personal injury or illness	53	29. Revision of personal habits	24
7. Marriage	50	30. Trouble with boss	23
8. Fired at work	47	31. Change in work hours or conditions	20
9. Marital reconciliation	45	32. Change in residence	20
10. Retirement	45	33. Change in schools	20
11. Change in health of family member	44	34. Change in recreation	19
12. Pregnancy	40	35. Change in church activities	19
13. Sexual difficulties	39	36. Change in social activities	18
14. Gain of new family member	39	37. Mortgage or loan less than $10,000	17
15. Business readjustment	39	38. Change in sleeping habits	16
16. Change in financial state	38	39. Change in number of family get-togethers	15
17. Death of close friend	37	40. Change in eating habits	13
18. Change to different line of work	36	41. Vacation	13
19. Change in number of arguments with spouse	35	42. Minor violations of the law	11
20. Mortgage over $10,000	31		
21. Foreclosure of mortgage or loan	30	Taken from Rahe, R. H. (1969) in *Psychotropic Drug*	
22. Change in responsibilities at work	29	*Response. Advances in Prediction*, May, P. R. A., and	
23. Son or daughter leaving home	29	Wittenborn, J. R., Illinois, p. 97.	

to begin after or at the time when life event scores increase, rather than at times when they are low (60, 61).

These studies deal with groups of individuals rather than with any single person; they are, therefore, subject to a logical error. It is a fallacy to believe that an association between two characteristics — the increased number of life events in an aggregation (population) of persons and illnesses and diseases (or any one of them) — will generalize to the same characteristics when measured across or in individuals (13, 62). In fact, some individuals with high life event scores seem impervious to illness and disease, while others with low scores do fall sick.

Furthermore, this line of investigation makes it impossible to predict the nature of the illness and disease from which the person will suffer. The S.R.E. also contains a tautology — illness, injury (and pregnancy) can be antecedents of illness, accidental injury, disease, and the complications of pregnancy!

The correlations in a large number of studies between the incidence and prevalence of symptoms of illnesses and diseases (including psychiatric ones) and life-change scores, although statistically reliable, are in the range of .2 to .3. They would, therefore, account for 4% to 9% of the variance. But this may be the wrong way of presenting the association of life events and illnesses. A better way is to calculate the population-attributable-risk percent. Using psychiatric cases only, 32% of psychiatric cases can be attributed to stressful life events; the figures rise to 41% when women patients are studied (63).

Because relatively little of the etiological variance of sickness is accounted for, it is not surprising that many authorities have concluded that this line of approach is unpromising (64, 65). Before coming to such a final conclusion, one might ask whether indeed there is any temporal relationship between life events and the onset of symptoms? This question arises because many deny the association which is based on retrospection: Subjects who are asked to look back one year in time in order to determine what has happened in their lives may be subject to all the familiar infirmities of human memory. Also, the spouses, or others, are often unable to remember the same set of events recalled by the subject (66, 67). The problems that an analysis of these investigations highlight are compounded by the fact that most studies have been cross-sectional and not longitudinal.

In order to circumvent these real difficulties, a prospective and longitudinal research strategy is called for — such as the one that was used by Grant and his colleagues (68). They compared and followed 72 psychiatric outpatients of a variety of diagnostic categories in a V.A. Mental Health clinic and 94 employees of the same facility (unfortunately not matched for age and socioeconomic status), for a period of three years. The S.R.E. and Symptom

Checklist were administered every two months. The data obtained were subjected to Fourier and spectral analyses. The results of this study show that in 42% of the patients and 31% of the control subjects symptoms increased and were time-locked with a rise in the number of undesirable life events. In another group of patients (8%) and subjects (12%), the two were 180° out of phase with each—a result which raises the question whether symptoms preceded life changes or followed them. In another group of patients and subjects, events were at times closely coordinated with an increase in symptoms; at other times they were not. Two groups remain: In one no coherent pattern emerges; in another life events changed but no symptoms were recorded.

Despite the limitations of such numerical assessment, the results of this study were impressive but not surprising. Many patients respond immediately with an increase in symptoms, but some do not; they only become more symptomatic after a time. The fact that the onset of symptoms is delayed in some persons should not be surprising. Some systems (e.g., the emotional and the immune systems) may respond with a significant latent period. Nor should it be surprising that some (9%) psychiatric patients do not respond at all to changes in their lives; they even seem impervious to certain categories of events in their lives.

The authors of this study are ruthlessly self-critical, forgetting that the nature of human nature is almost infinitely variable. It is this variation which confounds this particular line of research. Rather than abandoning it, a more constructive approach is to seek out those specific variables that mediate life events and sickness, to ask: Who are those persons who do or do not become ill and what are their social, intellectual, and other personal resources? What buffers certain people against disease? Are some individuals predisposed to one disease and not another? Why do they become sick at a particular age or on a particular day? What is the interaction of events in their lives and their chronic, daily burdens?

Stressful life events are dramatic occurrences which are recorded as major changes in the lives of people. They are generally not considered to be the straw that breaks a person's back, but a club. Life can be boring or constantly irritating, frustrating, or distressing. Work or marriage can be chronically demanding or troubling. Bosses can be tyrants. For a poor woman to raise children and have to support them by working can be burdensome. In fact, most people lead lives of quiet desperation. (These chronic life situations are called "strains," not "stresses," for reasons not fully explained.) Very often some relatively minor specific event—of a personal or financial nature, increasing lack of privacy, or a minor illness—tips the scale, and sickness ensues. The interaction of "strains" with "stresses" has hardly been studied. A chronic background of strain and distress, irritation, and frustration can lead to poor morale, depression, and disease — associations that have only recently been the subject of investigation (69, 70).

Modifiers of the Impact of Stressful Life Events

When the questions enumerated above are asked, one finds a number of answers which begin to explain the low correlations obtained between life events and disease onset. People vary in their responses to demands and events by virtue of their genetic endowment, age, life experiences, intelligence, enterprise, capacity for human relationship, wealth, and the meaning that events have for them. These differences have been explored in a limited manner; they are the topics of current stress research and are studied under the following headings:

1) Coping — Why does the manner in which demands and changes are dealt with reduce their impact?
2) Social support — Does the help, love, encouragement, and advice that other human beings provide really reduce the impact of life events?
3) Meaning — What do events, changes or demands mean to individuals?
4) Personality — What are the personal characteristics of those who survive and those who succumb?
5) Age — Events may have more of an impact at some ages than at others. Why?

Coping. The responses and behaviors of the victims of natural disasters are examples of one kind of coping. At first, fear and danger arouse them to an emergency. They are protected from its full impact by feeling numb. They are then impelled to save themselves, their kin, and others. Once the emergency is past, they rebuild their destroyed homes and community with or without the assistance of others. Evidence has also been presented that those who perform (or cope) well in acutely dangerous or meaningful situations (e.g., examinations) have different physiological responses than those who do not.

Even in these dire situations of disaster, the tasks at hand — survival and rebuilding — are clear, and the operations to be performed are specific and defined.

In contrast, the survival of victims of terrorism and persecution is uncertain; ambiguity is maximal. All control over personal destiny is taken away. Passivity, capitulation, submission, identification, and massive denial are engendered and may be the only ways of coping with and surviving such a situation. To take steps to escape or to fight back is to court injury and death.

Embedded in these examples are the major components of what is meant by coping processes. In order to fully understand them we need to know the nature of the task, how it is appraised, the individual meanings it has for the person, and the strategies and behavioral programs employed to deal with it. The appraisal and the meanings of the task and the manner of dealing with it are individual; each person has his own style of doing so, which varies also with his age, intelligence, and sociocultural background.

The process of coping entails cognitive appraisal of and programmatic actions for dealing with and solving demands, tasks, events, and experiences with or without success (71, 72). The task may be deemed feasible or not. If it is, the person may master it or fail at it. Each of these outcomes is accompanied by specific emotional responses — hope, pride, shame, despair, helplessness, etc. — against which one person may in turn have to protect himself, by "indirect coping" maneuvers. Alternatively, a task may be appraised unrealistically, and excessive, unproductive actions may be brought into play. There may be no appropriate programs for ambiguous or constantly changing situations. Some persons confronted with a novel situation have no learned program. Additionally, some persons cannot learn from experience, and, therefore, they never have acquired appropriate programs of coping with a task or problem.

The fact that most persons cope with the tasks of their everyday lives with or without the aid of other lives is one reason why there is no linear relationship between life events and disease onset. But the fact remains that we still do not know how most people cope successfully with migration, unemployment, bereavement, marriage, divorce, illness, and disease. Our knowledge of the stressful nature of these events derives from observations of those who have failed to cope with them.

Each of these categories of experience have personal meanings that cannot be studied quantitatively. In the ensuing account we shall see that work means different things to different people; therefore, each person assays unemployment in a different manner and copes with it in a specific fashion to reduce economic hardship (strain), avert a fall in self-esteem, and the incidence of depression. If supported by others, the unemployed person's self-esteem suffers less and he has a sense of mastery over the situation (6): Coping and support act on separate aspects of the responses to unemployment.

Social support. For the last 10 years, a number of investigators have studied the presumed role of social supports in buffering the effects of life events to reduce their deleterious effects (73, 74, 75). It is claimed that the availability of supports lowers, for example, the correlation between high life event scores and the complications of pregnancy (76), psychiatric symptoms (77), the dose of steroid needed to control the symptoms of asthma (78), and the number of swollen arthritic joints following the loss of a job (75).

Any available resource (including an inanimate one, e.g., money) may be supportive. Social supports, however, have also been defined quantitatively by the frequency and number of social interactions or by the degree of love, trust, advice, or help the stricken person can obtain from others. The interactions do not have to be actual; comfort flows from the belief (or perception) that help or support is available. When that perception is impaired, the mortality of elderly persons is increased; it is about one-and-a-half times greater than in those to whom actual, social interactions or relationships are available (79).

The literature on social supports contains an additional puzzling feature in the form of a tautology. To be specific, if a spouse dies, a significant event is recorded in the S.R.E. At the same time, one (or an additional) source of support is lost. In order to avoid this circularity, it is necessary to determine the level of support available prior to or at the time of the event, and not after it has occurred or sickness has begun; only then can it be established that social supports truly soften the impact of adverse events. (In short, longitudinal studies are called for.)

Social support may buffer the impact of change in a variety of ways. In research of this kind, the quality, not only the quantity of support and the amount, kind, and source, all need to be measured (65). Because this strategy has not yet been employed, the important idea that support buffers the unfortunate against the winds of change has not yet been established.

Should the buffering hypothesis be confirmed, strong support would be lent to the idea that human relationships are critical for the maintenance of health, especially in those persons who most rely on them — children, the infirm, the aged, the sick, psychiatric patients, and those whose behavior is inappropriate to their age (80).

The meaning of some events and experiences. Physicians do not concern themselves with the healthy; they are predominantly interested in the sick. As a result of their interest in patients, we have learned that disease and sickness can have a variety of different meanings. By virtue of these meanings sickness may or may not be distressing or disturbing.

Sickness may act as a challenge to be mastered. It may be a source of comfort, like an old "friend." Suffering may be enjoyed. It may seem to appear as an enemy to be fought and conquered. Relief from everyday cares and problems can be obtained by being sick. Disease and ill-health may even be prized. Some sicknesses, however, are a source of shame or a form of punishment. They can cut short all hope for and expectations of the future. The disabled or sick may feel irreparably damaged or disfigured. A pervasive feeling of loss is present in some patients, especially in those in whom a particular function (e.g., memory, vision, athletic prowess) is especially prized (72, 81).

The meaning of sickness and disease may have important practical implications. The prognosis for those who need to suffer with a disease is poorer than for those who wish to rid themselves of suffering. The meaning of sickness will determine not only its outcome, but also what coping efforts are made and how help is obtained and utilized.

Additional personal factors. Life event research carries with it the implication that certain groups of persons are essentially untouched by events while others succumb to them. This implication is correct; it is borne out by long-term studies of adults in a similar occupation and over the same period of life. Hinkle (82) found marked differences in the amount of illness and disease experienced by the individual members of his cohort. Disease and illness were not independent events randomly distributed in a population. Not everyone of his subjects was at equal risk; some were more likely to fall ill than others, not only from one but several illnesses or diseases afflicting several of their organ systems. Furthermore, their disabilities, due to a variety of apparent causes, clustered over time; those who are disabled have several illness and disease episodes in some years and few in others.

These clusters of illness and disease coincided with increased demands upon them; with periods of unhappiness with their work, lot in life, and family lives; with difficulties in their relationships to others; in short, with discontent and disappointment. In contrast, the healthy subjects in Hinkle's cohort were people whose social backgrounds, personal aspirations, and interests coincided with the circumstances in which they found themselves. They fitted their environments, enjoyed their work, and liked their families and associates; they were, in other words, content.

Another kind of prospective study was carried out by Vaillant (83). This 30-year, longitudinal study of Harvard undergraduates found that age-inappropriate, adaptive-defensive patterns of coping with the environment and of defending against personal distress and problems enhanced the likelihood of a significant morbidity and mortality from a variety of diseases. The members of Vaillant's cohort did have similar educational opportunities but did not have similar backgrounds, occupations, or personal lives after graduation from college. Nonetheless, his study suggests that personal factors play a significant role in determining who remains healthy and who does not.

The kind of person who falls ill is less mature and has fewer coping skills: For different reasons, children, the mentally defective or impaired, widows, and the lonely and elderly do not have the education, information, knowledge, social supports, or interpersonal skills to cope with events and solve the problems created for them.

Many adult persons who are ill share certain psychological characteristics. Ruesch (84), in particular, stressed the age-inappropriate behavioral and psychological features of adult patients that made them particularly unadapted to and unable to cope with their environments. He listed their features as impaired or arrested social learning; a propensity for imitating rather than learning from others; a tendency to express thought and feeling in direct physical action; dependency on others; passivity; childlike ways of thinking; lofty and unrealistic aspirations; difficulties in assimilating and integrating life experiences; a reliance on securing love and affection from other persons; and, above all, an inability to master changes in their lives or to learn new techniques for overcoming challenge and the deprivation of their wishes. Additional psychological features have been described: Many patients are unable to be aware of their own emotions, which serve as alerting signals of danger and distress. They do not resort to constructive imagination in coping with and solving problems and are preoccupied with the concrete specifics, rather than the meaning and significance of events in their lives (85, 86, 87).

The more immature or adaptively inept the person is, the less capable he is of coping alone or appropriately, and the stronger the influence of the social field on him (88). Therefore, events alone do not linearly produce disease; they only do so in interaction with their meaning for the person, his manner of coping with it, and coping capacities.

Our understanding of the difference between those who fall ill and those who do not is enhanced when the psychological differences between the two groups are specified. The differences also have a history. Psychological maturity and adaptive capacities are maturational and developmental concepts; they are the product of genetic endowment, adequate nutrition and child-rearing practices, education, and learning, and of an "average expectable environment" (89). They are at base biological concepts that define man's transactions with his ever-changing social, economic, political, human, and nonhuman environment. Conversely, social stability is one factor that protects persons against illness and disease.

Age as a variable. The age of a person is an important variable in determining the nature and impact of life events. Certain events are more likely to occur at one period during the life cycle than at another. Children have to learn the dangerous nature of certain situations; they may not have learned coping programs or skills requisite to mastering demands and challenges. They usually do not know where to obtain needed information; if they do, they may reject advice. Finally, they usually become decreasingly reliant on others as they mature and develop. Later, in adolescence, there is a background of chronic academic and social concerns. Upon this are grafted dramatic events, such as injuries and accidents, falling in and out of love, and unwanted pregnancies.

Younger and less-skilled workers are more likely than older ones to lose their jobs. Younger people marry, and they divorce more than older ones who, in turn, are more likely to become sick or lose a spouse due to divorce or disease. The behavioral progams for coping with tasks and challenges are stored in memory. As memory fades with age, the programs can no longer be retrieved or are lost altogether.

Yet many elderly persons seem impervious to change but are vulnerable to hardships (90). As long as they have a modicum of good health and comfort, interests, and some meaningful activity, dignity, and control over their remaining years, they may not become ill. In fact there is a body of literature which suggests that there may be an inverse relationship between scores on the S.R.E. and age (91, 92). However, many older persons experience fatigue, loneliness, unsympathetic people, disappointments, and chronic infirmity, none of which are listed in the S.R.E. Lazarus (92) has pointed out that events, whether chronic or acute, are appraised differently at different ages. A disease such as cancer may be responded to with rage in the young and with less anxiety or with resignation or relief in older people.

Elderly persons tend to restrict their lives in order to avoid situations with which they cannot cope. Or they pretend that they are more capable than they know themselves to be. They may become irascible when challenged. In fact, the most frequent coping strategies of the elderly are avoidance, restriction, denial, minimization, confrontation, reminiscing, and somatization.

There is little longitudinal information about stress, meaning, coping, and supports throughout the life cycle; most of the information derives from cross-sectional studies. Furthermore, the same stressful event or strain may lead to disease at one age and not another, because the physiological response systems have or have not developed.

ECONOMIC CHANGE AS A STRESSOR

Our knowledge of the effects of specific stressful events, the manner with which they are coped, the roles played by personal factors, support systems, and the age of the subject, and their individual meanings is still incomplete.

Two of the events that have been most fully studied in their psychobiological panoply are 1) economic change and 2) loss, separation, and bereavement. Both are frequent occurrences and illustrate the need to specify with precision the nature of these changes and the complex nonlinear responses they engender. This very complexity and nonlinearity makes the stress concept meaningless because it is too general and because its explanatory power is vanishingly small.

The nature of the stressor — economic change — requires further specification, because it may:

1) Produce real job loss, reduction of income, ability to pay rent and other bills — all probably undesirable experiences — by virtue of a shrinking economy;
2) Lead to a new job opportunity, expansion of personal indebtedness, or relocation — all potentially stressful — at times of economic instability;
3) Lead to wished for promotions or new jobs, but enhance responsibility, work load, or success. (Despite their desirability, such events may contain the seeds of future stresses.) Such professional changes may occur at times of economic expansion.

Most studies deal with the consequences of economic contraction affecting the incidence of illness and injury by producing job loss and financial hardship. However, such studies will need to specify whether the associations hold across all socioeconomic and age groups.

It follows that economic change requires exact specification. The evidence to date shows that economic contraction is most likely to produce distress, illness, and disease in groups of persons, while economic instability may affect certain individuals only.

Unemployment as a Stressful Event

Forced unemployment uncovers the vital role of work in the lives of human beings. Work is valued for reasons other than earning a living. Work ensures mental and physical activity. It may heighten social status. The goals and purposes of work are shared. Work structures the day. It assures human contacts and friendships. It promotes shared experiences with persons outside the family.

Unemployment affects men less when they merely depend on their jobs to earn a living than it does to those who have to rely on good relationships with fellow workers, take pride in their skills, and work with others towards a common purpose. For some, work is an escape from marital discord, a source of pride and dignity, or a way of maintaining authority in the family. The psychosocial consequences of unemployment, therefore, have a greater impact on some men than do the economic ones (93).

Changes in Psychological Status With Unemployment

The loss of work is frequently followed by a grief reaction—a sense of shock and disbelief, followed by preoccupation with what work meant—in the several senses already enumerated. Anxiety, insomnia, fatigue, anorexia, and loss of weight may occur. Unemployment may also be followed in some but not all men by a genuine clinical depression accompanied by suicidal thoughts, requiring antidepressant treatment. Changes in behavior, including the increased use of alcohol and tobacco, occur. Bodily injury in various forms of accidents is increased, and unemployed men as a group perform more acts of violence (56, 94).

Changes in Health Status With Unemployment

The unemployed show a marked increase in visits to medical facilities. In the period between 1965-75 sickness certification was increased in one English study by 77%. (Conversely, unemployment was caused by sickness or disability in 21%.)

The nature of the complaints in British men 17-64 years of age ranged all the way from illness (94)—headaches, backaches, itching skin—to significant increases in mortality due to cardiovascular disease, suicide, and of accidents (Table 10). The prevalence of bronchial asthma, chronic bronchitis, obstructive lung disease, and ischemic heart disease (I.H.D.) was raised (95, 96). Even the threat of unemployment may raise the mortality from I.H.D. in men aged 55-64 years. In another study, the incidence of peptic duodenal ulcer increased following unemployment (94).

Men with prior histories of poor health or recurrent disabilities which they had overcome suffered relapses on losing their jobs. Maternal and infant mortality increased in the families of unemployed men.

Changes in Physiology With Unemployment

The metabolic changes that occur with unemployment are some of the very ones that place men at risk for ischemic heart disease. Kasl and Cobb (97) found that men who lost their jobs showed increases in their blood pressure. Even the anticipation of the closing of an industrial plant was associated with elevations of serum uric acid (SUA), but not of serum cholesterol levels (SCL).

TABLE 10
Men, 17–64 Years, England & Wales: Per 10^5

	Employed	Unemployed Seeking Work
Mortality		
All causes (standardized)	86	130
Circulatory Diseases	88	115
Accidents	93	222
Violence		
Suicide		

When new employment was found, SUA levels returned to normal. The greater the anguish occasioned by losing the job, the higher the SUA levels. Men who anticipated the closing of the plant by resigning and looking for new employment had high but stable SUA levels. SCLs only rose after the men had lost their jobs; they remained high during the entire period they were without work and only fell on reemployment (98). Saxena (99) reported additional changes: Involuntary unemployment was associated with an increase in serum levels of low density, and a fall in high density lipoproteins. (Changes in serum lipids, increases in blood pressure, alcohol consumption, cigarette smoking, and changes in diet all enhance the risk for ischemic heart disease.)

Effects on the Family

The wives of the newly unemployed, if themselves not working, were similarly affected in regard to their health as their husbands were. Additionally, an increase in the incidence of peptic duodenal ulcer occurred in these women (54). Yet, if they worked, their health improved.

Children under but not over the age of 12 are affected in several ways by their father's unemployment: Truancy from school; a fall in the quality of their school work; more physical injuries; and an increase in visits to the doctor occur (56).

Coping With Unemployment

Not all men who become unemployed become depressed, fall ill, or develop a disease and die. The correlation between job loss and depression is, nonetheless, significant ($r = .34$, $p = < .05$). In these studies (6) 19% of the variance is accounted for by unemployment. In those men who became depressed, a fall in income increased economic problems in their families, causing them to feel less of themselves and lowering their sense of mastery.

There are several ways of coping with unemployment that reduce the economic strain and loss of self-confidence, but they do *not* prevent the loss of mastery. Successful coping strategies entail seeking information about or looking for a new job, minimizing the importance of money and of income, reassuring oneself that one is not so badly off after all. On the other hand, some make increasing demands upon themselves, feel more pressured, and become more irritable (100).

Pearlin and his colleagues (6) also showed that the emotional support of family and friends does not reduce the strain of economic worry but prevents loss of self-confidence and of mastery in the unemployed. These studies demonstrate that coping and social support act on different aspects of job loss. Studies of the unemployed show that, depending on the meaning of work, differences in reactions occur. Nevertheless, many of the psychological reactions to job loss share certain common features with other kinds of losses. The unemployed often go through a stage of shock, followed by a stage of realization, reminiscent of grief reactions. The unemployed and their families are at risk for illness and disease (101, 102) and behavior change. Relevant psychological effects are seen that place such persons at risk for ischemic heart disease but may be different from those seen on bereavement and separation.

Loss, Separation, and Bereavement

The S.R.E. assigns the highest weighting to bereavements due to the death of an intimate relative. The study of patients after the onset of a variety of diseases provides abundant evidence that separation or bereavement is the context in which they begin. Human relationships, it seems, are crucial to the maintenance and restoration of physical health and of psychological well-being. Their disruption is a potent factor in ill-health and disease. It also seems likely that human relationships play a central role in the proper development, maintenance, and usual regulation of bodily systems; this assertion stems from the study of young animals in which premature separation affects every bodily system and places them at risk for a variety of diseases (57, 58). The range of disturbances produced are not predicted by stress theory.

Separation or bereavement may be especially poignant for adults if they recapitulate a loss in childhood. The usual or the aberrant responses to loss may also occur when prized attributes (e.g., beauty, dignity, youth, strength, income, wealth, intelligence, skills, memory, ideals, occupations, body functions or parts, health, and the sense of well-being) are lost. Loss may be anticipated, and mourning may be over by the time the actual loss occurs.

Grief

The usual response to loss is grief (103). As in the responses to natural disasters, the following phases occur:

1) Phase of shock (Protest). It begins immediately and lasts from one to 14 days and is usually not associated with anxiety but with disbelief, a sense of being numb, shocked, lost, bereft, or helpless. The grief-stricken person may grope about and not feel like eating or sleeping. The person cries. The throat feels tight. Sighs are expressed. Nausea and "hollowness" in the chest and abdomen are experienced. The full reality and impact of the loss are hidden by the sense of disbelief, numbness, and protest.

2) Phase of despair, realization, and grief (Duration: six to eight months). After about two weeks, the full impact and actuality of the loss hits the bereaved, as disbelief is dissipated. Crying may increase and come in waves. The bereaved feels drained; the world seems empty; nothing is very enjoyable; none of the basic life functions matter, and they (e.g., food intake, sleep) may be neglected or disrupted.

The bereaved constantly thinks of and frequently dreams about the departed person. The departed person's faults are forgotten; he is often idealized. Some survivors reproach themselves for not having done enough for or regret having held grudges against the lost one. Anger at, neglect of, and some guilt about the deceased may occur in the grieving person, but usually these feelings are transient. Brief periods of imagining that the departed person is still alive may occur; strangers may even be misidentified as the lost person.

Although this period is said to last six to eight months or longer (104), it may also last a lifetime; for example, a young couple who loses an only child may grieve for eternity. In other instances, grief recurs on the anniversary of the death or birthday of the deceased.

3) Phase of resolution (Duration: weeks or months). The bereaved person gradually resumes his life, interests, work, and relationships. The future no longer seems bleak. He returns to the world that seems fuller and more rewarding.

The bonds that held the survivor to the deceased are loosened, and his emotional currency is invested elsewhere. The reality of the loss is accepted; crying spells diminish; feelings of emptiness are dissipated. The recurrent memories of the departed fade.

The feelings of grief and the manner of coping with it (the disbelief, then the constant recall in memory of the past relationship, followed by the loosening of the bond that held it together) are attenuated by the support and empathy of other persons. All cultures make provisions for sharing bereavement by death through the agency of mourning rituals.

There are, however, other methods of handling grief: Men in our culture find it harder than women do to cry. In still others angry feelings may supplant grief. Physicians notoriously protect themselves against feeling it and prevent their patients from expressing it.

The consequence of not being permitted or encouraged to express grief may be dire: feelings of shame and depression; resorting to other measures (such as drugs and hypnotics); attempts at suicide; and physical symptoms designed to elicit attention, sympathy, and help.

Pathological Mourning and Grief

Loss and bereavement can also incite pathological mourning; it may begin in the immediate aftermath of the loss or may be delayed in onset. This form of mourning consists of a complex mixture of love, longing, and the need for the lost person, mixed with hatred, anger, and bitterness. Feelings of vengefulness produce a cascade of anguish, guilt, and fears of retribution and the need to make amends, or pleas for forgiveness. Pathological mourning can be anticipatory: It may also occur in childhood and is often again induced in adulthood by seemingly trivial losses (105, 106), or in persons incapable of expressing any feelings (107). Pathological mourning occurs when certain kinds of people (those described earlier, who rely on others and are not capable of mature relationships) are bereft by unexpected or unusual circumstances — murder, suicide, or disappearance (108, 109). The survivor's guilt stems from the belief that he wittingly or unwittingly drove the partner away (or to suicide).

Pathological mourning (distorted grief) is a major risk factor for depression and/or suicide, for the acquisition of the departed's symptoms and behaviors, and for a life of bitterness, social isolation, and pain. The mourner may distract himself with restless overactivity in order to remain oblivious to the profound sense of loss and the cascade of painful feelings it has engendered.

Grief and pathological mourning may not be expressed at all following a loss. The onset may be delayed; symptoms may occur only on key anniversaries or, as noted, after seemingly trivial losses, and be associated with the onset of disease. Survivors may deny the death of a relative and live in a make-believe world in which it never occurred. Other people disguise their grief in chronic anger or become touchy or impassive. They may be incapable of experiencing or expressing any feelings.

Major depressive syndromes may have their onset with a latent period of weeks or months after a loss or bereavement; such patients do not make causal connections between the event and the illness and deny that they feel sad. Or, delayed grief reactions may be transmuted into a variety of pain and hyperventilation syndromes.

Following the death of a relative, some survivors, rather than feeling grief, remarry quickly (after a spouse has died) or try to replace a dead child by becoming pregnant or by adopting one. Sooner or later they become symptomatic if they have never mourned their immediate loss.

Because of their age-inappropriate, psychological makeup, those who mourn pathologically are particularly needy for encouragement, ventilation of their complex feelings, and advice (110).

Psychobiology of Loss and Separation in Young Animals

Hofer (57), on the basis of his extensive experience, has pointed out that in both animals and man separation can be divided into two phases: The acute protest phase is seen in both infants and adults (Table 11*). Out of this phase a chronic, background disturbance develops. In the adult, the protest phase corresponds in time and quality with the phase of shock, despair, and realization (Table 12*).

We know a great deal more about the physiological changes in young animals following separation (Table 11) than about those in adults. Young animals show a variety of psychobiological responses to being prematurely separated from their mothers. A careful analysis of the effects of separation indicates that it is not a global experience. In fact, the experience of separation is highly discriminated: each behavioral or physiological system responds to a separate interaction between the mother and her infant; separation terminates the mother's inputs to her infant (Table 13*) (summarized in References 57, 58, 111, 112, 113). Rats separated at 15 days of age show increased motor activity in the form of self-grooming, rearing up, moving about, and squealing. These behaviors are suppressed by the physical presence of the mother who provides warmth and tactile stimulation. These young animals are unable to regulate their body temperature; when it falls, their activity declines. In separated rats with low body temperature the levels of their brains catecholamines, protein, and nucleoprotein fall (111).

---

*Tables 11, 12, and 13 are reprinted by permission of Elsevier Science Publishing Co., Inc. from Hofer, M.A.: Presidential address. Relationships as regulators: A psychobiological perspective on bereavement. *Psychosom. Med., 46*, p. 183, 1984.

TABLE 11
Infant Separation Responses

BEHAVIOR	PHYSIOLOGY
A. ACUTE – 'PROTEST' PHASE, LASTING MINUTES-HOURS.	
AGITATION	↑HEART RATE
VOCALIZATION	↑CORTISOL
SEARCHING-INACTIVITY	↑CATECHOL AMINES
B. CHRONIC – SLOW-DEVELOPING 'DESPAIR' PHASE, LASTING HOURS-DAYS.	
↓SOCIAL INTERACTION, ↓PLAY	↓BODY WEIGHT
MOUTHING, ROCKING	SLEEP DISTURBANCE:
HYPO – OR HYPER-RESPONSIVE	↓REM ↑AROUSALS
↓OR ↟FOOD INTAKE	METABOLIC:
POSTURES AND FACIAL EXPRESSION	↓CORE TEMP
OF SADNESS	↓O_2 CONSUMPTION
	CARDIOVASCULAR:
	↓CARDIAC RATE,↑RESISTANCE
	↑ECTOPIC BEATS
	ENDOCRINE:
	↓GROWTH HORMONE (↓ODC)

TABLE 12
Bereavement — Human Adult

BEHAVIOR   PHYSIOLOGY

A. ACUTE EPISODES - WAVES OF DISTRESS, LASTING MINUTES

   AGITATION   TEARS

   CRYING   SIGHING RESPIRATION

   AIMLESS ACTIVITY-INACTIVITY   MUSCULAR WEAKNESS

   PREOCCUPATION WITH IMAGE OF
      DECEASED

B. CHRONIC, BACKGROUND DISTURBANCE, LASTING WEEKS-MONTHS

   SOCIAL WITHDRAWAL   ↓BODY WEIGHT

   ↓CONCENTRATION, ↓ATTENTION   SLEEP DISTURBANCE

   RESTLESS, ANXIOUS   MUSCULAR WEAKNESS

   ↓OR ↑FOOD INTAKE   CARDIOVASCULAR:

   POSTURES AND FACIAL EXPRESSIONS   ENDOCRINE:
      OF SADNESS

   ILLUSIONS....HALLUCINATIONS   IMMUNOLOGICAL:

   DEPRESSED MOOD

TABLE 13
Infant Behavioral and Bodily Symptoms Which Are Regulated by Specific
Inputs Provided by the Mother

INFANT SYSTEMS		MATERNAL REGULATIONS
BEHAVIORAL		
ACTIVITY LEVEL	↑↓	BODY WARMTH
NOVELTY		TACTILE AND OLFACTORY
SUCKING		
-NUTRITIVE	↓	MILK (DISTENTION)
-NON-NUTRITIVE	↓	TACTILE (PERIORAL)
NEUROCHEMICAL		
CNS: NE, DA	↑	BODY WARMTH
CNS: ODC	↑	TACTILE (DORSAL)
METABOLIC		
O_2 CONSUMPTION	↑	MILK (SUGAR)
SLEEP-WAKE CYCLES		
REM	↑	PERIODCITY MILK AND TACTILE
AROUSALS	↓	" " " " "
CARDIOVASCULAR		
HEART RATE (BETA-ADRENERGIC)	↑	MILK (INTEROCEPTORS)
RESISTANCE (ALPHA-ADRENERGIC)	↓	" "
ENDOCRINE		
GROWTH HORMONE	↑	TACTILE (DORSAL)

Specific areas of the infant rat's body are stimulated by the mother. She licks the back of the neck of the infant. She picks them up by the scruff of the neck. When not stimulated at this site, levels of growth hormone and ornithine decarboxylase in the heart and brain fall (114, 115, 116).

The touch of the nipple on the infant's lips increases non-nutritive sucking which is diminished in the mother's absence. The sense of smell is critical to the attachment of the infant to the nipple, because the areolar glands appear to produce a chemically-unidentified pheromone which attracts the infant. This substance is under the control of oxytocin, which in turn is released in the mother rat by suckling. When this pheromone is washed off, or the olfactory epithelium of the infant is destroyed, the infant does not attach itself to the nipple and begins to demonstrate the motor behaviors seen in separated infants.

Nutritive suckling in infants declines in separated rats and is restored when milk distends the stomach. The heart and respiratory rate of baby rats falls 30% within two to four hours following separation. Only feeding milk, not the physical presence of the mother, restores the heart rate. This effect is mediated by a reflex whose efferent loop is the beta-adrenergic, sympathetic, cardioaccelerator nerve. Milk also regulates the peripheral resistance of young animals, which rises with an increase in alpha-adrenergic, sympathetic tone in the separated rats deprived of milk (111).

These infant animals on separation also show a profound sleep disturbance, consisting of a delay in the onset of sleep, frequent awakenings, and a decrease in activated (rapid eye movement) sleep. The intermittent infusion of milk restores sleep to normal in separated 15-day-old rats.

Milk restores the metabolic rate of separated animals and assures the normal development of thermoregulation of young rats. While still poikilothermic, their body temperature is also regulated by the temperature of the nest, which in turn is determined by the mother's and litter mates' body temperatures. Proper nutrition may also regulate the usual development of immune function, and levels of the catecholamine-synthesizing enzymes in the adrenal medulla are reduced in weaned mice when they are separated and socially isolated (117, 118, 119). Separated infant monkeys rock themselves, presumably to provide their own vestibular stimulation of which they have been deprived in the absence of a mother who rocked them while transporting them (120).

These observations document the validity of Beach's (14) injunction, previously quoted, and cast serious doubt on a global and vague concept such as "stress." Because separation is cited as a major stress for human beings, our understanding of its psychobiology will only be advanced by a refined analysis of its effects. Future studies will have to ask the question about what specific facets of the interaction between two or more human beings or animals are altered by separation. What is the bereaved person bereft of? Is it the touch, sound, smell, sight, love, hatred, support, or income of the departed person? And how do these deprivations specifically affect the bereaved?

Psychobiology of Loss and Separation in Adults

The psychobiological correlates of separation in adult persons or animals have not yet been investigated in depth or in detail. (An extensive literature exists on the psychobiology of depressed mood states; it will not be reviewed here.)

In a pioneer investigation, Wolff and his colleagues (121) studied the parents of children who were dying of leukemia. After an initial period of shock, disbelief, and grief on being told about their child's illness, these parents gradually came to accept it by inquiring about it. Their sense of responsibility for the illness could be dispelled by a frank discussion of its nature, by information about treatment, and, finally, by advice and sympathy concerning the anticipated loss of their child.

At each stage of this process, Wolff and his colleagues accurately predicted the 17-OHCS levels in the parents. Their criteria for predicting these levels were the "integrity" of inferred psychological defenses (such as repression, denial, isolation, and identification) and the extent of emotional arousal (especially of unpleasant feelings).

They studied the characteristic differences among individual parents, with the hypothesis in mind that the more effectively a person defends himself against impending loss, the lower will be his mean 17-OHCS excretion rate. In 23 of the 31 instances, predictions were made from the psychological data obtained of the levels of 17-OHCS excretion. The results supported the hypothesis that the more effective the defenses, the lower the mean 17-OHCS excretion level. Therefore, one of the implications of this study is that the baseline level of an individual's 17-OHCS excretion may reflect the effectiveness of psychological defenses or other ways of coping. And, indeed, the same conclusion was reached for many years by many investigators (122). However, it may not be correct in the sense that both adrenal cortical excretion levels (or cortisol production and secretion) and coping strategies, although correlated, may reflect two separate abiding characteristics of persons; therefore, they are not causally related.

Nonetheless, loss and bereavement do have significant effects on the immune system. Bartrop and his coworkers (123) studied the stimulation of phytohemaglutinin and concavalin A — both mitogens — on the incorporation of thymidine into the lymphocytes of widows and an age-matched control population. The lymphocyte responses in the widows were lower and took six weeks to show themselves. The same result was obtained in a longitudinal study on men, 33 to 76 years of age, whose wives were dying of breast cancer (124). (Idoxuridine incorporation after mitogen stimulation was used in this study.) There were significant changes in the spouses after the wife's death. Idoxuridine incorporation was significantly lower after the first month following the spouse's demise and not before it. Recovery of function began after that and was partially completed after one year. This study also demonstrated that B- and T-cell numbers were not altered. Follow-up reports on these widowers have not appeared to date. It would be most interesting to know if this suppression of T-cell function is clinically meaningful — whether for example they showed an increase in morbidity, infections, or malignant diseases.

Immunoglobulin levels may be affected by combinations of the stress of examinations and by maintenance of personal relationships or not. Salivary secretory immunoglobulin A is higher in students who maintain close, supportive ties with each other and falls less during examinations than in students who are mainly interested in grades and power. In this second group, the immunoglobulin levels continued to decline even after the examination was over (125).

Elderly persons languishing in institutions frequently do not interact with relatives, friends, fellow inmates, and staff. The effects of such deprivation, isolation, and loss can be devastating psychologically, physiologically, and medically. Systematic attempts at reversing this form of deprivation have now been made. As the result of reversing the social isolation of persons (with an average age of 78 years), physical and hormonal changes occurred when they were compared with similar persons who were allowed to remain by themselves. Specifically, the treated group did not lose physical stature; they remained at the same height. Estradiol and testosterone levels fell continuously in the men who remained by themselves, whereas their levels increased in men in the experimental group. Plasma growth hormone levels increased. Dehydroisoandrosterone levels rose significantly in the first three months of increasing human contact and then fell in the socially stimulated group but continued to fall in those in whom human contact continued to remain minimal. The same trends in hormonal levels were seen in the women who became less isolated, but the hormonal changes were not as great (126).

These results are relevant to the topic of loss and bereavement. They show that human relationships alter hormonal levels even in the elderly.

The Onset of Illness and Disease in the Setting of Loss

For not only scientific but preventive reasons, the role of bereavement in disease onset should become a central concern of every health worker. Abundant observations have been recorded that the health of about 67% of widows declines within one year of bereavement (127, 128), and psychiatric morbidity increases. Parkes (129), in a study of patients admitted to a psychiatric hospital, found that the number of patients whose illness followed the loss of a spouse was significantly greater than anticipated for people of that age and social group. Major depressions are particularly frequent in bereaved persons; in one study 45% became severely depressed within one year after their loss (130, 131). Such depressions enhance the risk of suicide, which then becomes another (but not the only) cause for the known increases in mortality observed in survivors six months after the loss (132, 133, 134).

Bereaved persons not only show a decline in health, and an increase in morbidity and mortality, but they also change their habits. They smoke more cigarettes and drink more alcohol—known risk factors for a variety of diseases—and use more "tranquilizers" (128).

Less believable to many physicians are the observations that losses are the settings in which major medical diseases begin. Schmale (135), postulating that object loss and depression are often the setting in which disease occurs, studied 42 patients, selected for age (18–45 years) and to some extent for social class, who were admitted to a general medical service with diagnoses ranging from hysterical conversion symptoms to aseptic meningitis. Shortly after admission each patient was interviewed using the conventional, open-ended psychiatric interview. Special attention was paid to a history of loss or change in relationship with a highly valued object, and the nature of the loss was operationally divided into four categories: 1) actual loss; 2) threatened loss; 3) "symbolic" loss; and 4) no loss. In 16 of 42 instances, either the patient reported or the investigator inferred that a loss, or significant change in relationships to others, had occurred within 24 hours of the appearance of symptoms of the disease. In another 15 patients, such loss or change occurred within the week prior to the onset of illness. Thus, 31 of 42 patients experienced the onset of an illness within one week of a significant loss. Another eight patients gave a similar history for the month prior to the onset of illness. Schmale also noted that 35 of the 42 patients experienced real or threatened loss in the first 16 years of their lives. Many of these persons had unresolved conflicts with respect to these events, which were rekindled by their present illness.

A number of studies of specific diseases and the setting in which they begin have supported Schmale's observations. Real or threatened separation and bereavement have been cited as one specific factor contributing to the onset of a variety of diseases – anorexia nervosa and bulimia (136, 137), autoimmune diseases (106), bronchial asthma (138), malignancies (139, 140), diabetes mellitus (141, 142), peptic duodenal (143) and gastric ulcer (144), leukemia (145), Graves' disease (146), essential hypertension (143, 147), congestive heart failure (148), myocardial infarction (133), abdominal pain (149), ulcerative and granulomatous colitis (150), tuberculosis (151), the complications of pregnancy (76), postpartum depression (152), and most major psychiatric illnesses (77, 131). The prognosis of myocardial infarction is considerably worse in widowers than in age-matched married men (153).

Young and his colleagues (154), studying mortality among widowers, found that 213 of 4,486 widowers, 55 years old and older, died within the first six months of the loss of their spouse, an increase of about 40% above that expected for married men of the same age. Kraus and Lilienfeld (155) noted that the mortality rate of persons of both sexes, who had lost a spouse, was increased, and that there was a mortality in excess of that expected in those under 35 years of age.

In a recent study by Helsing and his colleagues (156), Young and his colleagues', but not Kraus and Lilienfeld's, observations were confirmed. It is now quite clear that, at least, widowers are considerably more likely to die between the ages of 55 and 74 years. The death of a spouse in that age group of men enhances the risk of death, especially of ischemic heart disease, for reasons and by mechanisms that we do not understand. It is very likely that bereavement acts as a "permissive" factor in patients with already present coronary artery disease. Loss may play a more direct pathogenetic role in the onset of other diseases.

In all of these studies it is still not certain what form of grief is more likely to be correlated with disease onset. Is it the fully developed grief reaction or pathological mourning in its delayed or distorted forms?

Developing Schmale's work in the area of giving up and its primary feelings of hopelessness and helplessness, Engel (157) has hypothesized that the "giving-up, given-up complex" is the emotional setting in which most disease occurs. He estimates that this "complex" precedes the onset of illness in 70% to 80% of patients. As with all stressful stimuli, Engel notes that it is difficult to appreciate which external stimulus will be critical to a particular person; the determining factor will be how the individual responds – i.e., just what constitutes a loss or threatened loss will depend upon the individual's past experience and present capacity for coping with loss. Where a serious loss is suffered or threatened, the predisposed person may react by giving up, leading to a state of having given up. The most characteristic feature of this is the sense of psychological impotence — a feeling that for a period of time one is unable to cope with any task. Clinically, the complex is manifested by: 1) feelings of helplessness and hopelessness; 2) low self-esteem; 3) an inability to enjoy the company of other people, one's work, hobbies, etc.; 4) disruption of the sense of continuity in one's past, present, and future; and 5) a reactivation of memories of earlier periods of giving up. Engel believes that this state of mind may last for varying periods of time, and that it is commonplace for people to experience this complex several times during a lifetime; in situations in which prompt resolution is impossible and periods of struggling alternate with periods of giving up, illness may occur.

Engel's conclusions are based on his studies of patients with ulcerative colitis and on Greene's (145) and Schmale's (135) observations. Paulley (106), however, finds that pathological mourning specifically antecedes a variety of autoimmune diseases — rheumatoid arthritis, giant cell arteritis, systemic lupus erythematosus, polymyalgia, Sjögren's syndrome, and autoimmune thyroid disease.

Clearly, this area of stress research and its relationship to particular diseases is waiting to be carried forward. Specific questions await answers. Are grief reactions, states of helplessness, or states of pathological mourning associated with different psychobiological patterns which either play indirect, "permissive" roles, or more direct ones in the onset and, therefore, the pathogenesis of disease?

The "Choice" of Disease Following Bereavement

Linear theories of disease causality would predict that an agent, stimulus, or challenge to man or animal would produce a specific disease. After all, the streptococcus does incite erysipelas, but it only does so if the host is also immunosuppressed. Many other factors — the dose of the infectious agent, the age of the patient, the integrity of the immune system, and bereavement — play a role in determining disease onset; a host-agent interaction must occur.

Those who hold to a linear, causal hypothesis of the pathogenesis of disease refute the observation that losses and bereavement are associated with the onset of a variety of diseases. Why, they ask, do such events not incite one disease along? The answer is that neither bereavement nor the streptococcus specifies a particular disease. (This bacterium is also associated with boils, tonsillitis, rheumatic fever, acute glomerulonephritis, meningitis, etc.) The characteristics of the host determine the outcome.

Specific predispositions of a particular disease decide its nature or challenge. They specify the "choice" of the disease with which the bereaved or infected person will fall ill—if indeed he does. They are the source of the variability of outcome. In addition, most diseases are not uniform entities. Various sub-forms exist whose predispositions differ.

These predispositions may be genetically determined. In the case of peptic duodenal ulcer, elevated levels of the pepsinogen I isoenzyme are a risk factor in about 60% of all patients with the disease, and they are inherited as an autosomal dominant trait (155). The remainder of patients with duodenal ulcer have normal levels of this enzyme. Others have elevations of the pepsinogen II isoenzyme (58, 158).

The predisposition may not only be genetically determined, despite the fact that diseases tend to run in families. The normotensive son of one hypertensive parent has a more reactive cardiovascular system than one who has normotensive parents (159). Many diseases run in families (122, 143)—a fact that is usually explained on a genetic basis, but more goes on in families than the vertical transmission of genes. In fact, intrauterine (160) or postnatal experiences such as premature separation (see below) places animals at risk for disease by permanently altering levels of enzymes and disrupting rhythmic processes that regulate sleep and body temperature.

Nevertheless, the predisposition to disease takes many forms. Immunodeficiency is a risk factor for infection and for malignancies. The capacity to form immunoglobulin-E (IgE) is associated with various diseases—atopic dermatitis, allergic rhinitis, and bronchial asthma, but bronchial asthma will not develop unless bronchial hyperreactivity is also present. Both these tendencies are permanent characteristics of asthmatic persons. Yet attacks of the disease are intermittent and are incited by many factors including personal loss and the grief it engenders (143). Autoimmune factors play a role in Graves' disease and rheumatoid arthritis, but also, threat in the acute form of Graves' disease and losses in the latter are associated with their onset (143).

In one form of early, essential hypertension, increased sympathetic discharge accounts for the increased cardiac output, cardiac contractility, heart rate, plasma catecholamine and renin levels, but a normal peripheral resistance (161). These patients with this sub-form also differ in their psychological makeup (162) and in their responses to challenge (163). Psychological differences have also been described in two forms of rheumatoid arthritis (164, 165).

Such observations suggest that the responses to bereavement or separation will not be uniform. The various predispositions will determine the disease with which the person will fall ill—the choice of the disease. Patients with the various sub-forms of the diseases describe differences in their psychological sensitivities and their capacities to cope, which in turn will determine their response to specific events and the way they can cope with them.

In other words, bereavement may play a greater role at the onset of one sub-form because of the specific nature of the psychobiological makeup of the host. In another sub-form it may play less of a determining role (or none at all). This suggestion is supported by Strober's (137) observations that patients with anorexia nervosa who are also involved in binge eating experienced significantly more life stress in a six-month period than either those patients who remorselessly restricted their food intake, or normal adolescents.

Age as a Factor in Disease Onset

The association of separation or bereavement and disease onset is in part age-dependent and, in part, a product of earlier experiences. However, the psychobiological responses to loss observed at a prior age in one particular system are not necessarily the same as those seen in that system at a later age. In fact, the problem of the relationship of the responses to prior experiences of separation and of responses to equivalent experiences later in the life of a person remains largely unsolved. No a priori reason exists for believing that the later psychobiological responses should have the same conformation as the earlier ones. One possible explanation for this discrepancy is the trans-formations with age that occur in every organ system. They, in turn, determine its response tendencies. For this reason alone bereavement may account for just a part of the pathogenetic variance in one particular age group—in en-hancing, for example, the mortality of widowers of between 55 and 74 years of age.

Age-related changes have been described in:

1) The endocrine system. The hypothalamic pituitary ovarian axis (166) and the hypothalamic pituitary adrenal axes (with a low dehydroisonan-drosterone to cortisol ratio prior to adrenarche [167]) go through maturational sequences, and, after the menopause, gonadotrophin levels rise. In anorexia nervosa (A.N.), including that brought on by separation, both gonadotro-phins and the adrenal hormones revert to premenarchal and preadrenarchal patterns of secretion. Amenorrhea without A.N. may also follow a young girl's leaving home—another separation.

It follows that retrogressions of hormone patterns following separation depend in part on their previous maturation. For that reason alone, the peak age of incidence of anorexia nervosa is at about puberty, although its onset may occasionally occur before then or later.

2) The immune system. The thymus increases in size during childhood and then progressively shrinks. Eventually, it fails as an endocrine organ, producing less and less thymopoeitin after the age of 30–40 years. After that age, more and more immature T-cells appear peripherally, particularly T-helper cells. Cellular immune responses are impaired. Other branches of the immune system also show age-dependent changes; responses to a specific antigen are less vigorous. And autoantibodies – rheumatoid factors, antinuclear, and antithyroglobulin antibodies – become more prevalent. Aging is not the only variable altering immune function. Bereavement in middle age, as we have seen, also depresses T- and B-cell function with a latent period of four to six weeks (123, 124). Such a suppression also appears to occur in infants who languish in institutions. They are prone to opportunistic infections, especially viral ones, suggesting that their cellular immune system has become impaired.

Older people are prone to a variety of infections and are at markedly increased risk for malignancies, presumably because of decreases in immune surveillance over transformed cells. Bereavement has also been cited as an onset condition for malignancy. An interaction between bereavement and impaired immune function in the elderly is, therefore, suggested.

3) The stomach. At least in rats, the main control mechanisms of gastric secretion – acetylcholine, gastrin, and histamine – go through a maturational sequence. Gastrin levels, for example, rise just before normal weaning occurs. Gastric acid secretion also goes through maturational changes. These changes may be altered by premature separation, which partly explain the finding that (prematurely separated) animals do not begin to develop gastric ulceration under the challenge of restraint until 22 days of age. Yet they are particularly prone to do so between 30 and 40 days of age. Later they become decreasingly susceptible to restraint (168).

4) The brain. Both apical and circumferential dendrites in many areas of the brain grow and branch, then fade, and eventually disappear altogether (169). Brain volume begins to shrink after the age of 40 years; and cognition declines. Despite this, major behavioral manifestations of the aged brain may not appear until a separation or bereavement occurs.

5) Circadian rhythms. Additionally, the endocrine, immune, central nervous, and gastric systems and others have their own time periodicities with their own maturational sequences. To date, the circadian periodic function has been studied most. Rhythmic changes occur in neurotransmitter and hormone levels, B- and T-cell function, the excretion of electrolytes and metabolites (citric acid, beta-hydroxybutyric acid, and ammonia), the effects of drugs and antigens, heart rate, blood pressure, gastric secretion, temperature regulation, attention, and dreaming. But the development of these rhythmic patterns is not well-known. These processes are under the control of a hierarchy of oscillators and pacemakers. The pacemakers require daily synchronization by "Zeitgebers" such as light and personal relationships (57, 170).

Circadian rhythms determine hours of maximal or minimal resistance to pathogenic agents such as infection and restraint. Constraining animals at the height of their activity cycle is a potent factor in gastric ulceration (171). The topic of the interaction of time—periodic systems, which have their own development and separation experiences at different ages, is of major interest.

The question of the age and timing of disease onset is complex. It can in part be understood by alterations in rhythmic time, periodic systems, and in part as the result of disrupted personal relationships.

Experimental Evidence that Separation is a Risk Factor in Disease Onset

The psychobiological effects of separation on infant animals are permanent, and they also place them at risk for disease in every organ system studied to date. This generalization carries with it a provision that the factor of the age of the animal at the time of challenge must be taken into account. The results of studies on separation in animals demonstrate that it has immediate psychobiological conseqences which may differ in kind from those that occur with challenges at a later age.

These contentions are borne out by the following data:

1) Development of high blood pressure. Henry and his colleagues (117) studied the effects of social confrontations with members of the animal's own species in animals with different previous experiences. They showed that the effects of mixing males from different boxes, of aggregating them in small boxes, of exposing mice to a cat for many months, and of producing territorial conflict in mixed males and females resulted in sustained elevations of systolic blood pressure, arteriosclerosis, and an interstitial nephritis; higher levels of systolic blood pressure were achieved by male rather than by female mice, who also failed to reproduce under such conditions. If male mice were castrated, minimal elevations in blood pressure occurred, while in those given reserpine, minimal decreases in blood pressure resulted. Previous experiences of living together attenuated the effects on blood pressure of experimentally induced aggregation and territorial conflict. On the other hand, isolation of animals from each other after weaning and to maturity exacerbated the effects of crowding on blood pressure levels.

Axelrod et al. (118) and Henry et al. (117, 118, 119) later reported that the socially isolated male mice showed a decreased activity of tyrosine hydroxylase and phenylethanolamine N-methyl transferase activity in the adrenal gland in the baseline state. When these animals were now crowded together, the effect was to increase the activity of these enzymes — an increase significantly greater than in those accustomed to crowding. The activity of both enzymes, of monoamine oxidase, and the contents of noradrenaline and adrenaline in the adrenal gland were greater in these previously isolated animals who were later in constant contact with each other than in animals who were conventionally housed, i.e., crowded, but never isolated. In other words, the levels of the catecholamine-synthesizing enzymes in the adrenal medulla of socially isolated male animals are lower than in animals of the same age housed together, and, under social stress, a marked reactive "overshooting" in their activity occurs.

The previously isolated male mouse becomes the dominant animal in the colony. It pays the price for its social position in the hierarchy by developing elevations of systolic blood pressure and an interstitial nephritis. Separation has not only changed the social behavior of these animals but also placed them at risk for systolic hypertension and fatal kidney disease.

2) Disturbances in pulse rate. Hofer and Weiner (172, 173) showed that a 40% fall in heart rate occurs (despite an increase in behavioral activity) when 15-day-old rats are separated from their mothers — an effect observable four hours following separation. Starting at 20 days, the heart rate of normally weaned rats falls from a level of about 420 to about 300 beats per minute. The prematurely separated animal's heart rate, having initially fallen, begins to climb and by 28 days is significantly higher (350 beats per minute) than in its normally weaned peer (111).

3) Disturbances in sleep and body temperature regulation. Both in the 15-day-old rat and six-month-old monkey, separation (which is followed by not eating) produces a profound sleep disturbance (174, 175, 176). Sleep onset is delayed; activated sleep is lost; rapid transitions occur between the two sleep stages; sleep is fragmented; awakenings are frequent; and the animal has an overall decrease in sleep time. This sleep disturbance still occurs if the body temperature of 15-day-old rats is maintained within the normal range. Recovery of sleep patterns occurs by 30 days of age in these rats; they have the same ones as normally weaned rats.

When the prematurely separated animal is food deprived or restrained at 30 days, it initially falls asleep: An increase in sleep occurs mainly due to slow wave sleep — changes which are not seen in normally weaned animals and are independent of changes in body temperature. Following this, the former show a fall in body temperature, either when food deprived or restrained, at which time they progressively lose sleep, mainly at the expense of slow wave sleep (8).

Prematurely separated animals initially respond to separation and not eating with one kind of sleep disturbance. At 30 days another kind of change in sleep pattern occurs when the animals are not fed, despite the fact that prior to not feeding these patterns were normal. In addition, not feeding or restraint elicits a disturbance in temperature regulation not present before challenge. These results suggest that the same challenge at two different times in the life of a separated rat produces different sleep disturbances and also elicits a disturbance in temperature regulation which had lain dormant (177). The separated rat at 30 days of age on challenge reverts to its previous poikilothermic state.

4) Gastric erosions. Prematurely separated rats when restrained or not fed (or both) at 22 and 30 days develop gastric erosions with an incidence of 80%–95% (168). (The incidence in normally weaned animals is 10%.) This effect is mediated by the aforementioned fall in body temperature (177). These animals do not ulcerate when separated at 17 days of age. After 30 days the incidence of gastric erosions declines, and is 20% by 200 days of age. The effects of a challenge in prematurely separated animals is, therefore, age-related. The initial separation does not produce erosions, but places animals at profound risk for the lesions on subsequent challenge at a later age.

5) Disturbances in immune function and development of opportunistic infection. Keller and his colleagues (178) have reported that the T-cells of 40-day-old rats prematurely separated at 15 days of age from their mothers have a significant suppression of the absolute value of thymidine incorporation into their lymphocytes after a mitogenic stimulus. The ultimate outcome of this experiment was totally unexpected. By 100 days of age 50% (80% of the males and 20% of the female rats) of the prematurely separated animals had died of opportunistic — apparently viral — infections of the lungs.

6) Disturbances in the regulation of enzyme levels. The enzyme, ornithine decarboxylase (ODC), is crucial to polyamine synthesis and, therefore, to growth and maturation of organs such as the heart and brain. Growth hormone is one of several regulators of its levels. Premature separation of rats for one hour at 10 days of age lowers levels of both the hormone and enzyme. After two hours of separation, the enzyme becomes permanently unresponsive to the stimulatory effects of administered growth hormone, although it remains responsive to cyclic AMP and insulin administration (179).

7) Growth disturbances. Fifteen-day-old rats do not usually feed themselves during the 48 hours following separation. They lose weight and body temperature because they are still poikilothermic at that age. These animals are underweight and have less brown fat at 30 and 40 days of age (178, 180). Their body weight is permanently lower than their normally weaned peers.

8) Disturbances of catecholamine and nucleoprotein content of the brain. After three days of separation, the brains of 15-day-old pups raised at room temperature contained lower levels of catecholamines, protein, DNA, and RNA. When maintained at ambient temperatures of about 35°C, the levels of norepinephrine and dopamine in the brain actually were raised, but the levels of protein, DNA, and RNA continued to be depressed in the cerebrum and cerebellum, and their body weights remained lower than their non-separated peers (181). Whether the diminished levels of proteins and nucleoproteins continued for the duration of the lives of these animals is not known.

These observations demonstrate that separation has a variety of effects that place animals at risk for disease when later exposed to social, viral, nutritional, or physical (restraint) challenges. They add substance to the belief that separation is a potent risk factor for later disease at least in animals.

CONCLUSION

The Status of the Concept of Stress

The purpose of this chapter has been to carry out an analysis of the concept of stress. The concept is not a new one; it is an updated version of the Greek belief that disease is an outcome of the dynamic interactions of man with his environment (182) — that events (other than bacteria, toxins, and extremes of climate) external to a person can influence the onset and course of illness and disease. Selye, the modern proponent of this view, initiated a long line of investigations that has produced about 150,000 publications in 50 years, and has engendered extensive debate and controversy.

The emphasis in this line of research has been on stressful events that culminate in disease. Selye first studied the generalized, bodily responses to a variety of noxious agents. It needs to be emphasized again that these agents were directly damaging to the physical integrity of the organism. They were inescapable. They could not be fended off. And they produced a syndrome of nonspecific responses — shock, inflammation, and the outpouring of adrenocortical and adrenomedullary hormones.

It is true that these physiological responses are elicited by very many circumstances, challenges, and diseases. But, as we have seen, it is also true that the unique feature of the organism is not that its responses to the environment are general and nonspecific but that they are highly discriminated and specific. Survival is guaranteed by the exquisite specificity and appropriateness of the response to a particular threat, not to any threat. In fact, when the threat is poorly defined – when an experience is ambiguous – an appropriate response cannot be given. Fear is engendered because survival cannot be assured in the absence of a behavioral program designed to overcome the threat.

Calamities brought about by natural, but especially by man-made disasters, often preclude a response; the behavioral programs underlying it may be punished, disallowed, or lead to disastrous pain or injury. If the concept of stress is to be applied at all to less dire circumstances – the vicissitudes of daily living – it should either be defined anew or be dispensed with altogether. What is stressful is the absence or unavailability of behavioral programs for coping with or solving a task or problem or meeting a demand. These programs may not be available or appropriate because they have never been learned, or cannot be carried out because the social environment will not permit it. And novel or ambiguous situations preclude the person from knowing which of several potential programs to carry out.

Even the most dire situations do not necessarily produce the same responses. Not everyone develops acute or chronic stress syndromes – only about 75% of a population does. Nor does fear, ambiguity, loss, or injury produce the same responses. A broken ankle and a grief reaction are responses of a very different nature! Pain, novelty, fear, or loss may induce corticosteroid responses in some but certainly not in all. In fact, even in situations of real or imagined danger, no corticosteroid response may be seen, especially in persons who find them thrilling (49).

Any attempt to define stress in terms of its physiological correlates is fraught with peril. This line of thinking has been pursued to the point of absurdity; some have even considered that any physiological change is a criterion of stress. If that were so, rising every morning from bed would be considered a stress because it is accompanied by an increase in blood pressure as levels of aldosterone rise in blood plasma. Also, the same kind and degree of physiological changes occur daily and are occasioned by a system of oscillators, which are only partly under external control (170), and by the withdrawal of stimulation (183, 184). For these reasons alone it becomes evident that to call every behavioral or psychobiological response to a change or event in the environment "stress" is to beg the question of its nature.

The question of stress is even more vexing when one considers that Selye originally believed that the body's responses in the second phase of the G.A.S.

were designed to restore homeostasis. A close examination of his data fails to bear out his contention; his restrained rat was permanently altered anatomically. In fact, the data reviewed in this chapter suggest that the organism never returns to its previous state. The person subjected to the mindless violence of nature or man is never again the same; the event is forever after burned into his memory and may even eventually disrupt it. Grief is eternal in the former inmate of a concentration camp. The lymphocyte is permanently altered after its first encounter with a specific antigen; it "remembers." The prematurely separated rat is changed psychobiologically in every system so far studied.

These observations accord much more closely with modern concepts in physics than the concept of homeostasis. Organisms are not simple systems like billiard balls. When simple systems interact, they immediately partition their energy atomistically. The energy is dissipated. Complex systems are made of mobile fluid or semi-fluid components contained within a membrane. When complex systems interact, or boundary conditions at the membrane are altered, the external momentum changes. Some hormones or transmitter substances appearing at membrane receptors are transduced, and the message is carried to the nucleus of the cell. The membrane is a thermodynamic engine, controlling the admission of ions and the effects of hormones and transmitter substances. These processes, and those which underlie conformational changes in complex structures (such as cells), are the necessary conditions for the internal time delay that characterizes the responses of biological systems and forms the basis of memory (185). Although these statements are phrased in molecular terms, they also apply to whole organisms. The phenomena described in this chapter accord more with this model than a homeostatic one.

The Future of Stress Research

The concept of stress, despite its stimulus to investigation, should be either modified or altogether dispensed with. The modifications entail:

1) The need for a classification. Selye's original intent should be followed. Only directly damaging stimuli or events should fall under the rubric of stress. They not only produce physical damage but also preclude any immediate response, because they are directly applied to the organism; they cannot be avoided. In this category, extreme physical conditions and natural and man-made disasters might be included, but the vicissitudes of everyday life should not.

2) The need for specification. In order to further stress research, it has become increasingly necessary to: Extract the salient features of the change in the environment, which requires a behavioral response or not on the part of the organism; analyze the correlated and integrated patterns of physiological responses; understand the mechanisms that enhance, modify, or attenuate both the behavioral and physiological (i.e., psychobiological) responses; identify the sources of individual differences in psychological responses; study the acute and long-term consequences of the changes in the psychobiology of the organism (including changes in health status) at different ages and throughout the life cycle; and observe the usual responses to change and challenge that do not lead to illness and disease. (Man rises to and meets challenges and is not necessarily defeated and damaged by them.)

A psychobiology of everyday life is called for which goes beyond the preoccupation in stress research with disease and illness onset.

REFERENCES

1. Selye, H.: The evolution of the stress concept — stress and cardiovascular disease. In: L. Levi (Ed.), *Society, Stress and Disease. Vol. 1. The Psychosocial Environment and Psychosomatic Disease.* London and New York: Oxford University Press, 1971.
2. Selye, H.: A syndrome produced by diverse nocuous agents. *Nature* (Lond.), 148:84–85, 1936.
3. Selye, H.: The general adaptation syndrome and the diseases of adaptation. *J. Clin. Endocrinol.*, 6:117–196, 1946.
4. Selye, H., and Fortier, C.: Adaptive reactions to stress. *Res. Publ. Assoc. Nerv. Ment. Dis.*, 29:3–18, 1950.
5. Wolff, H. G.: *Stress and Disease.* Springfield, IL: Charles C Thomas, 1953.
6. Pearlin, L. I., Lieberman, M. A., Menaghan, E. G., and Mullan, J. T.: The stress process. *J. Health Soc. Behav.*, 22:337–356, 1981.
7. Kagan, A.: Epidemiology and society, stress and disease. In: L. Levi (Ed.), *Society Stress and Disease. Vol. 1. The Psychosocial Environment and Psychosomatic Disease.* London and New York: Oxford University Press, 1971.
8. Ackerman, S. H., Hofer, M. A., and Weiner, H.: Sleep and temperature regulation during restraint stress in rats is affected by prior maternal separation. *Psychosom. Med.*, 41: 311–319, 1979.
9. Tyhurst, J. S.: The role of transition states — including disasters — in mental illness. In: *Symposium on Preventive and Social Psychiatry.* Washington, D.C.: Walter Reed Army Institute of Research, 1953.
10. Rioch, D. McK.: Transition states as stress. In: L. Levi (Ed.), *Society, Stress and Disease. Vol. 1. The Psychosocial Environment and Psychosomatic Disease.* London and New York: Oxford University Press, 1971.
11. Grinker, R. R., and Spiegel, J.: *Men Under Stress.* Philadelphia: Blakiston, 1945.
12. Hinkle, L. E., Jr.: The concept of "stress" in the biological and social sciences. *Sci. Med. and Man*, 1:31–48, 1973.

13. Arthur, R. J.: Life stress and disease: An appraisal of the concept. In: L. J. West and M. Stein (Eds.), *Critical Issues in Behavioral Medicine*. Philadelphia: J. B. Lippincott, 1982.

14. Beach, F. A. Discussion. *Res. Publ. Ass. Nerv. Ment. Dis.*, 29:674–675, 1950.

15. Frederick, C. J.: Effects of natural versus human induced violence upon victims. *Evaluation and Change* (Special Issue), 71–75, 1980.

16. Frederick, C. J.: Violence and disasters: Immediate and long-term consequences. Paper, Working Group Conference on the Psychosocial Consequences of Violence. W.H.O., Geneva, Switzerland, 1981.

17. Tyhurst, J. S.: Psychological and social aspects of civilian disasters. *Can. Med. Assoc. J.*, 76:385–393, 1957.

18. Popovic, M., and Petrovic, D.: After the earthquake. *Lancet*, 2:1169–1171, 1964.

19. Erickson, K. T.: Loss of communality at Buffalo Creek. *Amer. J. Psychiat.*, 133:302–305, 1976.

20. Kasl, S. V., Chisholm, R. F., and Eskenazi, B.: The impact of the accident at Three Mile Island on the behavior and well-being of nuclear workers. *Amer. J. Publ. Health*, 71: 472–495, 1981.

21. Bromet, E.: Three Mile Island: Mental health findings. N.I.M.H. Contract No. 278–279, 0048 (SM). 1980.

22. Askevold, F.: Personal communication, 1983.

23. Eitinger, L.: Acute and chronic psychiatric and psychosomatic reactions in concentration camp survivors. In: L. Levi (Ed.), *Society, Stress and Disease. Vol. 1. The Psychosocial Environment and Psychosomatic Disease*. London and New York: Oxford University Press, 1971.

24. Eitinger, L.: *Concentration Camp Survivors in Norway and Israel*. New York: Humanities Press, 1965.

25. Chodoff, P.: Psychiatric aspects of the Nazi persecution. In: S. Arieti (Ed.), *American Handbook of Psychiatry. Vol. 6*. New York: Basic Books, 2nd Ed., 1975.

26. Ruskin, A., Beard, O. W., and Schaffer, R. L.: "Blast hypertension": Elevated arterial pressure in victims of the Texas City disaster. *Amer. J. Med.*, 4:228–235, 1948.

27. Gelshteyn, E. M.: Clinical characteristics of hypertensive disease under wartime conditions. *Klin. Med.* (Moskova), 21:10–15, 1943.

28. Ehrstrom, M. D.: Psychogene blutdrucksteigerung in Kriegshypertonien. *Acta Med. Scand.*, 122:546–561, 1945.

29. Graham, J. D. P.: High blood pressure after battle. *Lancet*, 1:239–240, 1945.

30. Henry, J. P., and Cassel, J. C.: Psychosocial factors in essential hypertension. Recent epidemiologic and animal experimental evidence. *Amer. J. Epidem.*, 90:171–193, 1969.

31. Harburg, E., Erfurt, J. C., Hauenstein, L. S., Chape, C., Schull, W. J., and Schork, M. A.: Socio-ecological stress, suppressed hostility, skin color, and black-white male blood pressure: Detroit. *Psychosom. Med.*, 35:276–296, 1973.

32. Stewart, D. N., and Winser, D. M. R. de.: Incidence of perforated peptic ulcer. Effect of heavy air raids. *Lancet*, 1:259–261, 1942.

33. Alpers, D. H.: Functional gastrointestinal disorders. *Hosp. Practice*, 18:139–153, 1983.

34. Bram, I.: Psychic trauma in the pathogenesis of exophthalmic goiter. *Endocrinology*, 11:106–121, 1927.

35. Iversen, K.: *Temporary Rise in the Frequency of Thyrotoxicosis in Denmark, 1945*. Copenhagen: Rosenkilde & Bagger, 1948.

36. Lacey, J. I.: Somatic response patterning and stress. In: M. Appley and R. Trumbull (Eds.), *Psychological Stress*. New York: Appleton-Century-Crofts, 1967.

37. Miller, B. V., and Bernstein, D. A.: Instructional demand in a behavioral avoidance test for claustrophic fears. *J. Abn. Psychol.*, 80:206-210, 1972.
38. von Uexküll, T., and Wick, E.: Die Situationshypertonie. *Arch. fur Kreislauf Forschung.*, 39:236-242, 1962.
39. Bogdonoff, M. D., Estes, E. H., Harlan, W. R., Trout, D. L., and Kirsher, R.: Metabolic and cardiovascular changes during a state of acute central nervous system arousal. *J. Clin. Endocrin. Metab.*, 20:1333-1340, 1960.
40. Bloch, S., and Brackenridge, C.: Psychological performance and biochemical factors in medical students under examination stress. *J. Psychosom. Res.*, 16:25-33, 1972.
41. Syvälahti, E., Lammintausta, R., and Pekkarinen, A.: Effect of psychic stress of examination on serum growth hormone, serum insulin, and plasma renin activity. *Acta Pharmacol. et Toxicol.*, 38:344-352, 1976.
42. Dimsdale, J., and Moss, J.: Plasma catecholamines in stress and exercise. *J.A.M.A.*, 243:340-342, 1980.
43. Taggart, P., Carruthers, M., and Somerville, W.: Electrocardiogram, plasma catecholamines, and lipids, and their modification by oxprenolol when speaking before an audience. *Lancet*, 2:341-346, 1973.
44. Taggart, P., and Carruthers, M.: Endogenous hyperlipedemia induced by emotional stress of racing driving. *Lancet*, 1:363-366, 1971.
45. Dimsdale, J., and Herd, A.: Variability of plasma lipids in response to emotional arousal. *Psychosom. Med.*, 44:413-430, 1982.
46. Fenz, M. D., and Epstein, S.: Gradients of physiological arousal of experienced and novice parachutists as a function of an approaching jump. *Psychosom. Med.*, 29:33-51, 1967.
47. Fenz, M. D., and Jones, G. B.: Individual differences in a physiological arousal and performance in sport parachutists. *Psychosom. Med.*, 34:1-18, 1972.
48. Noel, G. L., Dimond, R. C., Earll, J. M., and Frantz, A. G.: Prolactin, thyrotropin, and growth hormone release during stress associated with parachute jumping. *Aviation, Space and Env.*, 47:543-547, 1976.
49. Ursin, H., Baade, E., and Levine, S.: *Psychobiology of Stress. A Study of Coping Men.* New York: Academic Press, 1978.
50. Hilton, S. W.: Ways of reviewing the central nervous control of the circulation — old and new. *Brain Res.*, 87:213-219, 1975.
51. Rubin, R. T., Rahe, R. H., Arthur, R. J., and Clark, B. R.: Adrenal cortical activity changes during underwater demolition team training. *Psychosom. Med.*, 31:553-564, 1969.
52. Miller, R. G., Rubin, R. T., Clark, B. R., Poland, R. E., and Arthur, R. J.: The stress of aircraft carrier landings. I: Corticosteroid responses in naval aviators. *Psychosom. Med.*, 32:581-588, 1970.
53. Rubin, R. T., Miller, R. G., Clark, B. R., Poland, R. E., and Arthur, R. J.: The stress of aircraft carrier landings. II: 3-methoxy-4-hydroxyphenylglycol excretion in naval aviators. *Psychosom. Med.*, 32:589-597, 1970.
54. Bourne, P. G., Rose, R. M., and Mason, J. W.: Urinary 17-OHCS levels. Data on seven helicopter ambulance medics in combat. *Arch. Gen. Psychiat.*, 17:104-110, 1967.
55. Bourne, P. G., Rose, R. M., and Mason, J. W.: 17-OCHS levels in combat. Special forces "A" team under threat of attack. *Arch. Gen. Psychiat.*, 19:135-140, 1968.
56. Farrow, S. C.: Unemployment and health: A review of methodology. E.E.C. Workshop, February, 1983, Bad Hamburg, Germany. In press, 1984.
57. Hofer, M. A.: Presidential address. Relationships as regulators: A psychobiological perspective on bereavement. *Psychosom. Med.*, 45: In press, 1984.

58. Weiner, H.: What the future holds for psychosomatic medicine. Address to the Plenary Session of the VII World Congress of the International College of Psychosomatic Medicine. In press, 1984.
59. Holmes, T. H., and Rahe, R. H.: The social readjustment scale. *J. Psychosom. Res.*, 11:213–218, 1967.
60. Dohrenwend, B. S., and Dohrenwend, B. P. (Eds.): *Stressful Life Events.* New York: Wiley, 1974.
61. Gunderson, E. E. E., and Rahe, R. H. (Eds.): *Life Stress and Illness.* Springfield, IL: Charles C Thomas, 1974.
62. Kasl, S. V.: Mortality and the business cycle: Some questions about research strategies when utilizing macrosocial and ecological data. *Amer. J. Publ. Health*, 64:784–788, 1979.
63. Cooke, D. J., and Hole, D. J.: The aetiological importance of stressful life events. *Brit. J. Psychiat.*, 143:397–400, 1983.
64. Rabkin, J. G., and Struening, E. L.: Life events, stress and illness. *Science*, 194:1013–1020, 1976.
65. Thoits, P. A.: Conceptual, methodological and theoretical problems in studying social support as a buffer against life stress. *J. Health Soc. Behav.*, 23;145–159, 1982.
66. Horowitz, M., Schaeffer, C., Hiroto, D., Wilner, N., and Levin, B.: Life event questionnaires for measuring presumptive stress. *Psychosom. Med.*, 39:413–431, 1977.
67. Schless, A. P., and Mendels, J.: The values of interviewing family and friends in assessing life stressors. *Arch. Gen. Psychiat.*, 35:565–567, 1978.
68. Grant, I., Yager, J., Sweetwood, H. L., and Olshen, R.: Life events and symptoms: Fourier analyses of time series from a three year prospective inquiry. *Arch. Gen. Psychiat.*, 39: 598–605, 1982.
69. DeLongis, A., Coyne, J. C., Dakof, G., Folkman, S., and Lazarus, R. S.: Relationship of daily hassles, uplifts and major life events to health status. *Health Psychol.*, 1:119–136, 1982.
70. Kanner, A. D., Coyne, J. C., Schaefer, C., and Lazarus, R. S.: Comparison of two modes of stress measurement: Daily hassles and uplifts versus major life events. *J. Behav. Med.*, 4:1–39, 1981.
71. Lazarus, R. S.: *Psychological Stress and the Coping Process.* New York: McGraw-Hill, 1966.
72. Lipowski, Z. J.: Physical illness, the individual, and the coping process. *Psychiatry Med.*, 1:91–102, 1970.
73. Antonovsky, A.: *Health, Stress and Coping.* San Francisco: Jossey-Bass, 1979.
74. Cassel, J.: The contribution of the social environment to host resistance. *Amer. J. Epidemiol.*, 104:107–122, 1976.
75. Cobb, S.: Social support as a moderator of life stress. *Psychosom. Med.*, 38:300–314, 1976.
76. Nuckolls, K. B., Cassel, J., and Kaplan, B. H.: Psychosocial assets, life crisis, and the prognosis of pregnancy. *Amer. J. Epidemiol.*, 95:431–441, 1972.
77. Brown, G. W., and Harris, T.: *Social Origins of Depression: A Study of Psychiatric Disorder in Women.* New York: Free Press, 1978.
78. de Arauyo, G., Van Arsdel, P. P., Holmes, T. H., and Dudley, D. L.: Life change, coping ability and chronic intrinsic asthma. *J. Psychosom. Res.*, 17:359–363, 1973.
79. Blazer, D. G.: Social support and mortality in an elderly community population. *Amer. J. Epidemiol.*, 115:684–694, 1982.
80. Mueller, D. P.: Social networks: A promising direction for research on the relationship of the social environment to psychiatric disorder. *Soc. Science Med.*, 14A:147–161, 1980.

81. Yager, J., and Robinson, J.: Stress and coping in illness. In: L. Jarvik and C. Eisdorfer (Eds.), *Behavioral Science for the Clinician*. In press, 1984.
82. Hinkle, L. E., Jr.: The effect of exposure to culture change, social change and changes in interpersonal relationships on health. In: B. S. Dohrenwend and B. P. Dohrenwend (Eds.), *Stressful Life Events: Their Nature and Effects*. New York: Wiley, 1974.
83. Vaillant, G.: *Adaptation to Life*. Boston: Little, Brown, 1977.
84. Ruesch, J.: The infantile personality: The core problem of psychosomatic medicine. *Psychosom. Med.*, 10:133–144, 1948.
85. Marty, P., and de M'Uzan, M.: La pensée opératoire. *Rev. Franc. Psychoanal.*, 27: Supp. 1345, 1963.
86. McDougall, J.: The psychosoma and the psychoanalytic process. *Int. Rev. Psychoanal.*, 1:437–450, 1974.
87. Nemiah, J. C., and Sifneos, P. E.: Affect and fantasy in patients with psychosomatic disorders. In: O. W. Hill (Ed.), *Modern Trends in Psychosomatic Medicine – 2*. London: Butterworths, 1970.
88. Bettelheim, B., and Janowitz, M.: *Social Change and Prejudice*. New York: Free Press, 1964.
89. Hartmann, H.: *Ego Psychology and the Problem of Adaptation*. New York: International Universities Press, 1958.
90. Pearlin, L. I.: The life cycle and life strains. In: H. M. Blalock (Ed.), *Sociological Theory and Research: A critical appraisal*. New York: Free Press, 1980.
91. Goldberg, E. L., and Comstock, G. W.: Epidemiology of life events: Frequency in general populations. *Amer. J. Epidemiol.*, 111:736–752, 1980.
92. Lazarus, R. S., and DeLongis, A.: Psychological stress and coping in aging. *Amer. Psychologist*, 38:245–254, 1983.
93. Jahoda, M., and Rush, H. Work employment and unemployment. University of Sussex. *Science Policy Research Unit Report*, 12, 1980.
94. Farrow, S. C.: Unemployment and health: A review of methodology. In: J. Cullen and J. Sigerist (Eds.), *Psychological and sociological parameters in studies of breakdown in human adaptation*. Amsterdam: Elsevier, 1984 (in press).
95. Cook, D. G., Cummings, R. O., Bartley, M. J., and Shaper, A. S.: The health of unemployed middle-aged men in Great Britain. *Lancet*, 1:1290–1291, 1982.
96. Fox, A. J., and Goldblatt, P. O.: Longitudinal Study, 1971–1975. O.P.C.S. London: Her Majesty's Stationery Office, 1982.
97. Kasl, S. V., and Cobb, S.: Blood pressure changes in men undergoing job loss: A preliminary report. *Psychosom. Med.* 32:19038, 1970.
98. Kasl, S. V., Cobb, S., and Brooks, G. W.: Changes in serum uric acid and cholesterol levels in men undergoing job loss. *J.A.M.A.*, 206:1500–1503, 1968.
99. Saxena, K.: Physiological effects of job loss. Paper presented at the Annual Meeting of the International Society for the Prevention of Stress, 1980.
100. Sigerist, J.: Personal communication, 1983.
101. Weiner, H.: Gesundheit, Krankheitsgefühl, und Krankheit – Ansatze zu einem integrativen Verständnis. *Psychother. Med. Psychol.*, 33:15–34, 1983.
102. Lloyd, G.: Medicine without signs. *Brit. Med. J.*, 287:539–542, 1983.
103. Brown, J. T., and Stoudemire, G. A.: Normal and pathological grief. *J.A.M.A.*, 250: 378–382, 1983.
104. Parkes, C. M.: The first year of bereavement. *Psychiatry*, 33:444–467, 1970.
105. Bowlby, J.: Pathological mourning and childhood mourning. *J. Am. Psychoan. Ass.*, 11:500–541, 1963.

106. Paulley, J. W.: Pathological mourning: A key factor in the psychopathogenesis of auto-immune disorders. Paper presented at the 14th European Congress on Psychosomatic Research, Hamburg, Germany, 1982.
107. Lindemann, E.: Symptomatology and management of acute grief. *Amer. J. Psychiat.* 101:141-148, 1944.
108. Parkes, C. M.: Determination of outcome following bereavement. *Proc. Roy. Soc. Med.*, 64:279, 1971.
109. Raphael, B.: Preventive intervention with the recently bereaved. *Arch. Gen. Psychiat.*, 34:1450-1454, 1977.
110. Raphael, B.: The management of pathological grief. *Aust. N.Z.J. Psychiat.*, 9:173-180, 1975.
111. Hofer, M. A.: Toward a developmental basis for disease predisposition: The effects of early maternal separation on brain, behavior, and cardiovascular system. In: H. Weiner, M. A. Hofer, and A. J. Stunkard (Eds.), *Brain, Behavior and Bodily Disease.* New York: Raven Press, 1981.
112. Hofer, M.A.: On the relationship between attachment and separation processes in infancy. In: R. Plutchick (Ed.), *Emotion, Theory, Research and Experience: Emotions in Early Development — 2.* New York: Academic Press, 1982.
113. Weiner, H.: The prospects of psychosomatic medicine: Selected topics. *Psychosom. Med.*, 44:488-517, 1982.
114. Butler, S. R., Suskind, M. R., and Schanberg, S. M.: Maternal behavior as a regulator of polyamine biosynthesis in brain and heart of developing rat pups. *Science*, 199:445-447, 1978.
115. Kuhn, C. M., Butler, S. R., and Schanberg, S. M.: Selective depression of serum growth hormone during maternal deprivation in rat pups. *Science*, 201:1035-1036, 1978.
116. Evoniuk, G. E., Kuhn, G. M., and Schanberg, S. M.: The effect of tactile stimulation on serum growth hormone and tissue orinthine decarboxylase activity during maternal deprivation in rat pups. *Comp. Psychopharmol.*, 3:363-370, 1979.
117. Henry, J. P., Meehan, J. P., and Stephens, P. M.: The use of psychosocial stimuli to induce prolonged systolic hypertension in mice. *Psychosom. Med.*, 29:408-432, 1967.
118. Axelrod, J., Mueller, R. A., Henry, J. P., and Stephens, P. M.: Changes in enzymes involved in the biosynthesis and metabolism of noradrenaline and adrenaline after psychosocial stimulation. *Nature* (London), 225:1059-1060, 1970.
119. Henry, J. P., Stephens, P. M., Axelrod, J., and Mueller, R. A.: Effect of psychosocial stimulation on the enzymes involved in the biosynthesis and metabolism of noradrenaline and adrenaline. *Psychosom. Med.*, 33:227-237, 1971.
120. Mason, M. A., and Berkson, G.: Effects of maternal mobility on the development of rocking and other behaviors in rhesus monkeys. *Develop. Psychobiol.*, 8:197-211, 1974.
121. Wolff, C.T., Friedman, S. B., Hofer, M. A., and Mason, J. W.: Relationship between psychological defenses and mean urinary 17-hydroxycorticosteroid excretion rates. I. A predictive study of parents with fatally ill children. *Psychosom. Med.*, 26:576-591, 1964.
122. Katz, J. L.: Three studies in psychosomatic medicine revisited. *Psychosom. Med.*, 44:29-42, 1982.
123. Bartrop, R. W., Luckhurst, E., Lazarus, L., Kiloh, L. G., and Perry, R.: Depressed lymphocyte function after bereavement. *Lancet*, 1:834:836, 1977.
124. Schleifer, S. J., Keller, S. E., Camarino, M., Thornton, J. C., and Stein, M.: Suppression of lymphocyte stimulation following bereavement. *J.A.M.A.*, 250:374-377, 1983.
125. Jemmott, J. B., III, Borysenko, M., Chapman, R., Borysenko, J. Z., McClelland, D. C.,

Meyer, D., Benson, H.: Academic stress, power motivation, and decrease in secretion rate of salivary secretory immunoglobulin A. *Lancet*, 1:1400-1402, 1983.

126. Arnetz, B. B., Theorell, T., Levi, L., Kallner, A., and Eneroth, P.: An experimental study of social isolation of elderly people: Psychoendocrine and metabolic effects. *Psychosom. Med.*, 45:395-406, 1983.

127. Maddison, D., and Viola, A.: The health of widows in the year following bereavement. *J. Psychosom. Res.*, 12:297-306, 1968.

128. Parkes, C. M., and Brown, R. J.: Health after bereavement. *Psychosom. Med.*, 34:449-461, 1972.

129. Parkes, C. M.: Recent bereavement as a cause of mental illness. *Br. J. Psychiat.*, 110: 198-204, 1984.

130. Clayton, P. J., Herjanic, M., Murphy, G. E., and Woodruff, R., Jr.: Mourning and depression: Their similarities and differences. *Can. J. Psychiat.*, 19:309-312, 1974.

131. Bornstein, P. E., Clayton, P. J., Halikas, J. A., Maurice, W. L., and Robins, E.: The depression of widowhood after 13 months. *Br. J. Psychiat.*, 122:561-566, 1973.

132. Rees, W. D., and Lutkins, S. G.: Mortality of bereavement. *Br. Med. J.*, 4:13-16, 1967.

133. Parkes, C. M., Benjamin, B., and Fitzgerald, R. G.: Broken heart: A statistical study of increased mortality among widowers. *Br. Med. J.*, 1:740-743, 1969.

134. Jacobs, S., and Ostfeld, A.: An epidemiological review of the mortality of bereavement. *Psychosom. Med.*, 39:344-357, 1977.

135. Schmale, A. H., Jr.: Relation of separation and depression to disease: I: A report on a hospitalized medical population. *Psychosom. Med.*, 20:259-277, 1958.

136. Garfinkel, P. E., and Garner, D. M.: *Anorexia Nervosa: A multidimensional perspective.* New York: Brunner/Mazel, 1982.

137. Strober, M.: Stressful life events associated with bulimia in anorexia nervosa: Empirical findings and theoretical speculations. *Int. J. Eating Disorders.* In press, 1985.

138. Rees, L.: The importance of psychological, allergic and infective factors in childhood asthma. *J. Psychosom. Res.*, 7:253-262, 1964.

139. Bahnson, C. B.: Psychophysiological complementary in malignancies: Past work and future vistas. *Ann. N.Y. Acad. Sci.*, 164:319-334, 1969.

140. Kissen, D. M.: Psychological factors, personality, and lung cancer in men aged 55-64. *Br. J. Med. Psychol.*, 40:29-43, 1967.

141. Hinkle, L. E., Jr., and Wolf, S.: A summary of experimental evidence relating life stress to diabetes mellitus. *J. Mt. Sinai Hosp.*, 19:537-570, 1952.

142. Stein, S. P., and Charles, E.: Emotional factors in juvenile diabetes mellitus: A study of early life experience of adolescent diabetics. *Amer. J. Psychiat.*, 128:700-704, 1971.

143. Weiner, H.: *Psychobiology and Human Disease.* New York: Elsevier, 1977.

144. Peters, M. N., and Richardson, C. T.: Stressful life events, acid hypersecretion and ulcer disease. *Gastroenterol.*, 84:114-119, 1983.

145. Greene, W. A., Jr.: Psychological factors and reticulo-endothelial disease: I. Preliminary observations on a group of males with lymphomas and leukemias. *Psychosom. Med.*, 16:220-230, 1954.

146. Lidz, T.: Emotional factors in the etiology of hyperthyroidism. *Psychosom. Med.*, 11:2-10, 1949.

147. Reiser, M. F., and Ferris, E. B.: Life situations, emotions and the course of patients with arterial hypertension. *Psychosom. Med.*, 13:133-142, 1951.

148. Perlman, L. V., Ferguson, S., Bergum, K., Isenberg, E. L., and Hammarstein, J. F.: Precipitation of congestive heart failure: Social and emotional factors. *Ann. Intern. Med.*, 75:1-7, 1971.

149. Drossman, D. A.: Patients with psychogenic abdominal pain: Six years observation in the medical setting. *Amer. J. Psychiat.*, 139:1549–1557, 1982.
150. Engel, G. L.: Studies of ulcerative colitis. III. The nature of the psychologic processes. *Amer. J. Med.*, 19:231–243, 1955.
151. Day, G.: The psychosomatic approach to pulmonary tuberculosis. *Lancet*, 1:1025–1028, 1951.
152. O'Hara, M. W., Rehm, L. P., and Campbell, S. B.: Postpartum depression. A role for social network and life stress variables. *J. Nerv. Ment. Dis.*, 171:336–341, 1983.
153. Chandra, V., Szklo, M., Goldberg, R., and Tonascia, J.: The impact of marital status on survival after an acute myocardial infarction: A population-based study. *Amer. J. Epidemiol.*, 117:320–325, 1983.
154. Young, M., Benjamin, B., and Wallis, C.: The mortality of widowers. *Lancet*, 2:454–456, 1963.
155. Kraus, A. S., and Lilienfeld, A. M.: Some epidemiological aspects of the high mortality in a young widowed group. *J. Chronic Dis.*, 10:207–217, 1959.
156. Helsing, K. J., Szklo, M., and Comstock, G. W.: Factors associated with mortality after widowhood. *Amer. J. Public Health*, 71:802–809, 1981.
157. Engel, G. L.: A life setting conducive to illness: The giving-up, given-up complex. *Arch. Intern. Med.*, 69:293–300, 1968.
158. Rotter, J. I., Sones, J. Q., Samloff, I. M., Richardson, C. T., Gursky, J. M., Walsh, J. H., and Rimoin, D. L.: Duodenal-ulcer disease associated with elevated serum pepsinogen I: An inherited autosomal dominant disorder. *New Engl. J. Med.*, 300:63–66, 1979.
159. Light, K. C.: Cardiovascular responses to effortful coping: Implications for the role of stress in hypertension development. *Psychophysiology*, 18:216–228, 1981.
160. Skolnick, N. J., Ackerman, S. H., Hofer, M. A., and Weiner, H.: Vertical transmission of acquired ulcer susceptibility in the rat. *Science*, 208:1161–1163, 1980.
161. Julius, S., and Esler, M. D.: Autonomic nervous cardiovascular regulation in borderline hypertension. *Amer. J. Cardiol.*, 36:685–692, 1975.
162. Esler, M. D., Julius, S., Randall, O. S., Ellis, C. N., and Kashima, T.: Relation of renin status to neurogenic vascular resistance in borderline hypertension. *Amer. J. Cardiol.*, 36:708–715, 1975.
163. Lorimer, A. R., McFarlane, P. W., Provan, G., Duffy, T., and Lawrie, T. D. V.: Blood pressure and catecholamine responses to stress in normotensive and hypertensive subjects. *Cardiovasc. Res.*, 5:169–175, 1971.
164. Rimon, R.: A psychosomatic approach to rheumatoid arthritis. *Acta Rheum. Scandinav.*, 13:1–59, 1969.
165. Vollhardt, B. R., Ackerman, S. H., Grayzel, A. I., and Barland, P.: Psychologically distinguishable groups of rheumatoid arthritis patients: A controlled, single blind study. *Psychosom. Med.*, 44:353–362, 1982.
166. Boyar, R. M., Katz, J. L., Finkelstein, J. W., Kapen, S., Weiner, H., Weitzman, E. D., and Hellman, L.: Anorexia nervosa: Immaturity of the 24-hour luteinizing hormone secretory pattern. *N. Engl. J. Med.*, 291:861–865, 1974.
167. Rich, B. H., Rosenfield, R. L., Lucky, A. W., Helke, J. C., and Otto, P.: Adrenarche: Changing adrenal response to adrenocorticotropin. *J. Clin. Endocrinol. Metab.*, 52:1129–1135, 1981.
168. Ackerman, S. H., Hofer, M. A., and Weiner, H.: Age at maternal separation and gastric erosion susceptibility in the rat. *Psychosom. Med.*, 37:180–184, 1975.
169. Scheibel, M. E., Tomiyasu, U., and Scheibel, A. B.: The aging human Betz cell. *Exp. Neurol.*, 56:598–609, 1977.

170. Moore-Ede, M. C., Sulzman, F. M., and Fuller, C. A.: *The Clocks That Time Us*. Cambridge: Harvard Univ. Press, 1982.

171. Ader, R.: Gastric erosions in the rat. Effects of immobilization at different points in the activity cycle. *Science*, 145:406–407, 1964.

172. Hofer, M. A., and Weiner, H.: Mechanisms for nutritional regulation of autonomic cardiac control in early development. *Psychosom. Med.*, 34:472–473, 1972.

173. Hofer, M. A., and Weiner, H.: Physiological mechanisms for cardiac control by nutritional intake after early maternal separation in the young rat. *Psychosom. Med.*, 37:8–24, 1975.

174. Hofer, M. A.: The organization of sleep and wakefulness after maternal separation in young rats. *Develop. Psychobiol.*, 9:189–206, 1976.

175. Reite, M., Kaufman, I. C., Pauley, J. D., and Stynes, A. J.: Depression in infant monkeys: Physiological correlates. *Psychosom. Med.*, 36:363–367, 1974.

176. Reite, M., and Short, R.: Nocturnal sleep in separated monkey infants. *Arch. Gen. Psychiat.*, 35:1247–1253, 1978.

177. Ackerman, S. H., Hofer, M. A., and Weiner, H.: Early maternal separation increases gastric ulcer risk in rats by producing a latent thermoregulatory disturbance. *Science*, 201:373–376, 1978.

178. Keller, S. E., Ackerman, S. H., Schleifer, S. J., Schindledecker, M. A., Camerino, M. S., Hofer, M. A., Weiner, H., and Stein, M.: Effect of premature weaning on lymphocyte stimulation in the rat. *Psychosom. Med.*, 45:75, 1983.

179. Kuhn, C. M., and Schanberg, S. M.: Loss of growth hormone sensitivity in brain and liver during maternal deprivation in rats. (abstract) *Soc. Neurosci.*, 5:168, 1979.

180. Ackerman, S. H.: Premature weaning, thermoregulation and the occurrence of gastric pathology. In: H. Weiner, M. A. Hofer, and A. J. Stunkard (Eds.), *Brain, Behavior and Bodily Disease*. New York: Raven Press, 1981.

181. Stone, E., Bonnet, K., and Hofer, M. A.: Survival and development of maternally deprived rats: Role of body temperature. *Psychosom. Med.*, 38:242–249, 1976.

182. Rosenberg, C. E.: The therapeutic revolution: Medicine, meaning and social change. *Perspect. Biol. Med.*, 20:485–506, 1977.

183. Zuckerman, M., Levine, S., and Biase, V. D.: Stress response in total and partial perceptual isolation. *Psychosom. Med.*, 26:250–260, 1964.

184. Levi, L.: Stress and distress in response to psychosocial stimuli. *Acta Med. Scand.*, 191 (Suppl. 528):1–166, 1972.

185. Iberal, A.: A proposal for a force essential to biological organization. *Perspect. Biol. Med.*, 18:399–408, 1975.

Part II

IMMUNITY AND GENETICS

3

Frontiers of Stress Research: Stress and Immunity

Marvin Stein, M.D.,
and Steven J. Schleifer, M.D.

IMMUNE RESPONSE

Before considering specific aspects of stress effects on immune function, it is important to have a general understanding of the various components of the immune system. The immune response is responsible for the maintenance of the integrity of the organism in relation to foreign substances, such as bacteria, viruses, tissue grafts and organ transplantation, and neoplasia.

The immune system can be divided into two major aspects: cell-mediated immunity and humoral immunity. The basic cellular unit of both cell-mediated and humoral immunity is the lymphocyte; however, there are differences in the lymphocytes in each immune component. The T lymphocyte is primarily involved in cell-mediated immunity, and the B lymphocyte is primarily involved in humoral immunity. Both T and B lymphocytes derive from pluripotent stem cells in the bone marrow with T cell maturation in the thymus. Several subsets of T cells have been described and include helper T cells, suppressor T cells, and effector T cells. In addition to T and B lymphocytes, a number of other cell types are involved in immune processes and include monocytes, macrophages, mast cells, and neutrophils.

The authors' studies were supported in part by project grant MH37774 from the National Institute of Mental Health and by the Chernow Foundation.

In the development of an immunologic response, antigens — substances recognized as foreign — attach to lymphocytes genetically programmed to recognize a specific antigen. When antigens bind to the surface of lymphocytes, division of the cells occurs, resulting in lymphocyte proliferation and effector responses. Upon reexposure to the antigen, a more rapid and extensive secondary response occurs, due to the induction of memory developed in a subset of lymphocytes during the proliferative component of the primary response.

In humoral immunity, sensitized B lymphocytes, following activation by signals from macrophages and T helper cells, proliferate and differentiate into plasma cells which synthesize antigen-specific antibodies (Figure 1). Antibodies are immunoglobulins (Ig) and include five major classes: IgG, IgM, IgA, IgE and IgD. The immunoglobulins IgM and IgG are produced in response to a wide variety of antigens, with the production of relatively small amounts of IgM soon after antigenic stimulation, followed by large amounts of IgG. The function of IgA involves protection of external surfaces of the body, and IgA is found in mucous secretions of the gut and respiratory tract and in colostrum and milk. IgE is the reaginic antibody which binds to mast cells and, when a specific antigen combines with IgE, the mast cells release the mediators of immediate hypersensitivity. These mediators include histamine, kinins, and slow reacting substance (leukotrienes).

The primary protective function of humoral immunity is against infections by encapsulated bacteria, e.g., streptococcus. At times, however, the response can be pathological such as in anaphylaxis, asthma, and, occasionally, in response to the organism's own tissues, in an autoimmune disorder such as systemic lupus erythematosus.

In contrast to the B cell whose role is primarily secretory, the T cell participates itself in the cell-mediated immune response (Figure 1). Genetically controlled T lymphocytes passing through the tissues are sensitized to a specific antigen peripherally and then progress to a local lymph node, where they enter the free areas of the cortex follicles. The T cells proliferate and are transformed into larger lymphoblasts. After several days the T lymphocytes become immunologically active, and one subpopulation of effector T lymphocytes mediates delayed type hypersensitivity such as occurs in chemical contact sensitivity or in the tuberculin reaction. Another subpopulation of T cells involved in cell-mediated immunity is cytotoxic and, upon contact with the antigen, releases lymphokines such as macrophage migration inhibitory factor (MIF), chemotactic factors, cytotoxic factors, and interferon. The lymphokines are involved in the destruction of the foreign antigen. Cell-mediated immune responses include protection against viral, fungal, and intracellular

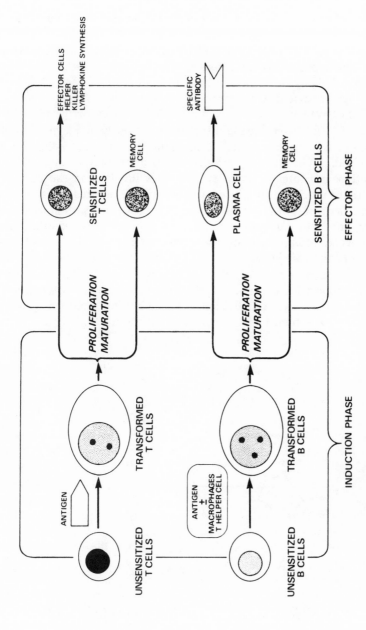

FIGURE 1. The development of an immune response. Reproduced, with permission, from Stites, D. P., Stobo, J. D., Fudenberg, H. H., and Wells, J. V. *Basic and Clinical Immunology, 4th Edition.* Lange Medical Publications: Los Altos, California, 1982, p. 279.

bacterial infection; transplantation reactions; and immune surveillance against neoplasia.

The classical division of the immune system into cellular and humoral immunity is oversimplified. Recent research has revealed that the immune system consists of highly fine tuned and self-regulatory processes with T to T and T to B lymphocyte interdependence and interactions. These regulatory functions may have both protective and pathological effects on the organism.

Many of the studies reported in this chapter utilized lymphocyte stimulation as an in vitro correlate of cellular immunity. Lymphocyte stimulation (Figure 2) is an in vitro technique which is commonly used to assess the in vivo function and interaction of lymphocytes involved in the immune response. In the procedure, sensitized lymphocytes are cultured and activated with specific antigens, or non-sensitized cells are activated with nonspecific stimulants, known as mitogens. A number of plant lecithins and other substances have been utilized as mitogens. Phytohemagglutinin (PHA) and concanavalin A (ConA) are predominantly T cell mitogens, and pokeweed mitogen (PWM) stimulates primarily B lymphocytes.

When lymphocytes are stimulated, there is an increase in DNA synthesis which eventually results in cell division and proliferation. The measurement of DNA synthesis is made by labeling stimulated cultures with a radioactive

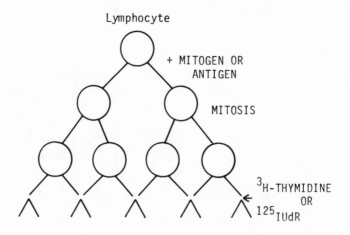

Lymphocyte

+ MITOGEN OR ANTIGEN

MITOSIS

^{3}H-THYMIDINE
OR
^{125}IUdR

Δ CPM = CPM in Stimulated Culture - CPM in Unstimulated Culture

FIGURE 2. Lymphocyte stimulation. Adapted by permission from Criep, L. H. *Allergy and Clinical Immunology*. Grune and Stratton: New York, 1976, p. 15.

nucleoside precursor which is incorporated into newly synthesized DNA. The determination of the amount of precursor incorporated provides a measure of DNA synthesis and is employed as the standard measure of lymphocyte responsiveness. The radioactive incorporation data are expressed as counts per minute (CPM) and, as shown in Figure 2, the CPM in unstimulated cultures are subtracted from the stimulated CPM and provide a stimulation index (ΔCPM).

STRESS AND HUMORAL IMMUNE RESPONSES

A variety of stressors have been found to alter humoral immune responses in animals. Early studies indicated that avoidance learning stress can decrease the susceptibility of mice to passive anaphylaxis (1) and that the production of a specific antibody could be suppressed in a variety of species by distressing environmental stimuli such as noise, light, movement, or housing conditions (2, 3, 4). Both primary and secondary antibody responses could be suppressed (5). However, exposure to other stressors such as repeated low voltage electric shock were found to enhance antibody responses (5, 6).

More recent studies have tended to support the observation that, while acute exposure to a stressor can suppress humoral immune responses, repeated exposure results in an apparent adaptation of the animals to the stressor and, in some cases, an enhanced response. Gisler (7) found that restraint or crowding, presented in a single session of varying lengths, induced suppression of antibody responses, but that after three days of repeated presentation of the stimulus, the response had returned to prestress levels. Monjan and Collector (8), assessing B lymphocyte activity using the mitogen lipopolysaccharide (LPS) to stimulate splenic lymphocytes, found that exposure of mice to sound stress for up to 20 days suppressed the response, but more extended exposure resulted in an enhanced response. The complexity of stress effects on humoral immunity were further highlighted by Joasoo and McKenzie (9), who found differential effects of different stresses on antibody responses in rats depending upon the sex of the animal. These studies suggest that the effect of stress on the humoral immune system are related to the nature and intensity of the stimulus, as well as biological and social characteristics of the organism.

Only a few reports suggest that there may be alterations in humoral immunity in relation to psychological conditions in man (10, 11). These studies measured total Ig levels rather than Ig production in response to specific antigens, and nonspecific effects on proteins may explain the findings. More recently, associations between stress and T dependent B cell function in man have been demonstrated using lymphocyte proliferative responses and will be described below.

STRESS AND CELL MEDIATED IMMUNE RESPONSES

A series of animal studies have begun to investigate stress and cell-mediated immune processes. Monjan and Collector (8) investigated the effect of sound stress on the response of murine splenic lymphocytes to the mitogen ConA. Parallel to findings with the B cell mitogen LPS, they found suppression of the response following short-term exposure to the stressor and enhancement with extended exposure. Reite and coworkers (12) have developed a model for studying immune function following separation experiences in primates and found decreased T cell mitogen lymphocyte stimulation responses following peer separation for two weeks in a pair of pigtailed monkeys raised together from early infancy. Mitogen responses returned to baseline within several weeks of reunion. Studies from our laboratory have demonstrated a relationship between the intensity of an acute stressor and the degree of suppression of T lymphocyte function in rats. A graded series of stressors, applied over 18 hours, including restraint in an apparatus, low-level electric tail shock, and high-level shock, produced a progressively greater suppression of both the number of circulating lymphocytes and PHA-induced stimulation of peripheral blood lymphocytes (13).

Laudenslager and Ryan (14) have recently reported that stress-induced suppression of lymphocyte stimulation is related to the psychosocial state of the animal. They found that PHA and ConA stimulation of lymphocytes was suppressed in rats subjected to a tail shock paradigm which had been found to induce opioid analgesia. Animals exposed to inescapable, uncontrollable electric tail shock for 80 minutes, followed 24 hours later by several minutes of tail shock, were found to have decreased mitogen responses. Animals receiving the same total amount of shock, using a yoked paradigm but able to terminate the stressor, did not have decreased lymphocyte activity. These studies are consistent with hypotheses suggesting that the ability to cope with a stressor protects against its noxious effects.

BEREAVEMENT AND LYMPHOCYTE FUNCTION

Conjugal bereavement is one of the most potentially stressful of commonly occurring life events and has been associated with increased medical morbidity and mortality (15). In our laboratory we have investigated the effect of bereavement on immunity in a prospective longitudinal study of spouses of women with advanced breast carcinoma (16). Lymphocyte stimulation responses were measured in 15 men before and after the death of their wives. As can be seen in Figures 3–5, lymphocyte stimulation responses to the mitogens PHA, ConA, and PWM were significantly lower during the first two months post-bereavement compared with pre-bereavement responses. The number of peripheral blood lymphocytes and the percentage and absolute number of T and B cells obtained during the pre-bereavement period were not significantly different from the post-bereavement period. Follow-up during the remainder of the post-bereavement year revealed that lymphocyte stimulation responses had returned to pre-bereavement levels for the majority but not all of the subjects. These findings demonstrate that suppression of mitogen-induced lymphocyte stimulation is a direct consequence of the bereavement event.

The processes linking the experience of bereavement with effects of lymphocyte activity are complex and remain to be determined. Changes in nutrition, activity, and exercise levels (17), sleep (18), and drug use (19, 20, 21) often found in the widowed (22) could influence lymphocyte function. Our subjects, however, did not report major or persistent changes in diet or activity levels or in the use of medication, alcohol, tobacco, or other drugs, and no significant changes in weight were noted. Further study is required to determine if subtle changes on these parameters are related to the effects of bereavement on lymphocyte function.

The effects of the death of a spouse on lymphocyte function could result from centrally mediated stress effects. Stressful life experiences may be related to changes in CNS activity associated with a psychological state such as depression. Bereaved subjects have been characteristically described as manifesting depressed mood (23, 24), and a subgroup of bereaved individuals has been reported as having symptom patterns consistent with the presence of a major depressive disorder (23).

DEPRESSION AND IMMUNITY

Several studies have assessed immune parameters in clinically depressed individuals. The frequency of antinuclear antibodies, which may reflect autoimmune processes, has been reported to be increased in patients with depression (25, 26, 27, 28). More recently, investigators have begun to evaluate general measures of lymphocyte function in depression. Cappel et al. (29) reported that lymphocyte stimulation responses to PHA were lower in a group of psychotically depressed patients during the acute phase of their illness than following clinical remission. PHA responses in the depressed group did not

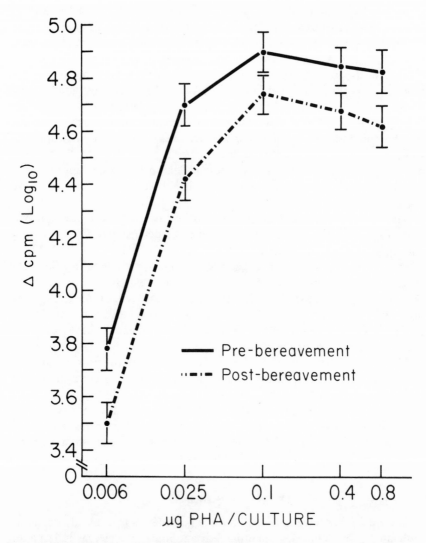

FIGURE 3. PHA-induced lymphocyte stimulation before and after (one to two months) bereavement. Each point represents group mean ± SEM (n = 15) of each subject's mean log change in counts per minute (ΔCPM) for each period. From S. J. Schleifer et al. (16), by permission. Copyright 1983, American Medical Association.

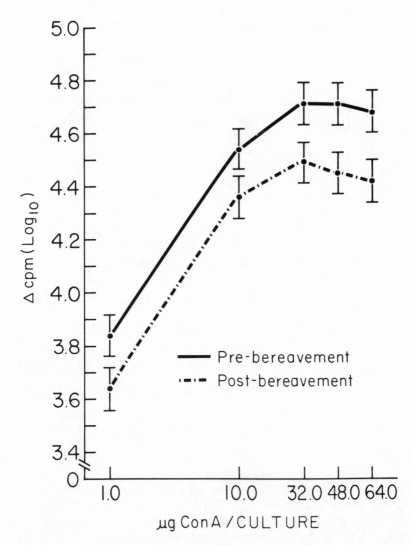

FIGURE 4. ConA-induced lymphocyte stimulation before and after (one to two months) bereavement. Each point represents group mean ± SEM (n = 15) of each subject's mean log change in counts per minute (ΔCPM) for each period. From S. J. Schleifer et al. (16), by permission. Copyright 1983, American Medical Association.

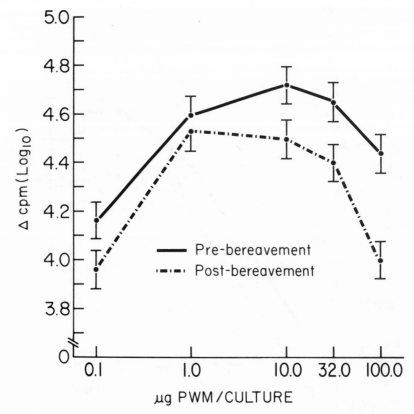

FIGURE 5. PWM-induced lymphocyte stimulation before and after (one to two months) bereavement. Each point represents group mean ± SEM (n = 15) of each subject's mean log change in counts per minute (ΔCPM) for each period. From S. J. Schleifer et al. (16), by permission. Copyright 1983, American Medical Association.

differ, however, from those of control subjects at either time, making interpretation of the findings difficult. Kronfol and coworkers (30) recently reported that melancholic patients had lower lymphocyte responses to PHA, ConA, and PWM than groups of non-melancholic psychiatric patients and normal controls. These studies have been limited by the lack of age- and sex-matched controls being studied on the same day as the depressed patients and by potential interactions between medication effects and lymphocyte function.

We have conducted a series of studies to determine if depressive disorders are associated with altered immunity. Mitogen-induced lymphocyte stimulation responses and the absolute number of lymphocytes were measured in a group of inpatients and outpatients with major depressive disorders. Each subject was studied on the same day with an age- and sex-matched, apparently healthy control. Depressed subjects were included if they met Research Diagnostic Criteria (RDC) (31) for Major Depressive Disorder, had a Hamilton Depression Scale score of 18 or greater (32), were free of acute or chronic medical disorders associated with immune alterations, and were drug free.

In the severely depressed hospitalized patients with Major Depressive Disorder we found evidence of altered immunity (33). As can be seen in Figure 6, lymphocyte stimulation by PHA, ConA, and PWM was significantly lower in the group of hospitalized depressives than in the controls. The total number of T and B cells was also lower in the depressives, but the percentage of the cell types did not differ between the groups. These findings demonstrate that the functional activity of the lymphocyte, as well as the number of circulating immunocompetent cells, are decreased in individuals hospitalized with acute major depressive disorder.

In order to determine if altered immunity is associated specifically with depression and not related to hospital effects or nonspecifically to other psychiatric disorders, we investigated lymphocyte function in ambulatory patients with Major Depressive Disorder and in patients hospitalized with schizophrenic disorders. Lymphocyte stimulation responses were similar among depressed outpatients and controls for PHA, ConA, and PWM. The findings of no significant differences in mitogen responses between ambulatory depressives and controls, in contrast to our previous findings of suppressed responses to the same mitogens in hospitalized depressives, suggest that the decreased mitogen responses in the inpatient depressives may be related to hospitalization or to severity of the depression.

A group of hospitalized schizophrenic patients were, therefore, studied, and we found no differences between the hospitalized schizophrenic patients and their controls on any of the lymphocyte measures. These findings suggest that hospitalization on a psychiatric unit is not in itself sufficient to result in a change in mitogen responsivity or the number of peripheral blood lymphocytes. It is possible that schizophrenic inpatients are not directly comparable to inpatient depressives since they may have atypical responses to hospitalization, and further investigation is required.

The decreased mitogen responses in hospitalized patients with Major Depressive Disorder but not in ambulatory patients with Major Depressive Disorder suggest the altered immunity in depression may be related to severity of depressive symptomatology. The ambulatory patients had lower Hamilton scores as compared to the hospitalized depressives. This preliminary finding of an association between an immune alteration and severity of depression

Stress in Health and Disease

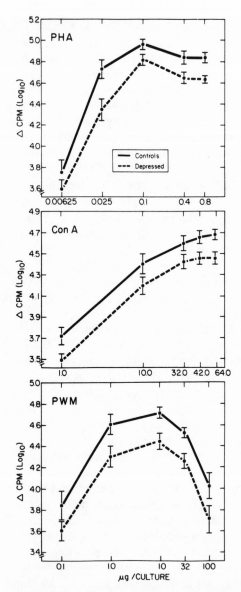

FIGURE 6. Mitogen-induced lymphocyte stimulation in depressed subjects and controls. Each point represents mean change in counts per minute (ΔCPM) $\pm$ SEM (n = 18) log transformed for each group. From S. J. Schleifer et al. (33), by permission. Copyright 1984, American Medical Association.

suggests that immune changes may be related to underlying biological processes in depression.

MEDIATION OF STRESS EFFECTS ON IMMUNE FUNCTION

A variety of factors may be involved in mediating the associations among stress, depression, and immunity. The endocrine system is highly responsive to both life experiences and psychological state and has a significant although complicated effect on immune processes. The most widely studied hormones are those of the hypothalamic-pituitary-adrenocortical axis. A wide range of stressful experiences is capable of inducing the release of corticosteroids (34–39), and cortisol secretion has also been shown to be increased in Major Depressive Disorder. Corticosteroids have extensive and complex effects on the immune system. Of particular interest in relation to our findings of decreased numbers of lymphocytes and lower mitogen responses in depression is the demonstration that pharmacological doses of glucocorticosteroids diminish mitogen-induced lymphocyte stimulation (40–43) and induce a redistribution of T cells from the circulating pool to the bone marrow (42, 44). Several reports have demonstrated that the recirculating lymphocyte traffic in humans is sensitive to endogenous corticosteroids and varies in relation to endogenous cortisol levels (45, 46) as does the response to PHA lymphocyte stimulation (46, 47).

Secretion of corticosteroids has long been considered to be the mechanism of stress-induced modulation of immunity and related disease processes (48, 49). The regulation of immune function in response to stress, however, may not be limited to corticosteroids. As previously noted, we have shown in rats that unpredictable, unavoidable electric tail shock suppressed immune function, as measured by the number of circulating lymphocytes and PHA stimulation (13). In an effort to determine if the adrenal is required for stress-induced suppression of lymphocyte function in the rat, we investigated the effect of stressors in adrenalectomized animals (50). Four groups of rats were studied and consisted of non-operated, adrenalectomized, sham-adrenalectomized, and adrenalectomized animals with a corticosterone pellet. The four treatments—home-cage control, apparatus control, low-shock, and high-shock animals—were identical to those used in our previous study. There was a progressive increase in corticosterone with increasing stress in both of the groups with adrenals; no corticosterone was detected in the adrenalectomized group; and the concentration of corticosterone in the adrenalectomized group that received the corticosterone pellets was constant.

In both the non-operated and sham-adrenalectomized group, there was a significant, progressive stress-induced lymphopenia. There were no stress-related changes in the numbers of lymphocytes in the adrenalectomized group or in the adrenalectomized with pellet group. These results demonstrate that stress-induced lymphopenia in the rat occurs in association with stress-induced secretion of corticosteroids and can be prevented by adrenalectomy. The stressful conditions suppressed stimulation of lymphocytes by PHA in the adrenalectomized animals. The stressors similarly suppressed PHA-induced lymphocyte stimulation in non-operated animals, replicating the data of our earlier study. Suppression of lymphocyte stimulation also occurred in the sham-adrenalectomized group and in adrenalectomized animals with steroid replacement. These results demonstrate that stress-related adrenal secretion of corticosteroids and catecholamines are not required for stress-induced suppression of lymphocyte stimulation.

The findings of adrenal-dependent, stress-induced lymphopenia, as well as adrenal independent effects on lymphocyte stimulation, indicate that stress-induced modulation of immunity is complex and multifaceted.

Changes in thyroid hormones, growth hormones, and sex steroids have been associated with stress, and all have been reported to modulate immune function (51). Furthermore, we (52, 53) and others (54), have shown that the hypothalamus, which plays a central role in neuroendocrine function, modulates both humoral and cell-mediated immunity. These findings suggest that a range of neuroendocrine processes may be involved in stress-induced altered immunity.

There is good evidence that influences other than hormonal are involved in CNS regulation of immunity. It has been demonstrated in hypophysectomized rats that anterior hypothalamic lesions result in an increase in the number of thymic lymphocytes and a decrease in mitogen response (54). A direct link between the CNS and immunocompetent tissues has been suggested by the demonstration of nerve endings in the thymus, spleen, and lymph nodes (55–58). The thymus has also been shown to receive direct innervation from the nucleus ambiguus (56). These findings, taken with the presence of adrenergic and cholinergic receptors on the lymphocyte surface (59, 60), further support the possibility of a direct link between the CNS and immune response to stressors and in association with psychological states such as depression.

Recently, it has been demonstrated that there is decreased norepinephrine turnover in the hypothalamus of the rat at the peak of an immune response, and it has been suggested that the immune response exerts an inhibitory action on central noradrenergic neurons as a result of mediators released by immunological cells (61). Furthermore, it has been shown that the lymphocyte can secrete an ACTH-like substance following viral infection (62). These findings suggest the presence of a neuroendocrine-immunoregulatory feedback process associated with aminergic circuits within the CNS.

CONCLUSIONS

Considerable evidence demonstrating a relationship between stress and immune function is accumulating. This chapter suggests that an extensive network of CNS and endocrine system processes may be involved in the modulation of the immune system in response to stressors which in turn may alter the development, onset, and course of a range of illnesses.

REFERENCES

1. Rasmussen, A. F., Jr., Spencer, E. T., and Marsh, J. T.: Decrease in susceptibility of mice to passive anaphylaxis following avoidance-learning stress. *Proc. Soc. Exp. Biol. Med.*, 100: 878–879, 1959.
2. Petrovskii, I. N.: Problems of nervous control in immunity reactions. II. The influence of experimental neuroses on immunity reactions. *Zh. Mikrobiol. Epidemiol. Immunobiol.*, 32: 63–69, 1961.
3. Hill, C. W., Greer, W. E., and Felsenfeld, O.: Psychological stress, early response to foreign protein, and blood cortisol in vervets. *Psychosom. Med.*, 29:279–283, 1967.
4. Vessey, S. H.: Effects of grouping on levels of circulating antibodies in mice. *Proc. Soc. Biol.*, 115:252–255, 1964.
5. Solomon, G. F.: Stress and antibody response in rats. *Int. Arch. Allergy*, 35:97–104, 1969.
6. Hirata-Hibi, M. Plasma cell reaction and thymic germinal centers after a chronic form of electric stress. *J. Retculoendo. Soc.*, 4:370–389, 1967.
7. Gisler, R. H.: Stress and the hormonal regulation of the immune response in mice. *Psychother. Psychosomat.*, 23:197–208, 1974.
8. Monjan, A. A., and Collector, M. I.: Stress-induced modulation of the immune response. *Science*, 196:307–308, 1977.
9. Joasoo, A., and McKenzie, J. M.: Stress and the immune response in rats. *Int. Arch. Allergy Appl. Immunol.*, 50:659–663, 1976.
10. Fessel, W. J.: Mental stress, blood proteins, and the hypothalamus. *Arch. Gen. Psychiat.*, 7:427–435, 1972.
11. Pettingale, K. W., Greer, S., and Tee, D. E.: Serum IgA and emotional expression in breast cancer patients. *J. Psychosom. Res.*, 21:395–399, 1977.
12. Reite, M., Harbeck, R., and Hoffman, A.: Altered cellular immune response following peer separation. *Life Sciences*, 29:1133–1135, 1981.
13. Keller, S., Weiss, J., Schleifer, S., et al.: Suppression of immunity by stress: Effect of a graded series of stressors on lymphocyte stimulation in the rat. *Science*, 213:1397–1400, 1981.
14. Laudenslager, M. L., and Ryan, S. M.: Coping and immunosuppression: Inescapable but not escapable shock suppresses lymphocyte proliferation. *Science*, 221:568–570, 1983.
15. Helsing, K. J., Szklo, M., and Comstock, G. W.: Factors associated with mortality after widowhood. *Am. J. Public Health*, 71:802–809, 1981.

16. Schleifer, S. J., Keller, S. E., Camerino, M., Thornton, J. C., and Stein, M.: Suppression of lymphocyte stimulation following bereavement. *J. Amer. Med. Assoc.*, 250:374–377, 1983.

17. Bistrian, B. R., Blackburn, G. L., and Serimshaw, N. S.: Cellular immunity in semistarved states in hospitalized adults. *Am. J. Psychiat.*, 28:1148–1155, 1975.

18. Palmblad, J., Petrini, B., Wasserman, J. et al.: Lymphocyte and granulocyte reactions during sleep deprivation. *Psychosom. Med.*, 41:273–278, 1979.

19. Baker, G. A., Santalo, R., and Blumenstein, J.: Effect of psychotropic agents upon the blastogenic response of human T-lymphocytes. *Biol. Psychiat.*, 12:159–169, 1977.

20. Sherman, N. A., Smith, R. S., and Middleton, E., Jr.: Effect of adrenergic compounds, aminophylline and hydrocortisone, on in vitro immunoglobulin synthesis by normal human peripheral lymphocytes. *J. Allergy Clin. Immunol.*, 52:13–22, 1973.

21. Tennenbaum, J. I., Ruppert, R. D., and St. Pierre, R. L. et al.: The effect of chronic alcohol administration on the immune responsiveness of rats. *J. Allergy*, 44:272–281, 1969.

22. Clayton, P. J.: The sequelae and nonsequelae of conjugal bereavement. *Am. J. Psychiat.*, 136: 1530–1534, 1979.

23. Clayton, P. J., Halikes, J. A., and Maurice, W. L.: The depression of widowhood. *Br. J. Psychiat.*, 120:71–78, 1972.

24. Parkes, C. M.: *Bereavement: Studies of Grief in Adult Life*. New York: International Universities Press, 1972.

25. von Brauchitsch, H.: Antinuclear factor in psychiatric disorders. *Am. J. Psychiat.*, 128: 102–104, 1972.

26. Deberdt, R., Van Hooren, J., Biesbrouck, M., and Amery, W.: Antinuclear factor-positive mental depression: A single disease entity. *Biol. Psychiat.*, 11:69–74, 1976.

27. Johnstone, E. C., and Whaley, K.: Antinuclear antibodies in psychiatric illness: Their relationship to diagnosis and drug treatment. *Brit. Med. J.*, 2:724–725, 1975.

28. Shopsin, B., Sathananthan, G. L., Chan, T. L., Kravitz, H., and Gershon, S.: Antinuclear factor in psychiatric patients. *Biol. Psychiat.*, 7:81–86, 1973.

29. Cappel, R., Gregoire, F., Thiry, L., and Sprecher, S.: Antibody and cell medicated immunity to herpes simplex virus in psychotic depression. *J. Clin. Psychiat.*, 39:266–268, 1978.

30. Kronfol, Z., Silva, J., Jr., Greden, J. et al.: Impaired lymphocyte function in depressive illness. *Life Sciences*, 33:241–247, 1983.

31. Spitzer, R. L., Endicott, J., and Robins, E.: Research diagnostic criteria: Rationale and reliability. *Arch. Gen. Psychiat.*, 35:773–782, 1978.

32. Endicott, J., Cohen, J., Nee, J. et al.: Hamilton depression rating scale. *Arch. Gen. Psychiat.*, 38:98–103, 1981.

33. Schleifer, S. J., Keller, S. E., Meyerson, A. T., Raskin, M. J., Davis, K. L., and Stein, M.: Lymphocyte function in major depressive disorder. *Arch. Gen. Psychiat.*, 41:484–486, 1984.

34. Coe, C. L., Mendoza, S. P., Smotherman, W. P., and Levine, S.: Mother-infant attachment in the squirrel monkey: Adrenal response to separation. *Behav. Biol.*, 22:256–263, 1978.

35. Tache, Y., DuRuisseau, P., Tache, J., Selye, H., and Collu, R.: Shift in adrenohypophyseal activity during chronic intermittent immobilization of rats. *Neuroendocrinol.*, 22:325–336, 1976.

36. Hofer, M. A., Wolff, C. T., Friedman, S. B., and Mason, J. W.: A psychoendocrine study of bereavement, Part 2: Observations on the process of mourning in relation to adrenocortical function. *Psychosom. Med.*, 34:492–504, 1972.

37. Wolff, C. T., Friedman, S. B., Hofer, M. A., and Mason, J.: Relationship between psychological defenses and mean urinary 17-hydroxycorticosteroid excretion rates. *Psychosom. Med.*, 26:576–590, 1964.

38. Katz, J. L., Weiner, H., Gallagher, T. F., and Hellman, L.: Stress, distress, and ego defenses. *Arch. Gen. Psychiat.*, 23:131–142, 1970.
39. Sachar, E. J.: Neuroendocrine abnormalities in depressive illness. In: E. J. Sachar (Ed.): *Topics in Psychoendocrinology*. New York: Grune and Stratton, 1975.
40. Berenbaum, M. C., Cope, W. A., and Bundick, R. A.: Synergistic effect of cortisol and prostanglandin E on the PHA response. *Clin. Exp. Immunol.*, 26:534–541, 1976.
41. Fauci, A. S.: Corticosteroids and circulating lymphocytes. *Transplant. Proc.*, 7:37–48, 1975.
42. Fauci, A. S., and Dale, D. C.: The effect of hydrocortisone on the kinetics of normal human lymphocytes. *Blood*, 46:235–243, 1975.
43. Goodwin, J. S., Messner, R. P., and Williams, R. C.: Inhibitors of T cell mitogenesis: Effect of mitogen dose. *Cell. Immunol.*, 45:303–308, 1979.
44. Claman, H. N.: Corticosteroids and lymphoid cells. *N. Eng. J. Med.*, 287:388–397, 1972.
45. Thomson, S. P., McMahon, L. J., and Nugent, C. A.: Endogenous cortisol: A regulator of the number of lymphocytes in peripheral blood. *Clin. Immunol. Immunopathol.*, 17:506–514, 1980.
46. Abo, T., Kawate, T., Ito, K., and Kumagai, K.: Studies on the bioperiodicity of the immune response. 1. Circadian rhythms of human T, B, and K cell traffic in the peripheral blood. *J. Immunol.*, 126:1360–1363, 1981.
47. Tavadia, H. B., Fleming, K. A., Hume, R. D., and Simpson, H.: Circadian rhythmicity of human plasma cortisol and PHA-induced lymphocyte transformation. *Clin. Exp. Immunol.*, 22:190–193, 1975.
48. Riley, V.: Psychoneuroendocrine influences on immunocompetence and neoplasia. *Science*, 212:1100–1109, 1981.
49. Selye, H.: *Stress in Health and Disease*. Boston: Butterworths, 1976.
50. Keller, S. E., Weiss, J. M., Schleifer, S. J., Miller, N.E., and Stein, M.: Stress-induced suppression of immunity in adrenalectomized rats. *Science*, 221:1301–1304, 1983.
51. Stein, M., Keller, S., and Schleifer, S.: The hypothalamus and the immune response. In: H. Weiner, M. A. Hofer, and A. J. Stunkard (Eds.), *Brain, Behavior and Bodily Disease*. New York: Raven Press, 1981, pp. 45–65.
52. Keller, S. E., Stein, M., Camerino, M. S., Schleifer, S. J., and Sherman, J.: Suppression of lymphocyte stimulation by anterior hypothalamic lesions in the guinea pig. *Cellular Immunol.*, 52:334–340, 1980.
53. Stein, M., Schleifer, S., and Keller, S.: The role of the brain and neuroendocrine system in immune regulation: Potential links to neoplastic disease. In: S. Levy (Ed.), *Biological Mediators of Behavior and Disease*. New York: Elsevier North Holland, 1982, pp. 147–168.
54. Cross, R. J., Brooks, W. H., Roszman, T. L., and Markesbery, R.: Hypothalamic-immune interactions. Effect of hypophysectomy on neuroimmunomodulation. *J. Neurol. Sciences*, 53:557–566, 1982.
55. Calvo, W.: The innervation of the bone marrow in laboratory animals. *Amer. J. Anat.*, 123:315–328, 1968.
56. Bulloch, K., and Moore, R. Y.: Central nervous system projections to the thymus gland—Possible pathways for the regulation of the immune response. *Anat. Rec.*, 196:25A, 1980.
57. Giron, L. T., Crutcher, K. A., and Davis, J. N.: Lymph nodes—A possible site for sympathetic neuronal regulation of immune responses. *Ann. Neurol.*, 8:520–555, 1980.
58. Williams, J. W., Peterson, R. G., Shea, P. A., Schmedtje, J. F., Bauer, D. C., and Felton, D. L.: Sympathetic innervation of murine thymus and spleen: Evidence for a functional link between the nervous and immune systems. *Brain Res. Bulletin*, 6:83–94, 1980.

59. Bourne, H. R., Lichtenstein, L. M., and Melmon, K. L.: Modulation of inflammation and immunity by cyclic AMP. *Science*, 184:9–28, 1974.
60. Pochet, R., Delesperse, G., Gauseet, P. W., and Collet, H.: Distribution of beta-adrenergic receptors on human lymphocyte subpopulations. *Clin. Exp. Immunol.*, 38:578–584, 1979.
61. Besedovsky, J., del Ray, A., Sorkin, E. et al.: The immune response evokes changes in brain noradrenergic neurons. *Science*, 221:564–566, 1983.
62. Smith, E. M., Meyer, W. J., and Blalock, J. E.: Virus-induced corticosterone in hypophysectomized mice: A possible lymphoid adrenal axis. *Science*, 218:1311–1312, 1982.

4

Interactions Between Stress and Genetic Processes

Seymour S. Kety, M.D.

Stress may be defined very broadly as an environmental deviation which evokes or produces a physiological or pathological change in an organism. Since the organism at every stage in its development is a product of the interaction between its genetic endowment and epigenetic environmental influences, the relationship between stress and genetic factors is an appropriate and interesting area of inquiry. Both stress and genetics are extremely broad categories, the latter including upwards of a million distinct genes, each determining a specific protein with particular structural or functional properties.

The term stress includes a comparable number of specific physical, chemical, microbial, social, and psychological factors. Moreover, the nature and intensity of a particular stress depends to a great extent on the past history of the organism to which it is applied. To most individuals, the word Buick is not a stress, but it is to a thief who has just stolen one. For purposes of this chapter, it is necessary to limit the topic to those in which psychological, as well as biological, processes are involved in the nature of the stress or in the physiological or pathological response.

In the area of psychosomatic problems, there are many examples of stresses which appear to operate through psychological processes in the etiology of a somatic disorder. The present generation of psychiatrists or psychosomaticists has made the field a science with well-controlled studies taking the place of elaborate hypotheses supported by anecdotal reports. This is especially seen in research which has attempted to elucidate the biological mechanism through which psychological changes mediate symptoms for the development of a somatic illness. As fundamental knowledge regarding the brain has advanced, we have seen successive concepts develop regarding the pathways from psychological process to somatic change. Those areas, richly supported in research, involve the autonomic nervous sytem, central neurotransmitters, neuroendocrine modulators, and, most recently, the complex immunological system. We have seen genetic and psychological deviations interacting in the development of peptic ulcers. Furthermore, we are beginning to understand how genetic factors, acted upon by environmental stress, which include psychological as well as chemical and physical stressors, evoke certain types of cancer depending on the state and activity of the immune system. The remainder of this essay will be devoted to the interaction of particular stressors with genetic factors in major mental disorders. While evidence for the operation of genetic factors is excellent, their modes of transmission, loci, and expression have not yet been specified.

The probability of an hereditary vulnerability to schizophrenia was recognized by Kraepelin and Bleuler who pointed out the tendency of the syndrome that they had described to cluster in particular families. That tendency has been consistently observed and quantified in well-controlled studies which made an exhaustive search for mental illness in these families. But a familial concentration of a disorder, although compatible with hereditary transmission, is not evidence for it unless non-genetic familial influences can be excluded. The 40% to 50% concordance for schizophrenia found in monozygotic twins, while the concordance in dizygotic twins is no higher than that in siblings, is more compelling evidence for genetic factors, but even better evidence for the importance of non-genetic or environmental factors. A disorder which was entirely genetic would have a 100% concordance in monozygotic twins, but, in schizophrenia, the concordance is rarely more than 50%.

The adoption strategy attempts to minimize the confounding of genetic- and family-dependent environmental influences in etiology through the separation of these factors which occur in the process of adoption. Three groups have examined the incidence of schizophrenia in the adopted-away offspring of schizophrenics (1–3), and each has found a higher incidence than that in the adopted-away offspring of control biological parents, comparable to the expected incidence in the non-adopted offspring of a schizophrenic parent. Another adoption strategy has been to examine the prevalence of schizophrenia in the biological and adoptive relatives of schizophrenic adoptees, as compared with the relatives of control adoptees. My colleagues and I have been conducting such studies in Denmark (4, 5) where the excellent records make possible almost complete ascertainment. The most recently published results of one study (6) are summarized in Table 1. Two independent diagnostic evaluations of the same set of data are tabulated, the data being extensive psychiatric interviews with the biological and adoptive relatives of 34 schizophrenic adoptees and 34 matched control adoptees in the Copenhagen sample. The relatives are divided into two groups on the basis of their genetic relationship to the schizophrenic adoptees. The biological relatives of the schizophrenic adoptees are the only group genetically related to them, while all of the adoptive relatives and the biological relatives of the controls would constitute the group not genetically related to the schizophrenic adoptees.

We found a significant difference in the concentration of chronic schizophrenia and in latent or uncertain schizophrenia, two syndromes which are related to schizophrenia symptomatically, in the people who were related genetically to the schizophrenic adoptees, even though they had not been reared by them or with them (5). These diagnoses were made blindly from extensive psychiatric interviews by Jacobsen and were based upon the descriptions of Kraepelin and Bleuler for dementia praecox or schizophrenia, and for what

TABLE 1

The Prevalence of Schizophrenic Illness in the Biological Relatives
of 34 Schizophrenic Adoptees (Genetically Related to Them) and in
Adoptive and Control Relatives (Genetically Unrelated to Them)

	Prevalence in Relatives (%)		
	Genetically Related Group	Genetically Unrelated Groups	p*
Diagnoses in relatives			
Chronic schizophrenia (DSM-II)**	4.2	0.9	= .05
Schizophrenia (DSM-III)***	2.9	0	= .03
Latent or uncertain schizophrenia (DSM-II)	16.1	4.9	< .001
Schizotypal personality dis. (DSM-III)	10.5	1.3	< .001
Total (DSM-II)	20.3	5.8	< .0001
Total (DSM-III)	13.3	1.3	< .0001

*Fisher's exact probability, one tailed, in this and subsequent tables
**Diagnoses based on DSM-II by Kety, Rosenthal and Wender (5)
***Diagnoses based on DSM-III by Kendler, Gruenberg and Strauss (7)

Bleuler called latent schizophrenia. Our diagnoses used the characterizations and terminology of DSM-II, and with the publication of DSM-III and its emphasis on operational diagnoses, standardized by some agreement among psychiatrists, it seemed useful to have the same interviews rated independently by another group using DSM-III diagnostic categories. This was accomplished by Kendler, Gruenberg, and Strauss (7). They found, as we had, no increase in affective disorder in the biological relatives of the schizophrenic adoptees, but confirmed with even greater discrimination a strong concentration of schizophrenia spectrum disorders in that group. Their results are also presented in Table I. Certain components of the schizophrenia spectrum were renamed in DSM-III. Schizotypal personality disorder is equivalent to our diagnoses of latent and uncertain schizophrenia from which it was largely derived. Kendler and his associates also found that paranoid personality disorder, as defined in DSM-III, tended to cluster in the individuals genetically related to the schizophrenic adoptees.

Thus there is rather compelling evidence that genetic factors operate in a significant proportion of schizophrenic illness, but it cannot be emphasized too often that these findings do not exclude the operation of environmental influences in etiology and pathogenesis.

The psychosocial milieu of the nuclear family, which 20 years ago occupied a dominant position among etiological theories regarding schizophrenia, still represents an influence of obvious importance in acculturation and personality development, although its role in the genesis of schizophrenia remains to be unequivocally demonstrated. The observations which contributed to its early prominence consisted of various indications of severe psychopathology in the parents of schizophrenic individuals. More compelling, however, was a study which avoided subjective bias on the impact of the schizophrenic upon his family by evaluating records and psychiatric interviews from parents of problem children or adolescents seen in outpatient clinics. Significantly more psychopathology, communication deviance, and marital stress were found in those whose children were to become schizophrenic some years later (8). This approach, as the authors recognized, was unable to rule out genetic factors shared between parents and offspring. In an effort to correct that deficit, studies of adoptive parents of schizophrenics have been conducted which have revealed no gross pathology in them comparable to that which is found in the biological parents of schizophrenics (9).

In blind evaluations of the Rorschach protocols of adoptive and biological parents of schizophrenics, however, Singer has found comparable degrees of communication deviance in parents who have reared a schizophrenic individual whether or not they were genetically related to the patient (10). If it were possible to rule out the effects of the experience of rearing a child who became schizophrenic on the parents' personalities and responses to psychological tests (11–13), the etiologic significance of parental communication deviance or other characteristics identifiable in the Rorschach response would be enhanced. This could be accomplished by applying the design of Waring and Ricks (8) to adopted children or by utilizing the strategy of Jacobsen and Kinney (14) to control the effects of having reared a schizophrenic individual.

It is difficult to believe that the deviances that have been found in the rearing parents of schizophrenics could produce in a normal child anything more than a pallid suggestion of the severe cognitive and behavioral disturbances that are seen in chronic schizophrenia. Perhaps more plausible hypotheses can be developed that are based upon an interaction between a deviant parental milieu and an infant or child made vulnerable by a genetic or other constitutional deficiency (15). The risk for schizophrenia in genetically vulnerable children, however, is remarkably insensitive to quite drastic extremes of rearing milieu. Heston and Denney (16) found no significant difference in the prevalence of schizophrenia or other psychopathology between children at high genetic risk for schizophrenia reared by foster families or in foundling institutions. Higgins (1) studied 50 young adults, all born of schizophrenic mothers, half of whom had been reared by their mothers, the other half separated from their mothers early in life and reared by agents without history of psychiatric illness. Four chronic schizophrenics were found in each group, and other types of psychopathology were no higher in the group reared by their schizophrenic mothers. Individuals born of normal biological parents but reared by adoptive parents with severe psychopathology or psychosis did not show an increased risk for schizophrenia spectrum disorders (17).

The biological and adoptive siblings of schizophrenic adoptees offer a valuable means of examining the relative influence of genetic and rearing factors on the risk for schizophrenia. If rearing factors were significant influences, one would expect the adoptive siblings reared by the same parents to show some increase in risk, whereas the biological siblings reared in a different family should show a diminished risk. This prediction is not borne out in the two studies of which I am aware. Karlsson (18) in his extensive study in Iceland found eight schizophrenics reared in foster families. These had 20 biological full siblings reared apart from them of which six became schizophrenic, and 28 foster siblings reared with them of whom none became schizophrenic. Our study of the national sample of adult adoptees in Denmark has identified 12 who became schizophrenic and had both biological and adoptive full siblings. Again, the biological siblings showed a high risk for schizophrenia whereas the adoptive siblings showed none.

The twofold higher prevalence of schizophrenia in the lower socioeconomic classes of large cities has suggested a number of environmental stresses that might exist to a greater extent in those classes. A large number of social and psychological stressors are associated with poverty, pertaining to status, role perception, values, and child-rearing practices. These provide a number of etiological hypotheses pertinent to schizophrenia which require further evaluation.

Certain biological hazards associated with lower social class should also be considered. To the extent that perinatal injuries, malnutrition, and infection may play roles in the environmental etiologies of schizophrenia, their impact would be exaggerated in the lower socioeconomic class in large cities. Several infectious diseases, especially those of viral origin, occur significantly more frequently in lower socioeconomic classes. Some of these, like cytomegalovirus, are known to be congenitally transmitted and to be latent in the central nervous system, eventually giving rise to deafness or mental retardation (19).

There are some perinatal stressors that may operate in schizophrenia and for which the evidence is quite good. McNeil and Kaij (20) found a significantly higher number of obstetrical complications attending the birth of subjects who eventually became schizophrenic, and this was confirmed in an independent study by Jacobsen and Kinney (14). That psychological stress during pregnancy could play an etiological role in schizophrenia was indicated by an ingenious study carried out by Huttunen (21) in Finland. He followed up a substantial number of the offspring of women whose husbands had died during their pregnancy, comparing them with a very ingeniously selected group of controls, i.e., the offspring of women whose husbands had died in the year following the birth of the child, so that the only systematic difference between the two groups was stress during or immediately after pregnancy. Seven of these offspring became schizophrenic and six were in the stress-during-pregnancy group. This was statistically significant even though the number of schizophrenics was small; moreover there was twice the prevalence of psychiatric disorder generally in the index group as in the controls (p = .025). It would be very worthwhile if such a study could be repeated. A form of social stress represented by expressed emotion in the home has been found in several studies in England and elsewhere to be related to the severity of symptoms and the rate of relapse in schizophrenia, if not to etiology (22).

In the field of depression, a substantial number of retrospective and inadequately controlled studies of an earlier period in psychiatry elicited an association between various stressful life events, such as parental death or separation, loss of a job, financial problems, rejection, and the subsequent development of depressive illness. These studies were difficult to interpret rigorously without information on the incidence of such life events in a comparable control population who did not develop depression. However, more recently, a number of well-controlled studies have been carried out in this area and have often found evidence for such an association. But, just as often, the apparent effect was quite small, leading Andrews and Tennant (23) to summarize the situation in 1978 this way: "The size of the association between life events and depression or schizophrenia is small, accounting for less than 10% of the variance and unlikely to have clinical or preventative importance." In the past year, however, Cooke and Hole (24), writing on the etiological importance of stressful life events, have pointed out a logical fallacy in this type of statistical analysis and have suggested the use of a relatively new statistical treatment and the calculation of what is called population attributable risk which can be defined as the percentage of cases in which the factor under consideration plays a crucial etiological role or, alternatively, as the percentage of cases which would disappear if the factor itself were removed. They calculated this statistic for a number of studies reporting on stressful life events and depression. They came up with values of 35% to 50% of cases in which life events played an important etiological role instead of the nine to 20% of variance explained by life events in previous approaches.

There are also genetic factors operating in depression, and, as in the case of schizophrenia, a high familial concentration of depressive illness has been observed over the years (25). There is also a high concordance rate for depressive illness in monozygotic twins (26), and an adoption study conducted in Belgium (27) reported a highly significant prevalence of manic-depressive illness in the biological parents of adoptees with major affective disorder.

My colleagues and I have been carrying out a study of depressive illness in the Danish adoption sample (27a) similar to the study of schizophrenia. We identified 71 adoptees in Denmark, adults adopted away at an early age, in whom we could agree on a diagnosis of affect reaction, neurotic depression, unipolar, or bipolar depression. After selecting 71 control adoptees, we identified the biological and adoptive parents, siblings, and half-siblings. Then blind diagnoses were made on the basis of hospital admission and discharge records. In our as yet unpublished results, we have found twice as much depressive illness in the biological relatives of the depressed adoptees as in the control adoptees (11.8 vs 6.1%, p = .004), whereas in schizophrenia we found four to five times as much schizophrenia or schizophrenia-related illness in the biological relatives of the ill adoptees. But also, in contradistinction to schizophrenia, we have found a higher prevalence of depressive disorder in the adoptive relatives of the depressed adoptees as opposed to the controls (8.0 vs 5.9,

N.S.). This is compatible with the possibility that in depressive illness there is an even greater heterogeneity than in schizophrenia and a greater input of cultural and other family-related environmental variables in the incidence of depressive disorders. Thus this study, as well as others in the field, indicates that genetic and environmental factors are not mutually exclusive but may be complementary.

Table 2 presents the prevalence of unipolar depression in the biological and adoptive relatives of the depressed adoptees and their controls. In eight out of 381, or 2.1% of the biological relatives of the depressed adoptees, we made a diagnosis of unipolar depression compared to 0.3% in the control relatives. The unipolar depression in the adoptive relatives did not differ between the index and the control series. Unipolar depression, however, is the only form of depression which showed so striking a concentration in the biological relatives and none in the adoptive relatives. This, of course, is the form of depression which was formerly called endogenous, because, in the minds of psychiatrists, external events did not appear to be operating, and the syndrome appeared to be generated almost exclusively by internal, endogenous processes. These findings would confirm that impression and indicate that unipolar depression (of all the depressions) is one which has the strongest input of genetic and constitutional factors and is least influenced by cultural variables or stressors.

TABLE 2

The Prevalence of Unipolar Depression and the Incidence of Suicide in the Biological and Adoptive Relatives of 71 Index Adoptees with Reactive, Neurotic, Unipolar or Bipolar Depression and 71 Control Adoptees

| | Prevalence or incidence in: | |
	Biological Relatives (%)	Adoptive Relatives (%)
In relatives of 71 index adoptees:		
Unipolar depression	2.1*	0.6
Suicide	3.7**	0.5
In relatives of 71 control adoptees:		
Unipolar depression	0.3	0.6
Suicide	0.3	1.2

*different from controls $p < .03$
**different from controls $p < .001$

Our most interesting and quite unexpected results were obtained in the case of suicide. Suicide is an example of deviant behavior where both environmental and genetic factors may be important or necessary, yet neither may be sufficient. We have known for a long time of a large number of socioenvironmental factors which are associated with suicide (28). There are marked differences in the rates for suicide according to age, religion, the country in which the study is carried out, the period of time in which the statistics are gathered, and the particular period in that country. These marked variations cannot be explained on the basis of genetic variance because the genes do not vary so widely from one country to another, nor do they vary within a country from one time to another. There are personal factors which are associated with suicide: marital status, financial status, unemployment, parental loss, and others which influence the risk. In addition, there are a large number of psychiatric risk variables: previous history of schizophrenia, of depression, of alcohol or drug dependence, and various types of personality disorder (29). Studies of suicide and mental illness in families have shown an association between the two but with a clear indication that the risk of suicide or attempted suicide is significantly enhanced where there has been a family history of suicide (30, 31).

We might expect that genetic factors would be better demonstrated by studies of twins, and it is interesting that Kallmann, who found such high concordance rates for schizophrenia and manic-depressive illness in monozygotic twins, found no concordance at all for suicide (32) and concluded from those studies that genetic factors did not operate significantly in suicide. However, Haberlandt (33), reviewing the studies to 1967, found an 18% concordance for suicide in a total of 51 monozygotic twin pairs and no dizygotic twins concordant for suicide. More recently, Jule-Nielsen (34) found a significant number of concordant monozygotic twin pairs with suicide. In no series is the concordance rate as high as it is for depression or schizophrenia; this is probably because the incidence of suicide itself in the population is quite low compared to schizophrenia or manic-depressive illness. Further, the crucial importance of an environmental stressor in suicide need not occur in both members of a pair of monozygotic twins. It is also possible that suicide in one monozygotic twin actually diminishes the possibility of suicide in the remaining twin for psychological reasons.

In the adoption studies which we carried out on depression, we expected to find a substantial number of suicides among the adoptees and also among their relatives. However, we were surprised at the remarkable concentration of suicide almost exclusively in the biological relatives of adoptees who were themselves depressed or who had committed suicide.

The prevalence of suicide in relatives of adoptees with depression and of control adoptees is presented in Table 2. There were 19 suicides in the relatives as a whole, 15 of which were in the biological parents, siblings, and half-siblings of the depressed adoptees. This highly significant concentration of suicide occurred in people who were related only genetically to adoptees with depressive illness. They did not rear them, were not reared by them, and in almost all cases were unaware of the whereabouts of the adoptee or what had happened to him. On the basis of this observation, Schulsinger searched our register of 5,483 adult adoptees in Denmark for any who had committed suicide. After that he sought the incidence of suicide in their biological and adoptive relatives and compared it to the incidence in relatives of matched control adoptees who had not committed suicide (35).

In the biological relatives of the adoptees who had committed suicide, there was a 4.5% incidence of suicide compared to an incidence of less than 1% in the control biological relatives. In the adoptive relatives of both groups there were no suicides. The psychiatric register was searched for indications of depression or other mental illness in those who committed suicide. In a significant segment, no such history was found. Although that does not exclude the possibility that a brief period of depression could have preceded the suicide, it was suggested that there is a type of suicide which is not associated with mental illness.

One would not, of course, conclude from these results that suicide is entirely a genetically determined pattern of behavior, since there is a vast literature which supports a number of crucial socioenvironmental factors operating in suicide (28). It is more likely that of all individuals who are subjected to some stressful life event, those who commit suicide have some genetic predisposition to do so. That raises the question: What might that predisposition be?

If we look for biochemical correlates of suicide, we find a number of studies suggesting biochemical processes which may be an expression of the genetic trait predisposing to suicide (36). A marked increase in cortisol secretion has been reported in subjects who have shortly thereafter committed suicide (37). This rise in cortisol secretion, however, was thought to be secondary to the stress which antedates the suicide and may be less a trait marker than an indication of psychological state. More interesting is the evidence supporting the hypothesis that serotonin metabolism may be involved and may be deficient in some way in individuals who commit suicide. There are studies carried out on the metabolites of serotonin in the cerebrospinal fluid of depressed patients, some of whom went on to commit suicide. Åsberg and her associates (38) have found that patients in whom the 5-hydroxyindolacetic acid was particularly low had a greater tendency to commit suicide than the others.

There was, in fact, a bimodal distribution in her observations with suicide, clustering in the individuals who had the lowest values of 5-hydroxyindolacetic acid. There have been studies on postmortem samples of brain from suicide victims compared with those who died suddenly of other causes. In such studies, by and large, there has been evidence for a diminution in serotonin synthesis and turnover and low levels of 5-hydroxyindolacetic acid (39).

More recently, there has been a study on imipramine binding in samples of cerebral cortex from suicide victims (40), reporting significantly lower values where death resulted from suicide than from other causes and suggesting a decrease in brain serotonin turnover associated with suicide. I find especially interesting a study carried out by scientists at the NIMH (40) on a group of college students at the University of Maryland. The students merely gave a blood sample and filled out a questionnaire. The blood sample was analyzed in the laboratory for platelet monoaminoxidase (MAO). The questionnaire was a rather comprehensive one, including questions about the individual's family and his patterns of behavior. The groups with the highest and the lowest levels of MAO in their platelets were then compared regarding their answers to the questionnaires. Among a number of findings, the most interesting one pertinent here is that those students with the lowest levels of this enzyme in their platelets had eight times the prevalence of suicide in their families compared to the students with high levels. Results such as those summarized above certainly suggest that serotonin metabolism may have some bearing upon suicide and possibly on the genetic factor involved. We can also ask what is the behavioral trait which is genetically transmitted. Is it depression itself which sometimes leads directly to suicide? This, of course, would be an easy conclusion to draw since there is such a high incidence of suicide in depression and also of depression preceding suicide. Robins (41), who studied 134 suicides exhaustively, found that a diagnosis of clinical depression could be made in the majority of such individuals. It has been pointed out, however (42), that whereas 62% of those over 60 years of age were diagnosed in that series with affective disorder, that was true for only 24% of those under 40 years. In the latter age group, 54% could be said to have had histories of violence or impulsivity.

If we break down the incidence of suicide in the biological relatives of depressed adoptees according to the type of affective disorder diagnosed in the adoptee (Table 3), we see that whether the adoptees' diagnoses were affective reaction, neurotic depression, bipolar or unipolar depression, there is a significant concentration of suicide in the biological relatives of each group. It is interesting that the very highest incidence of suicide was in the biological relatives of the adoptees with the very transient depressive syndrome called affect reaction. This was usually a serious suicide attempt followed by a

TABLE 3
The Incidence of Suicide in the Biological Relatives
of Depressive and Control Adoptees

	Incidence of Suicide in Biological Relatives		p
Diagnosis in adoptee			
Affective reaction	$\frac{5}{66}$	7.6%	.0004*
Neurotic depression	$\frac{3}{127}$	2.4%	.056
Bipolar depression	$\frac{4}{75}$	5.3%	.0036
Unipolar depression	$\frac{3}{139}$	2.2%	.067
No mental illness	$\frac{1}{361}$	0.3%	

*compared with biological relatives of control adoptees with no known history of mental illness

depression of very brief duration with no known recurrence. These individuals did not come back into the psychiatric register. It was apparently an impulsive act almost always precipitated by some stressful life event. There was more than three times as much suicide in the biological relatives of these adoptees than in those of the unipolar depressions, which would be the paradigm of severe, chronic, depressive illness. As noted earlier, Tsuang (30) has found a significantly higher incidence of suicide in the families of depressed patients who committed suicide than in the relatives of those who did not. Thus it is an interesting possibility that there is a genetic predisposition not only to depression but also to suicide through impulsive behavior of which suicide is a prime example. There have been a number of studies compatible with that suggestion. Brown and his associates (43) at the NIMH found diminished levels of 5-hydroxyindolacetic acid in the cerebrospinal fluid of individuals who were not at all depressed but were characterized by impulsive or sociopathic behavior. Lithium, which is effective particularly in the prophylaxis of bipolar depression, has also been found to be effective in impulsive and aggressive behavior (44). It would be difficult to find out in a controlled manner, but interesting to know, whether antidepressant drugs or precursors, which act primarily to enhance the activity of serotonin in the brain, are capable of suppressing suicidal tendencies specifically.

We cannot dismiss the possibility that the genetic factor in suicide is an inability to control impulsive behavior, while depression and other mental illness, as well as overwhelming environmental stressors, serve as potentiating mechanisms which permit or trigger the impulsive behavior, resulting in a suicidal outcome. In any case, suicide illustrates better than any of the other studies that have been discussed the very crucial and important interactions between genetic factors and environmental stressors, in which neither may be sufficient and both are necessary.

REFERENCES

1. Higgins, J.: Effect of child rearing by schizophrenic mothers. *J. Psych. Res.*, 4:153–167, 1966.
2. Heston, L. L.: Psychiatric disorders in foster home reared children of schizophrenic mothers. *Br. J. Psych.*, 112:819–825, 1966.
3. Rosenthal, D., Wender, P. H., Kety, S. S., Schulsinger, F., Welner, J., and Ostergaard, L.: Schizophrenics' offspring reared in adoptive homes. In: D. Rosenthal and S. S. Kety (Eds.), *The Transmission of Schizophrenia*. Oxford: Permagon Press, 1968.
4. Kety, S. S., Rosenthal, D., Wender, P. H., and Schulsinger, F.: The types and prevalence of mental illness in the biological and adoptive families of adopted schizophrenics. In: D. Rosenthal and S. S. Kety (Eds.), *The Transmission of Schizophrenia*. Oxford: Pergamon Press, 1968.
5. Kety, S. S., Rosenthal, D., Wender, P. H., Schulsinger, F., and Jacobsen, B.: Mental illness in the biological and adoptive families of adoptive individuals who have become schizophrenic: A preliminary report based on psychiatric interviews. In: R. R. Fieve, D. Rosenthal and H. Brill, (Eds.), *Genetic Research in Psychiatry*. Baltimore: The Johns Hopkins University Press, 1975.
6. Kety, S. S.: Mental illness in the biological and adoptive relatives of schizophrenic adoptees: Findings relevant to genetic and environmental factors in etiology. *Am. J. Psychiat.*, 140: 720–727, 1983.
7. Kendler, K. S., Gruenberg, A. M., and Strauss, J. S.: An independent analysis of the Copenhagen sample of the Danish adoption study of schizophrenia, II: The relationship between schizotypal personality disorder and schizophrenia. *Arch. Gen. Psychiat.*, 38:982–984, 1981.
8. Waring, M., and Ricks, D. F.: Family patterns of children who become adult schizophrenics. *J. Nerv. Ment. Dis.*, 140:351–364, 1965.
9. Wender, P. H., Rosenthal, D., Rainer, J. D., Greenhill, L., and Sarlin, B.: Schizophrenics' adopting parents: Psychiatric status. *Arch. Gen. Psychiat.*, 34:777–784, 1977.
10. Wynne, L. C., Singer, M. T., and Toohey, M. L.: Psychotherapy, family studies, research. In: J. Jorstad and E. Ugelstad (Eds.), *Schizophrenia 75*. Oslo: University of Oslo Press, 1976.
11. Schopler, E., and Loftin, J.: Thought disorders in parents of psychotic children. *Arch. Gen. Psychiat.*, 20:174–181, 1969.
12. Liem, J. H.: Effects of verbal communications of parents and children: A comparison of normal and schizophrenic families. *J. Cons. Clin. Psychol.,* 42:438–450, 1974.
13. Hirsch, S. R., and Leff, J. P.: *Abnormalities in Parents of Schizophrenics*. Maudsley Monograph No. 22. London: Oxford University Press, 1975.
14. Jacobsen, B., and Kinney, D. K.: Perinatal complication in adopted and non-adopted schizo-

phrenics and their controls: Preliminary results. *Acta. Psychiat. Scand. (Suppl.)*, 285:337–346, 1980.

15. Garmezy, N.: The experimental study of children vulnerable to psychopathology. In: A. Davids (Ed.), *Child Personality and Psychopathology: Current Topics, Vol. 1.* New York: Wiley, 1975.

16. Heston, L. L., and Denney, D.: Interactions between early life experience and biological factors in schizophrenia. In: D. Rosenthal and S. S. Kety (Eds.), *The Transmission of Schizophrenia.* Oxford: Pergamon Press, 1968.

17. Wender, P. H., Rosenthal, D., Kety, S. S., Schulsinger, F., and Welner, J.: Cross-fostering: A research strategy for clarifying the role of genetic and experiential factors in the etiology of schizophrenia. *Arch. Gen. Psychiat.*, 30:121–128, 1974.

18. Karlsson, J. L.: *The Biologic Basis of Schizophrenia.* Springfield, IL: Charles C Thomas, 1966.

19. Hanshaw, J. A., Scheiner, A. P., Moxley, A. W., Gaev, L., Abel, V., and Scheiner, B.: School failure and deafness after "silent" congenital cytomegalovirus infection. *N. E. J. Med.*, 295:468–470, 1976.

20. McNeil, T. F., and Kaij, L.: Obstetric factors in the development of schizophrenia: Complications in the births of preschizophrenics and in reproduction by schizophrenic parents. In: L. C. Wynne, R. L. Cromwell and S. Matthysse (Eds.), *The Nature of Schizophrenia.* New York: Wiley, 1978.

21. Huttunen, M. O., and Niskanen, P.: Perinatal loss of father and psychiatric disorders. *Arch. Gen. Psychiat.*, 35:429–431, 1978.

22. Birley, J. L. T., and Brown, G. W.: Crises and life changes preceding the onset of relapse of acute schizophrenia. *Brit. J. Psychiat.*, 116:237–333, 1970.

23. Andrews, S. G., and Tennant, C.: Life event stress and psychiatric illness. *Psychol. Med.*, 8:545–549, 1978.

24. Cooke, D. J., and Hole, D. J.: The aetiological importance of stressful life events. *Brit. J. Psychiat.*, 143:397–400, 1983.

25. Nurnberger, J. I., Jr., and Gershon, E. S.: Genetics of affective disorders. In: E. Paykell (Ed.), *Handbook of Affective Disorders.* London: Churchill Livingston, 1982.

26. Rosenthal, D.: *Genetics of Psychopathology.* New York: McGraw-Hill, 1971.

27. Mendlewicz, J., and Rainer, J. D.: Adoption study supporting genetic transmission in manic depressive illness. *Nature*, 268:327–329, 1977.

27a. Wender, P. H., Kety, S. S., Schulsinger, F., Rosenthal, D. et al. Affective illness in the biological and adoptive relatives of adoptees with a history of affect disorder. Unpublished manuscript.

28. Dublin, L.: *Suicide: A Sociological and Statistical Study.* New York: Ronald Press, 1963.

29. Roy, A.: Risk factors for suicide in psychiatric patients. *Arch. Gen. Psychiat.*, 39:1089–1095, 1982.

30. Tsuang, M. T.: Risk of suicide in the relatives of schizophrenics, manics, depressives and controls. *J. Clin. Psychiat.*, 44:396–400, 1983.

31. Roy, A.: Family history of suicide. *Arch. Gen. Psychiat.*, 40:971–974, 1983.

32. Kallmann, F., and Anastasio, M.: Twin studies on the psychopathology of suicide. *J. Nerv. Ment. Dis.*, 105:40–55, 1947.

33. Haberlandt, W.: Aportacion a la genetica del suicidio. *Folio Clin. Int.*, 17:319–322, 1967.

34. Jule-Nielsen, N., and Videbech, T.: A twin study of suicide. *Acta. Genet. Med. Gemellol.*, 19:307–310, 1970.

35. Schulsinger, F., Kety, S. S., Rosenthal, D., and Wender, P. H.: A family study of suicide. In: M. Schou and E. Stromgren (Eds.), *Origin, Prevention and Treatment of Affective Disorders.* New York: Academic Press, 1979.

36. van Praag, H. M.: Depression, suicide and the metabolism of serotonin in the brain. *J. Aff. Disorders*, 4:275-290, 1982.
37. Bunney, W. E., Jr., and Fawcett, J. A.: Possibility of a biochemical test for suicidal potential. *Arch. Gen. Psychiat.*, 13:332-339, 1965.
38. Åsberg, M., Träskman, L., and Thoren, P.: 5-HIAA in the cerebrospinal fluid: A biochemical suicide predictor. *Arch. Gen. Psychiat.*, 33:1193-1197, 1976.
39. Lloyd, K. G., Farley, I. J., Deck, J. H. N., and Hornykiewicz, O.: Serotonin and 5-hydroxy-indoleacetic acid in discrete areas of the brain stem of suicide victims and control patients. *Adv. Biochem. Psychopharmacol.*, 11:387-397, 1974.
40. Buchsbaum, M. S., Coursey, R. D., and Murphy, D. I.: The biochemical high-risk paradigm: Behavioral and familial correlates of low platelet monoamine oxidase activity. *Science*, 194:339-341, 1976.
41. Robins, E.: *The Final Months: A Study of the Lives of 134 Persons Who Committed Suicide.* New York: Oxford University Press, 1981.
42. Carlson, G. A.: More analysis of Eli Robins' suicide data. *Am. J. Psychiat.*, 141:323, 1984.
43. Brown, G. L., Ebert, M. H., Goyer, P. F., Jimerson, D. C., Klein, W. J., Bunney, W. E., and Goodwin, F. K.: Aggression, suicide and serotonin: Relationship to CSF amine metabolism. *Am. J. Psychiat.*, 139:741-746, 1982.
44. Shard, M., Marini, J., Bridges, C., and Wagner, E.: The effect of lithium on impulsive, aggressive behavior in man. *Am. J. Psychiat.*, 133:1409-1413, 1976.

Part III

SOCIOCULTURAL ASPECTS
OF STRESS

5

Environmental Stress and the Crisis of Psychiatry

*Leonard J. Duhl, M.D.,
and James J. Hynes, B.A.*

This chapter will outline some of the current sources of stress on the field of psychiatry and suggest how these stressors may dramatically shift psychiatry into an ecological, or systems, approach to mental health in the future. In so doing, stressors will be conceived as the on-going contributions of environmental research and the consequences (processes) of economic, political, and social change.

A summary (1) of environmental parameters in stress research concludes that environment often plays simultaneous roles as both stressor and mediator. This conceptualization is relevant both to the clinical aspects of psychiatric work and to understanding and coping with these stressors on the psychiatric profession as a whole. It seems likely that future psychiatrists will be heavily influenced by current stressors within our environment and that psychiatrists will find themselves increasingly working in environmental, political, and social change arenas. Coincident with this shift will be the increasing emergence of a systems, or ecological, orientation in psychiatry.

Psychiatrists generally have had scant training in these arenas. Despite the growing recognition that the old medical model simply will be insufficient in a changing world, little has been done at an institutional or educational level to narrow the gap between what psychiatrists have been trained to do and what they may soon be asked to do. This gap constitutes the current crisis in psychiatry.

As we know from clinical work, a developmental history of the sources of stress may sometimes aid in a search for ways to resolve it. With this in mind, we will explore some relevant facets of social change, as well as the development of environmental thinking in psychiatry. It may then be possible to suggest ways psychiatry can mediate the stress and adapt through a viable systems-oriented role. Figure 1 will clarify our thinking in this regard.

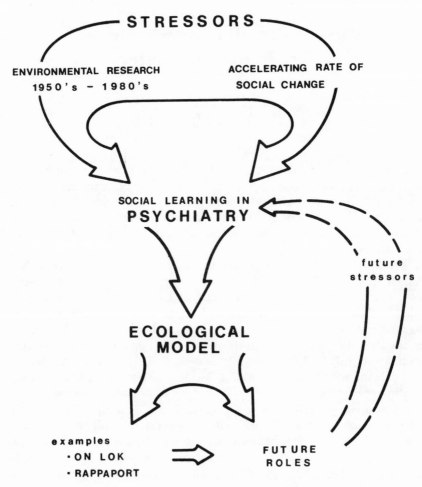

FIGURE 1.

Environmental Research

The post-World-War-II era was a time of tremendous optimism and concern about the environment (2). Walden II (3) is probably the best illustration of this type of optimism in the popular literature of the time. The optimism carried the notion that the environment was an appropriate intervention point through which both treatment and prevention of mental illness could occur.

Psychiatrists such as William Menninger (3a) and Greenwood (3b) began to conceptualize a view of mental health through their involvement with studies on the total environment of the military, corporations and other social systems, including the family. The Mental Health Act of 1946 stipulated the role of NIMH to be involved with not only the rehabilitation of the mentally ill but, perhaps more importantly, with the promotion of the mental health of the people of the United States. This legal definition of the scope of NIMH research activity coalesced with some of the insights of Menninger, and thus the NIMH became deeply involved with environment-related research. One aspect of this broader inquiry was an interest in studying the organizational characteristics of mental hospitals, resulting in the classic Stanton and Schwartz (4) study. Other studies, such as those by Caudill (5) and Goffman (6), added to the debate on environmental and social determinants of behavior. Dollard and Miller (7) even began an attempt to infuse traditional psychoanalytic theory with social learning theory, in a spirit of reconciliation between a rather dominant psychoanalytic school and a new arrival, the behaviorists. Further environmental-related work during the 1960s (8) helped influence the controversial writings of Kesey (9), Szasz (10), and Laing (11), who further influenced the view of a psychiatrist's role in society.

Lindemann's (12) seminal work on grief and bereavement stimulated NIMH to take a close look at an urban renewal project in order to see whether a community/systems level correlate of bereavement could be ascertained. And, as Gans (13) and Fried (14) found, indeed there was. "Grieving for a lost home" proved to be a significant cause of psychological pathology, as indicated in higher use of social service supports, such as welfare and police. This finding has been replicated elsewhere (15, 16), reinforcing the idea that networks and social supports that exist within communities may have more to do with mental health than anything that traditional psychiatry can offer.

Much of this thinking has been captured elsewhere (17), the product of a "recurring forum" (18) on the relationship between environment and mental health. The main point of the forum was that mental health and psychiatry were merely pieces of a much larger system. This recognition has endured and contributes to an ecological perspective to health. This type of systems approach heavily influences those psychiatrists and other mental health workers who study and treat families as a group (19).

Psychiatry had discovered the environment, but now it was beset with developing a concrete strategy for dealing with it. In some ways this has occurred. Speck and Attneave (20), as well as Wise (21), have innovatively responded to this need for a definite strategy by bridging family therapy and networking in the form of "network family therapy." This type of response is more or less rooted in the traditional paradigm of psychiatry. What it does not recognize is that much of what affects peoples' mental health lies beyond the traditional scope of psychiatry.

Other than the stressors within psychiatry itself, such as the increasing predominance of environmental explanations for behavior as opposed to psychosexual ones, there are external stressors as well. Lindheim and Syme (22) summarize some of the broader, more external social change characteristics that are presently affecting psychiatry. Psychiatry will increasingly be called upon to respond to these outside sources of stress. Some of the areas which these authors outlined are:

1) Living and working conditions. McLean, in this volume, has delineated roles of a psychiatrist in a corporate setting as something of a systems coordinator or social manager.

2) Hierarchical status.

3) Stigmatization, particularly the frequently observed tendency to place those in the lowest status in the worst environments.

4) The importance of participation and local control, which often does not occur.

5) The ability to command events that affect one's life. Seeley (23) has suggested that mental health depends on this ability.

6) A sense of connection to one's heritage and culture.

7) A sense of connection to nature.

8) The danger of isolating people from the life cycle.

9) The need for a sense of connection to a history and a place.

10) The implications of technological change and the accelerating pace of growth in our institutions.

In addition to these environmental stressors, which affect individuals and groups, there are pervading environmental stressors which affect nations and continents and threaten the mental and physical health of whole generations. The threat of thermonuclear war is a clear example of such a stressor, as are chemical pollutants, ionizing radiation, and the prospect of mass starvation, to name a few. Psychiatrists of the future will need to address the implications of these phenomena for the mental health of our people.

PSYCHIATRY AND SOCIAL CHANGE

The vast complexity of society has manifested itself at every level of human existence. Capra (24) has picked up this theme and has argued that Western society is at a "turning point." The extent of complexity has direct implications for psychiatry. As our world becomes more and more complex, we lose control over it. One can hardly escape the global impact of the oil embargo and the subsequent inflation and loss of jobs. The interconnectedness of global issues with mental health is becoming clear, yet a definite intervention strategy is lacking. Psychiatry is faced with developing means of dealing with social change issues. These societal changes will, in part, determine the future "gameboard" upon which psychiatry will play. Capra has pointed to a number of areas of social change that will have definite impact on the practice of psychiatry.

Major demographic changes, both in age and ethnicity, will have an effect on patient care and will prompt difficult questions as to the ways resources can be developed and organized to meet needed programs. The numbers of elderly are expected to soar between the years 2020 and 2040 (25) to the point where half of our resources will be expended on care for the elderly. Already 28% of the U.S. budget is spent on senior citizens. At the same time, the overall number of younger people is decreasing (25), with the exception of the poor, minority young. There are fewer and fewer higher paying jobs for them, yet they will someday be asked to carry the weight of an older, white population.

Increasing mobility of populations around the world continues to change the social and ethnic dimensions of communities. For example, because of the influx of Mexican immigrants, 60% of children starting school in Southern California do not speak English. This phenomenon, coupled with the new flow of Southeast Asian immigrants, demonstrates that geographical boundaries are somewhat ineffective in controlling populations. They simply do not correspond with social, economic, and political forces. The indirect effects of global population migration will invariably influence our social life as well as our mental and physical health. Because of this it is imperative that psychiatry become involved with understanding social change and its effects on health.

Aspects of the way society is changing are thoroughly and provocatively reported by Capra (24). In addition to population demographics, he discusses our decreasing ability to "control," the worldwide organization of economic activities, the roles of the sciences in social change, the expansion and the interconnection of every field of endeavor with every other. Capra clearly demonstrates that we are at a transition point, where even the basic values of society will change. In almost all spheres, more and more actors are arriving and wanting to participate in decision-making. A cogent and tangible example is the increase in participation on the part of women. Through this increased participation, we are seeing a change in the rules governing women's relationships with the environment. A new gameboard is being created in which all of the old rules about women's relationships to men, their relationships to each other, and their relationships to the world of work are no longer as viable. This is only one example of how the gameboard is changing, and it is changing all over. The field of psychiatry must recognize these changes and deal with them appropriately.

RESPONDING TO THE STRESS OF SOCIAL CHANGE

Social change is a source of stress on psychiatry and will influence the way psychiatrists define their role and practice, the science and art of their profession. It is not enough that they merely be aware of the dimensions of social change. The magnitude of the changes which are occurring require a systematic and conceptually integrated set of responses. They cannot be dealt with in a random manner, as if one stress were unrelated to other sources of stress. Some of the issues, changes, and stressors which will have to be dealt with are:

1) Decreasing support for psychiatric services from third-party payers.
2) Increase in competition from non-medically trained professionals.
3) Increase in the numbers of alternative healing practices outside the traditional realm of Western sciences.
4) Potential resolution through biological research of many of the issues psychiatrists have attempted to deal with through psychological and social interventions.
5) Psychiatric medications becoming generally available from other medical professionals.
6) Shortages of funds, raising ethical questions as to who should get treatment.
7) No major new direction set in government programs for 20 years.

Economics, as Brenner points out in this volume, is now, more than ever, determining the way psychiatry is practiced. The field is steadily moving towards capitation systems, either with Preferred Providers Organizations (PPOs) or Health Maintenance Organizations (HMOs), or some other as yet undeveloped mechanism. As capitation systems expand, psychiatry will be forced to reckon with the economic determinants of mental health services. Services are already responding with a "cost conscious" rationale, but instead, they really need to develop a "cost efficient" one. The need for this rationale increases as we see more and more programs cutting costs in order to provide the least expensive service, only to have to spend more money later on because of the problems which have been created by a presumably cost-conscious program. Psychiatry must be concerned with the economics of mental health services lest the field lose both credibility and opportunity.

SOCIAL LEARNING

Changes both within and outside of the psychiatric profession represent the environmental stressors which affect the practice of psychiatry. The ways psychiatrists deal with the inside and outside mediators will determine how we and our professional colleagues survive in the years ahead.

Psychiatry is at a turning point. It must develop new sets of values and paradigms on health, human services, welfare, participation, hierarchy, and control. This will involve a sharing of responsibility with other mental health professionals as well as with the consumers of our services. Psychiatrists must learn to share control, not merely for the sake of sharing, but, more important, because we realize we cannot control the breadth of these programs, and that by relinquishing some of our traditional control, we may gain a broader participation in the society which is emerging. Adapting, in this way, to the pressures of social and economic change is, as Leopold (26) points out, "a slow, essentially humanistic process in which there is little immediate gratification and many frustrations." It requires what Michael (27) calls "social learning." Social learning requires a new map, a new paradigm, and a way to respond to contemporary issues and changes in a non-controlling manner. Before social learning can happen, there must be acknowledgement that both individuals and institutions need to learn to behave in different ways. This is part of the current crisis for psychiatry. The profession has not yet acknowledged the need for a new paradigm. Yet, in order to respond to the crisis, there is a need for new models which will involve more cooperative roles with many others interested in the broad field of mental health.

Recently, The Communications Era Task Force (28) has explored many of the issues of social change and loss of control that have already been addressed in this chapter. Their findings have particular significance to the field of psychiatry. They cite the following as ways in which current and future stressors can be mediated:

1) Recognize and respond to the fact that individuals in general, and psychiatrists in particular, must reconnect themselves with neighborhoods and communities more so than in the past.
2) Psychiatrists must identify with those who may be under even more stress and, thus, less secure, and must act in ways which promote the security of all members of society.

Psychiatrists will, no doubt, continue in their clinical roles, but these will shift as social changes occur more and more rapidly. As The Communications Era Task Force (28) points out,

. . . the relationship between specialists and citizens will change dramatically. Specialists will no longer be the decision-makers, but will be the creators and communicators of tools, techniques, and knowledge. They will teach others how to be self-reliant. (p. 15)

In the near future one can likely expect the role of psychiatrists to change organizationally. As fee-for-service wanes and capitation waxes, the psychiatrist's logical response should be to work with teams and networks of people in the social management areas. In so doing, he will be developing different organizational roles which would be taking into account the "whole" milieu of mental health services. This on-going process is "social learning" and would involve redefining the meaning of "mental health" in ecological terms.

WAYS OF RESPONDING TO THE CRISIS—WHAT ARE OTHERS DOING?

McLean reports in this volume a rather specific example of the organizational and ecological changes in the role of the psychiatrist in the corporate environmental setting. Others within the broad field of psychiatry have always been involved with organizational, political, vocational, and social change issues with housing, industry, and job creation, as well as with the social structure of hospitals. The subjects of reconnection and disconnection have long been of interest to psychiatrists.

Recently in San Francisco, two interesting examples of "reconnected" institutions for the long-term care of the aged emerged. One is at On Lok in Chinatown, and the other is at the Mt. Zion Hospital. Many of the environmental qualities Lindheim and Syme (22) reported have been used in the development and design of On Lok. Lindheim, a leading figure in the field of health facilities architecture, was actively involved with its founding. On Lok is something of a Social HMO. It assumes responsibility for coordinating and integrating all the varied institutional pieces. For an old person, psychotherapy may be one piece of a complex set of needs. Medicine, housing, and welfare may be other pieces. If there is no integration of the pieces, the patient and the professional get lost. The most important consequences of more highly integrated arrangements such as On Lok are that effectiveness increases and costs decrease. A reconnecting strategy allows for the possibility that "less is more."

Another current response to the need for a changing psychiatric role is occurring at Alta Bates Hospital in Berkeley, California, where Rappaport is exploring a social, or case manager, role in his work with cancer and other chronically ill patients. Here the psychiatrist connects with community and social institutions in a manner similar to the psychiatrist's role in business and industry as described by McLean. This ecological model draws heavily on "liaison psychiatry." However, the ecological model differs from the corporate model in that the ecological one is generalizable to organizations and situations not necessarily corporate. Neither model is viable under a fee-for-service scenario. Thus, Rappaport, the psychiatrist, is salaried.

In conclusion, it should be mentioned that "Select Committees on Mental Health" have been and will be convened by state legislatures. Events at the legislative level will undoubtedly affect the way psychiatry is practiced. These Committees will look closely at how mental illness is being diagnosed and treated. They will explore precisely what are the needs of the patients, communities, and families, and develop a comprehensive map of the issues. The issues are, undoubtedly, biological, social, psychological, and economic. The solutions will involve decentralization, community organization, and broad participation. Once the issues are mapped out through this type of participation by many people across a state, new programs will be developed.

The implementation of these programs will involve psychiatrists with more capacity for teamwork. In order to reconnect people who have been previously disconnected, psychiatrists will have to work in a system of decentralized programs, more often than not in the local community rather than in centralized locations.

Although there is some pressure to refurbish the mental hospitals as a way to control the sick people on the streets, it is likely that more effort will be devoted to the community. This does not mean a uniform replication of the types of community mental health programs which occurred in the 1960s. Communities must be allowed to develop their own, unique, mental health programs. New, as yet unplanned, programs of care and prevention will undoubtedly arise.

CONCLUSION

In order to participate in the changing world around us, psychiatrists are not only required to know what's going on "out there," but also must know themselves as agents of change. Change is always greeted with resistance. Psychiatric professionals are as guilty as our patients in holding on to traditional ways as society changes. It is imperative that psychiatrists examine their strengths and limitations in order to adapt to the future needs of a changing society.

Psychiatry and psychiatrists will be subject to considerable stress, which is likely to increase in the future and will represent a crisis for psychiatry as a whole. It is important to keep in mind in the days ahead that resistance must be confronted before change can occur. Similarly, stress, and even crisis, may represent the opportunity needed for the future growth of our profession.

REFERENCES

1. Elliot, G. R., and Eisdorfer, C. (Eds.): *Stress and Human Health: Analysis and Implications of Research.* New York: Springer, 1982.
2. Mailer, N.: *The Naked and the Dead.* New York: Rinehart, 1948.
3. Krasner, L. (Ed.): *Environmental Design and Human Behavior: A Psychology of the Individual in Society.* New York: Pergamon Press, 1979.
3a. Menninger, W. C. *A Psychiatrist for a Troubled World.* New York: The Viking Press, 1967.
3b. Greenwood, E.: The role of residential treatment for children. *Am. J. Ortho.*, 15:692–696, 1955.
4. Stanton, A., and Schwartz, M.: *The Mental Hospital.* New York: Basic Books, 1954.
5. Caudill, W.: *The Psychiatric Hospital as a Small Society.* Cambridge: Harvard University Press, 1958.
6. Goffman, E.: *Asylums.* New York: Doubleday, 1961.
7. Dollard, J., and Miller, N. E.: *Personality and Psychotherapy: An Analysis in Terms of Learning, Thinking, and Culture.* New York: McGraw-Hill, 1950.
8. Salter, S.: *Towards a History of Community Mental Health in California.* Unpublished social welfare Ph.D. dissertation. University of California, Berkeley, 1982.
9. Kesey, K.: *One Flew Over the Cuckoo's Nest.* New York: Signet, 1967.
10. Szasz, T.: *The Myth of Mental Illness.* New York: Harper and Row, 1960.
11. Laing, R. T.: *The Politics of Experience.* New York: Pantheon Books, 1967.
12. Lindemann, E. *Beyond Grief.* New York: Aronson, 1979.
13. Gans, H.: *Urban Villagers.* Glencoe, IL.: The Free Press, 1963.
14. Fried, M.: Grieving for a lost home. In: L. J. Duhl (Ed.), *The Urban Condition.* New York: Basic Books, 1964.
15. Marris, P.: *Loss and Change.* Garden City, NY: Anchor Books, 1975.
16. Young, M.D., and Willmott, P.: *Family and Kinship in East London.* Glencoe, IL.: The Free Press, 1957.
17. Duhl, L. J. (Ed.): *The Urban Condition.* New York: Basic Books, 1964.
18. Calhoun, J. B. (Ed.): *Environment and Population: Problems of Adaptation.* New York: Praeger, 1983.

19. Duhl, B. S.: *From the Inside Out and Other Metaphors: Creative and Integrative Approaches to Training in Systems Thinking.* New York: Brunner/Mazel, 1983.

20. Speck, R., and Attneave, C. L.: *Family Networks.* New York: Vintage, 1973.

21. Rueveni, U., Speck, R., and Speck, J. (Eds.): *Therapeutic Intervention: Healing Strategies for Human Systems.* New York: Human Services Press, 1982.

22. Lindheim, R., and Syme, S. L.: Environments, people and health. *Am. Rev. Pbl. Hlth.,* 4:335–359, 1983.

23. Seeley, J.: *The Americanization of the Unconscious.* New York: International Science Press, 1967.

24. Capra, F.: *The Turning Point.* New York: Simon and Schuster, 1982.

25. Lecture by former Social Security Administration Director, Dorethea Rice, School of Public Health, University of California, Berkeley, 1983.

26. Leopold, R.: The Psychiatric Consultant: Can he act as social change agent? *Psychiat. Annals,* 13(2):115–123, 1983.

27. Michael, D. *On Learning to Plan and Planning to Learn: The Social Psychology of Changing Toward Future Responsive Societal Learning.* San Francisco: Jossey-Bass, 1973.

28. Communications Era Task Force. *At the Crossroads.* Spokane, WN: Communications Era Task Force, 1974.

6

The Corporate Environment
and Stress

Alan A. McLean, M.D.

Earlier chapters in this volume give us a magnificent exposure to the theoretical, biological, and some of the clinical substrates of stress and stress responses. The immediately preceding chapter by Duhl and Hynes introduces the broad sociocultural context.

This chapter represents a somewhat different perspective — a nonresearch viewpoint. It is written from the perspective of occupational psychiatry and as one concerned with the administration of occupational health programs. Even so, I will pick up on — and perhaps repeat — a number of points made earlier.

Certainly no clinical discussion of work stress can avoid concepts of loss or of age as independent variables. None can or should avoid the definitional issue. Eisdorfer has already pointed out that stress has been used as an independent, dependent, *and* intervening variable. He also quite rightly challenges the very concept of stress as a unifying, cohesive, theoretical or operational construct.

And Kety writes of stress as "environmental deviation producing pathological change." Reiser speaks of stress as the adaptive demand of the individual and differentiates it from *strain* which he feels is the effect which leads to pathological sequelae. Weiner goes back to Selye's original definition of stress and then discusses the changes in the concept and use of the term over the years.

I have no quarrel with any of the above conceptualizations of stress. So long as a writer defines his terms and sticks with the definition, we can get on with the discussion just as has been the case to this point. But it is important to know how writers are using terms relating to stress to understand their observations clearly. For the purposes of this chapter, stress, stressor, and stress reaction (or stress response) will be defined as follows:

Stress defines a process or a system which includes not only the stressful event and the reaction to it, but all the intervening steps between. The *stressor* is a stressful event or stressful condition that produces a psychological or physical reaction in the individual that is usually unpleasant and sometimes produces symptoms of emotional or physiological disability. The *stress reaction* concerns the consequences of the stimulus provided by a stressor. It is, in other words, the response to a stressor, and it is generally unhealthy. Most often, such reactions may be defined in rather traditional psychological terms, ranging from mild situational anxiety and depression to serious emotional disability.

Let me use my practitioner's perspective to open with two brief, anecdotal cases.

CASE EXAMPLES

Case #1

This case clearly illustrates the impact of stressors. I first heard about it more than 25 years ago from a colleague who was studying the operation of a paper-manufacturing plant. The circumstances are tragic, but the case is a perfect example of vulnerability to occupational stress reaction. The patient, a paper cutter about 60 years old, who had a long history of successful experience in a large manufacturing plant, began complaining of headaches. He consulted his private physician and the plant's physician, and both confirmed that he had developed moderately severe hypertension. The knowledge of this condition increased his vulnerability and made him more anxious. Then, one day, he fainted just after getting out of bed in the morning. This worried him further. Both his physician and the doctor at the plant advised that he seek an early retirement since there was increased likelihood that he might experience an accident on the job. A very favorable pension plan was arranged. Nonetheless, he had great misgivings. His friends were almost exclusively his co-workers. His job was the major part of his life. With a great deal of ambivalence, much hesitation, and considerable anxiety, he accepted his company's offer, even though he felt he would be lost without work. His last day on the job came. During the three final hours at his machine, despite all safeguards, he cut off his right hand. This was his first accident on the job.

The relationship between major vulnerability — such as the paper cutter's despair at losing his job — and accidents is clear: This accident was a symptom and a consequence of stress. Yet even in this case, which stemmed from such an obvious psychological foundation, it was almost impossible to predict such an outcome. No one could have predicted the failure of carefully designed safeguards against such an accident. But one *can* recognize that almost any engineering devices designed to prevent accidents can be bested by those who are intimately aware of their workings. With 20/20 hindsight, the paper cutter *should* have been removed from his job immediately once the decision had been made that he was a potential threat to himself or others. A desk job for the last few weeks at work may not have guaranteed against an accident, but it would have reduced the potential. Often we fail to act when someone's vulnerability soars and a potentially hazardous environment remains unchanged.

Case #2

On October 23, 1983, *The New York Times* carried a full-page article about changes at Rubbermaid Incorporated of Wooster, Ohio (1). Rubbermaid had been run by a local family for decades, had been a profitable company, and was virtually a household name in America. *The New York Times* reported that the board of directors recruited Mr. Stanley C. Gault in December of 1980 from his position as vice-chairman of the General Electric Company and brought him in as president. According to one Wall Street analyst,

> He was a local boy from Wooster who made good. He's a tough, tough guy.
>
> When he came to the company he saw Rubbermaid as "inadequately prepared for the recession." Quickly he began paring costs and speeding up new product development.
>
> Then in rapid succession he ordered a review of Rubbermaid's eight lines of business and lopped off half of them. . . . The remaining operations were reorganized into two main business lines. And in the resulting reorganization, Rubbermaid had a 50% turnover in its middle management.
>
> Mr. Gault then made even more aggressive moves: about 11% of Rubbermaid's white collar staff and 3% of its blue collar employees were fired. And a whole raft of GE employees was hired into key positions,

including Rubbermaid's president, chief financial officer, vice president for human resources, and international head. Also, Rubbermaid began to enter entirely new markets with completely different lines of distribution.

"We're not a GE alumni association, but we needed good people in critical slots and fast," said Mr. Gault. (1, p. 6)

While I am not aware of any studies of the Rubbermaid employee population during the past years, one can imagine the psychosocial disruption which at the same time allowed the organization to become economically more healthy.

The balance of this chapter will focus briefly on a few illustrative stressful events and conditions which have been identified as psychosocial stressors in the world of work and which have been held responsible for producing that psychopathology which has been termed "stress reactions" or "stress responses." The importance of both the context of an individual's life situation and his particular vulnerability at the time of the stressful event will be explored. Nonclinical issues such as Worker Compensation for job-related disability and the role of organizational support systems are important and will be discussed. Finally, the role of the psychiatrist in the work stress arena will be reviewed.

MEANING OF WORK

Central to my theme is that work has tremendous meaning for our patients. Work has the *potential* for many forms of gratification and challenge, harm, and the threat of harm. Indeed, it occupies a major part of most of our lives, both in time and in importance. It is not surprising that a great many find work life stressful at times. No wonder work stress is a contemporary issue.

Over the years, it is clear that the changing nature and meaning of work has been the cause of the greatest continuing restructuring of American lives of any force in our history. Few would argue that work is often a psychological anchor which, if seriously disturbed, can set the ship afloat.

STRESSORS

As we move to a consideration of stress issues, I think we can agree that one of the common denominators of stressful events in the world of work is change. Changes which are stressful often involve loss. The loss may be minor, such as giving up comfortable techniques when a work process changes. They may involve the irreversible destruction of social bonds when an esteemed supervisor leaves. It may be moving from a supportive work group to a more competitive or even hostile one. Or the loss may be one of self-esteem when a worker finds himself unable to perform a new and complicated routine.

Or, as Menninger (2) suggests, stressors have another common denominator, loss in a different sense: the loss of control.

> Sometimes we may actually *be* losing control—of events, of circumstances, of ourselves. . . . But, more often, stress reflects a *fear* of losing control (of events or outcome): performance anxiety before a speech; fears about the adequacy of one's work on an assigned task; fears of doing poorly in the face of very high expectations laid on by one's superior; situations which severely tax one's abilities and competence; or outcomes which fall significantly short of one's own standards of performance or expectations or hopes or desires.

In any event, whether stressful events involve change or loss or fear of losing control, they are, for almost everyone, a fact of life. I will examine several which have been reasonably well documented.

1) The rapid pace of technological advances in restructuring work operations causes stress. Workers often feel uneasy about their own status; the changing technology sometimes makes them redundant. As recent history has borne out, job loss and, more important, the threat of job loss are probably the most severe occupational stressors (3, 4).

2) Another stressful event, and one that is more subtle, is the nearly universal practice at work of being evaluated. How good a job are you doing? It is a built-in part of the work process, and evaluation is always a test of one's adequacy compared with others and has a lot to do with self-esteem. Work organizations, of course, are competitive societies, and they exist in a culture in which the child begins to experience evaluation threats in the form of examinations at a very early age. Marked anxiety about examinations is commonplace and carries over into adult work life (5).

3) Some practices and policies of employers tend to be at odds with the coping styles of individual employees. For example, consider the introverted person who had difficulties in social situations and who is pressured by an institutional custom to participate in frequent social functions.

4) The prospects of aging and retirement confront the person with a struggle between engagement and disengagement in the life process that work represents. Disengagement threatens the person with loss of independence and significance. As with all other psychosocial sources of stress, this one may have its most poignant expression on the job.

5) Increasing phenomena in the American economy are mergers, acquisitions, and dramatic management changes which often give new direction to every aspect of a work organization. Some are seen by employees at all levels as ruthless. Others represent necessary surgery to salvage an organization which has been allowed to deteriorate to the point of near bankruptcy. Still others come about as a result of takeovers by new investors coveting selected assets. And then there is bankruptcy itself.

Such macro-organizational revision may lead to massive job loss but, more often, to prolonged periods of uncertainty for all employees, a change in corporate values which may have been extant for generations, and the loss of deeply entrenched social support systems.

Consider how you might feel if you worked at Rubbermaid Incorporated in 1981 or 1982.

To briefly summarize, these illustrative stressors including coping with change and its attendant loss, reality-testing in the form of feedback known as evaluation, conflicts between individual and organizational values, aging and retirement issues, and unanticipated, organizational surgery. These will serve as examples of the host of traumatic events which may impact the lives of employees.

RESEARCH

There has been a vast amount of research on occupational stress. Much of it was reviewed in the Institute of Medicine study (6). I will include here only a brief comment. Although most research on occupational stress and health has been cross-sectional, rather than longitudinal or experimental, large differences in morbidity and mortality among occupations suggest that work stress can have an effect on health. One compelling type of evidence derives from comparisons of workers in high and low stress jobs, as determined by both external observers and self-reports of workers. Frankenhaeuser and Gardel (7) showed that workers in stressful blue-collar occupations, such as machine-paced jobs with short work cycles, exhibit more adverse psychological and physiological responses conducive to disease than workers in less stressful jobs.

But it is interesting that, from a clinical viewpoint, in occupational health settings one does *not* see significantly different numbers of stress-related *illnesses* based solely on *categories* of job assignment.

There have been very few prospective studies in the workplace in which persons free of disease are followed until they develop disease.

Worker Compensation

Worker compensation laws now tend to make an employer legally liable for an employee's mental illness, whatever its deep-seated or underlying cause, if it is aggravated, accelerated, precipitated, or triggered to the point of disability or need for medical care by *any* condition of the employment, most particularly, occupational stressors. This is true regardless of whether the employee himself was at fault. Actually, fault or absence from fault on the part of either the employer or the employee plays absolutely no part in determining the liability of the employer for the payment of worker compensation benefits or the entitlement of the employee to receive such benefits.

Increasingly, we have seen mental disorder held compensable. Increasingly, no physical injury is required to meet the definition of an accident. Held as compensable, for instance, has been emotional disability caused by physical trauma, physical disability caused by emotional stress, and emotional disability caused by emotional stressors.

One recent case, decided by the Supreme Court of the State of Michigan, concluded that if an employee "honestly believes" that any aspect of his work *caused* his disability, the employer must be held liable under Michigan's Worker Compensation Statutes (8). This extreme position has now also been adopted by a California court. Therefore, in both Michigan and California, an employee's subjective interpretation of the day-to-day events on a job as threatening (even though they may not be to anyone else at work) can occasionally lead to the employer's being held liable for any psychiatric or physical disability which that employee alleges stems from such a subjective reaction to customary work processes.

Modifiers

In a social and anthropological sense, no two work organizations are quite the same. This "corporate personality" represents a unique whole, so that in the mind of the individual worker there is an established concept of this wholeness and uniqueness as it relates to the organization. It represents the purposes, policies, practices, products, services, and values which define and symbolize the identity of the employer, be it a corporation, an institution, or an agency.

Those concerned with occupational mental health must clearly understand these organizational variables which define their corporate patient. Much can be done on behalf of the health of individual employees by influencing policies, procedures, and practices to be supportive of legitimate, work-related needs of workers at all levels. Each professional, therefore, must objectively study the system as it is before making suggestions for change. Indeed, one needs to become something of a cultural anthropologist. The real and symbolic roles played by members of the union hierarchy and by those at various levels in management clearly help to determine organizational function. Each enterprise sharply differs from the next, of course, none being the same in any real sense. One needs to study the variables that determine organizational individuality.

Such identification can also be made by reference to written policy statements and by procedural documents and investigation of the traditions, folklore, and rituals by which it is characterized. As Bakke (9) noted, "But its home is in the minds of members of the organization, and an imperfect reflection is in the minds of those who view the organization from outside" (p. 10). This characteristic personality of each organization presents a strong social pressure for each employee.

A worker may readily adjust to one company and have considerable difficulty in another. Some individuals, for instance, work much better in an organization which carefully spells out the expectations it has of its employees. At times, we may observe individuals presenting symptoms of anxiety or depression as they attempt to adjust to life with a new employer, even though the job content may be familiar. Some function well in a highly structured environment, others only when given considerable autonomy. Interestingly, *both* a rigid and controlling corporate personality *and* a permissive and flexible one can equally become known as "good places to work." The main point is the importance of being aware of the psychosocial force of the corporate organization and to recognize that it is not static but is ever-changing.

Social Support as a Buffer

There is available evidence which clearly indicates that the stress process may contribute to the development of a wide range of physical and mental disorders. Thus, a major preventive strategy for improving physical and mental well-being is to intervene in the process that contributes to these disorders. There are at least three major elements of a strategy for preventing the adverse effects of stress on health. *First*, the level of the stressors can be reduced. *Second*, techniques to bolster health can be provided. *Third*, the impact of stressors on health can be buffered.

For example, if work-related stressors contribute to an individual's depression, several things can be done. First, the work-related stressors could be reduced or eliminated through changes in the work situation. Second, efforts could be made to enhance the non-work aspect of the individual's life. Finally, the impact of work-related stressors on health could be blocked or reduced by doing something that necessarily neither reduces the level of the stressor nor improves health, but prevents stressors from having a deleterious effect on health. This "something" then would allow people to be exposed to stressors, with less likelihood that their health would be adversely affected. Many of us have recently become intrigued with the idea of *social support* as a buffering agent to lessen the impact of occupational stress on health. Social support appears capable of reducing the level of at least some occupational stressors and of directly promoting aspects of health as well. It does not promise to be a panacea for all problems of stress and health. But the quantity and quality of people's social relationships with spouses, friends, co-workers, and supervisors appear to have important bearings on the amount of stress they experience, their overall well-being, and on the likelihood that stress will adversely affect their overall well-being.

Social support can modify or counteract the more deleterious effects of stress in three ways. First, social support can directly enhance health and well-being because it meets important human needs for security, social contact, approval, belonging, and affection. That is, positive effects of support on health can offset or counterbalance negative effects of stress.

Second, support, at least from people at work, can directly reduce levels of occupational stress in a variety of ways and, hence, *indirectly* improve health. For example, supportive supervisors and co-workers can minimize interpersonal pressures or tensions; and the experience of support can satisfy work-related motivation for affiliation, approval, and accurate appraisal of the self and environment, generally leaving workers more satisfied with themselves and their jobs.

The third type of effect is the potential of social support to mitigate or buffer the impact of occupational stress on health. Here social support has no direct effect on either stress or health, but rather modifies the relationship between them, much as a chemical catalyst modifies the effect that one chemical has on another.*

Research has shown that support from spouses may soften the impact of job dissatisfaction on health by helping the person to recognize that the job is not so important in the total context of life and that dissatisfactions with it may be compensated for by satisfactions and accomplishments outside of work.

Considerable research clearly demonstrates that supportive behavior by work supervisors can improve both morale and productivity of workers and reduce many forms of organizational stress.

---

*The above material on social support borrows heavily from concepts of James House (10).

SIGNIFICANT VARIABLES

In order to organize my thinking around questions of work stress, I have proposed a frame of reference which may provide some cohesion for this discussion.

Two factors help to determine if a specific stressor will produce symptoms. The first is the *context* (or external environment) in which the interaction takes place. Even more important is the particular *vulnerability* of the individual at the time.

The social, physical, or psychological environment (or context) may be as broad as an economy or as small as a family unit. It may be industry-wide or limited to a single organization or one department of a plant within an organization. In a work setting, the context is also set by management policy and practice.

During times of economic uncertainty, for example, stressors may be much more significant to the individual than they would be when economic security is not threatened. The closing of a factory or sudden unemployment leads to vast disruption and changes in life-style. And activity of a family unit can be a supportive or a destructive environmental system.

If one's work and social situation are strongly supportive, a stressful event or stressful condition on the job may have relatively little impact. Its effects will, to some degree, be buffered. If the context itself is threatening, even a relatively minor stressful event or condition may produce a disabling stress reaction.

Individual vulnerability to specific stressors, of course, also varies widely and is even more important than context in determining reaction to factors in a work environment. The enduring personality characteristics of an individual are elements in setting the dimensions of vulnerability, and we must recognize both genetic and developmental influences, as well as the dynamic coping mechanisms which each of us uses to adapt and which stamp each of us as unique. At the same time, we clearly recognize that these characteristics will vary as other factors change. And the impact of life events upon the individual varies according to how these events are perceived and by the suddenness or unpredictability with which an event occurs.

Every age and every stage in life has its own unique vulnerabilities. The cocky 25-year-old has different susceptibilities than the 40-year-old, and the concerns of those in their sixties involve another set of problems.

There are many who are 40 and scared stiff by their organizational roles, and some by the threat of the loss of those roles. One of the myths of many organizations is that people who are defined by title and length of service and who are performing well are safe and secure. But much stems from the simple fact of aging. The fears of aging are incredible. The fears of being 40 and over in an organization and wondering where one is going to go can be extraordinarily threatening. What affects youth is not so important at mid-life, and the stressors of later life are unique to that era.

One way to illustrate the relationship between context, vulnerability, stressors, and symptoms is by the use of moving, at times overlapping, circles (Figure 1). The three circles here represent the three components I have been discussing. The area where all three overlap may be thought of as the individual's symptomatic response.

As one views the illustration, each circle should be thought of as moving away from and/or toward the others, depending on the importance of each of the three groups of variables. They are in constant and fluid motion. Each varies symbolically in size and with time. If the symbolic circle of vulnerability has shifted away from the others (to the right) so there is no overlap, there would be no symptoms. The same obtains for environmental factors if the context circle moves to the left. In this scheme, contextual or environmental factors obviously play a contributory role in the development of symptoms. One can withstand otherwise destructive stressors if the context is supportive and the vulnerability is low.

Consider again the case of the paper cutter and visualize the circle representing vulnerability as rapidly enlarging as he has his disabling headaches, further enlarging as his physician diagnoses hypertension, and becoming sufficiently large to overwhelm the two smaller circles of stressor and vulnerability as he learns that he must leave his work.

THE PSYCHIATRIST'S FUNCTION IN OCCUPATIONAL SETTINGS

Given the importance of work, occupational stressors, worker compensation decisions, employer differences, and the possibilities of organizational support systems, what can the psychiatrist contribute?

The most common role for psychiatrists in the work world is an extension of his clinical-consultative-liaison role. Frequently the psychiatrist's "place" within the organization is in the medical department, and the task consists of evaluating employees who are obviously dysfunctional, unable to work, and/or in treatment for medical reasons. The task is analogous to that performed by other medical consultants — namely, to evaluate the employee, to ensure that he is receiving appropriate treatment, and to ensure that the necessary information about the employee's work status is being conveyed to those who need to plan.

For example, with an employee who is experiencing a major depressive episode and is hospitalized, the psychiatrist's task would involve communicat-

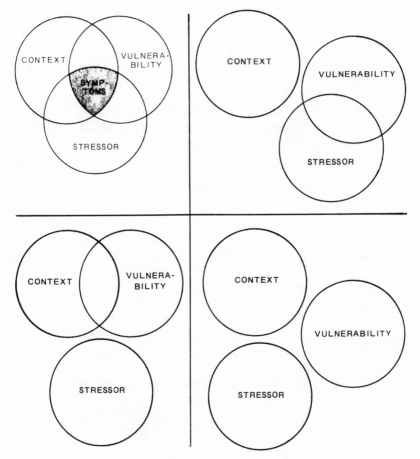

FIGURE 1. Symptomatic relationships between context, vulnerability, and stressors.

ing with the treating physician about the type and severity of the illness, the type of treatment being administered, and the prognosis, both in terms of extent and time. The psychiatrist would then inform the manager about when he can expect the employee to return to work and what limitations, if any, will affect the employee's ability to perform. No diagnosis would be discussed; only work restrictions would be suggested. This feedback enables the manager to make provisions for seeing that the necessary work is done while the employee is away, and assures a smooth transition and a feeling of being welcomed back when the employee returns.

The purposes of such "case management" are to maintain communication between employee and employer, to assure appropriate treatment, and to enhance efficiency at the job site by providing practical information with which management can make appropriate plans. Few cases are as straightforward as this example, but even in more complicated ones, the goal is to bring about a practical resolution that accommodates the needs of employee and employer. Thus, an employee who is inefficient because of growing senility can be spared constant frustration and helped to retire at his own pace. Or the alcoholic can be moved toward treatment rather than simply losing his job. Each of these examples would fall into the broad category of "case management."

Beyond this role lie multiple other tasks that the psychiatrist can perform in occupational settings. For example, he can and does advise managers about how to recognize changing performance and to deal with specific types of employee problems. He can train other occupational health professionals in such areas as crisis intervention, group dynamics, stress symptomatology and genesis, and the effects of drugs and alcohol on behavior. The consultant may be called on for comments concerning a variety of specific problems, such as the human factor in accident prevention or factors in the work environment which support healthy behavior; or he may be asked to gather demographic data on the incidence of mental illness in the company's work force. He can give advice on health insurance coverage for psychiatric illness or the implications of a liberal versus a frugal benefits package. And he can offer opinions to management about the implications for employee behavior of various types of change within the organization.

This latter role, however, occurs only over a significant period of time, after the psychiatrist has earned the trust and respect of his client. Perhaps this position as adviser/confidant is established not so much with direct patient contact as through behind-the-scenes work with other occupational physicians and members of the management hierarchy. As the psychiatrist helps these significant others to understand and cope with deviant behavior, the teaching process spreads his productivity.

Moving beyond the fundamental clinical role, the psychiatrist is responsible for *teaching* the management of work organizations at all levels. Mental health education can easily include informal periodic discussions with small groups of key executives to help members of management understand the role that feelings play in decision-making and to further group members' understanding of their own reactions to stressors at home and work. The sessions often increase management's sensitivity to interpersonal and intrapersonal issues involved in the operation of a work organization. During this process, the psychiatrist also acquires an increasingly sophisticated sense of how the organization operates and the implications of this management style for the productivity and well-being of the employee. For example, in the face of making a difficult decision that will have an unfortunate impact on one or more employees, an executive often responds, just as many of us do, with guilt, anxiety, withdrawal, and other defenses that can lead them to confuse their own feelings and needs with the feelings and needs of other people within the organization or of the organization itself. As the recent GAP report (11) on job loss notes, psychiatrists "can look for the hidden suffering in organizations and management teams just as they do with patients, families, or members of a therapeutic milieu team" (p. 56).

Once a psychiatric consultant has gained such acceptance, an employer may look to him to provide advice on broader issues of company policy, procedure, and practice. Such an influence can be extremely constructive for an entire employee group. For example, convincing administrators to move away from policies that tend to foster dependency and paternalistic behavior goes a long way toward making the work environment a healthier one. By studying the corporate subculture and using the traditional techniques of clinical study, assessment, diagnosis, and treatment, the psychiatrist can do much to enhance the health and reduce the disability of the people within that subculture.

In the occupational setting, a psychiatrist's perception is particularly valuable in view of the importance of the welfare of the organization as a whole. However, this utility extends only so far as these abilities are recognized as valuable and used appropriately. Those in authority in occupational settings vary widely in their inclination to recognize, value, and engage the services of psychiatrists. Some work organizations have a long tradition of psychiatric involvement; in many others such a tradition has never been established or seriously contemplated, and psychiatry is shrouded in the same stigma of misunderstandings as it is in much of the public at large.

CONCLUSIONS

Stress in the work environment has become a very special issue, an important and separate body of knowledge and concern. Both research and clinical experience in the world of work have identified both stressful events and stressful conditions unique to the occupational setting. The clinical and the legal systems are paying increasing attention. Social commentators and the lay press focus on actual and potential stressors. Researchers relate catecholamine levels to specific tasks. Social psychologists study support systems which can buffer the effect of stressors and thereby reduce stress response and the concomitant psychopathology. Occupational physicians, dealing at the front line, coordinate programs of preventive medicine, mental health education, and employee and management consultation.

Clearly, variables which must be considered in the stress-stress response chain include the nature of the stressor and its importance to the individual, that person's particular vulnerabilities at the time of the interaction, and the context (supportive or threatening) in which the transaction takes place. Finally, as the psychiatrist moves into the occupational setting to help deal with work stress issues, he must recognize the nature of the subculture that is the organization, and the role that is most appropriate for him to play in the best interests of both the individual and the organization.

COMMENT

It is not the intent of this chapter to give advice or make specific recommendations about stress management in the world of work. To close with a set of suggestions, however, does seem appropriate. Some years ago I asked Ralph Siu to make such recommendations to a conference on reducing occupational stress. Siu is best known as a neo-Taoist and neo-Buddhist. His publications have included *The Tao of Science* (12) and *The Master Manager* (13). He suggested the following proverbs as guidelines to the sophisticated, contemporary manager seeking to reduce the occupational stressors of those with whom he works.

Five proverbs for planning are:

1) The bird hunting the locust is unaware of the hawk hunting him.
2) The mouse with but one hole is easily taken.
3) In shallow waters, shrimps make fools of dragons.
4) Do not try to catch two frogs with one hand.
5) Give the bird room to fly.

Five proverbs for operations are:

1) Do not insult the crocodile until you have crossed the river.
2) It is better to struggle with a sick jackass than carry the wood yourself.
3) Do not throw stone at mouse and break precious vase.
4) It is not the last blow of the ax that fells the tree.
5) The great executive brings home not only the bacon but also the applesauce (14).

REFERENCES

1. *The New York Times*, October 23, 1983. Section F, p. 6.
2. Menninger, R.: Personal communication, June 1983.
3. Kasl, S. V., Gore, S., and Cobb, S.: Reports of illness and illness behavior among men undergoing job loss. *Psychosom. Med.*, 34(5):475, 1972.
4. Kasl, S. V., Gore, S., and Cobb, S.: The experience of losing a job: Reported changes in health, symptoms, and illness behavior. *Psychosom. Med.*, 37(2):106–122, 1975.
5. Lazarus, R. S.: Some thoughts about stress and the work situation. In: L. Levi (Ed.), *Society, Stress and Disease: Working Life.* New York: Oxford University Press, 1981.
6. Elliott, G. R., and Eisdorfer, C. (Eds.): *Stress and Human Health: Analysis and Implications of Research.* New York: Springer, 1982.
7. Frankenhaeuser, M., and Gardel, B.: Underload and overload in working life: Outline of a multidisciplinary approach. *J. Human Stress*, 2:35–46, 1976.
8. *McKenzie versus General Motors Corporation Fisher Body Division*, 48 Mich. App. 175, 210 N.W. 2D. 357, 1973.
9. Bakke, E. W.: *The Fusion Process.* New Haven, CT: Yale University Press, 1953.
10. House, J. S.: *Work Stress and Social Support.* Reading, MA: Addison-Wesley, 1981.
11. Group for the Advancement of Psychiatry, Committee on Psychiatry in Industry: *Job Loss—A Psychiatric Perspective.* New York: Mental Health Materials Center, 1982.
12. Siu, R. G. H.: *The Tao of Science.* Cambridge, MA: MIT Press, 1957.
13. Siu, R. G. H.: *The Master Manager.* New York: John Wiley, 1980.
14. McLean, A.: *Work Stress.* Reading, MA: Addison-Wesley, 1979.

7

Economic Change and the Suicide Rate: A Population Model Including Loss, Separation, Illness, and Alcohol Consumption

M. Harvey Brenner, Ph.D.

BACKGROUND

The theoretical and research literature on depression and suicide indicate that loss, especially substantial economic loss, is a major precipitating factor in suicide and clinical depression.

Following the classical sociological position of Durkheim (1), anomie (literally, the absence of societal norms), associated with cycles of economic activity, is related to suicide. Merton (2) elaborated the theory of anomie to refer to the absence of socially structured means to carry out activities that are highly socially valued. Thus, a state of anomie exists when the usual norms for carrying out socially desired actions are not operative. This condition exists for those who are caught in situations of loss during economic recession, when the economy ceases to provide to specified groups an access to income or the means to fulfill the basic requirements of the work role.

Following the traditional position of Freud and the early psychoanalytic school (3), depression is seen as a reaction to loss and separation. This is consistent with Freud's insistence on the central importance of work and love to mental health (4). The role of losses, in combination with predispositions based on early development, is central to much of the subsequent psychoanalytic literature on depression (5). Arieti (6), for example, specifies that one category of precipitating situation in chronic depressive psychosis and psychotic depression involves

> a severe disappointment in a relationship to an institution or work activity to which the patient had devoted his whole life, or the most important part of his time. This disappointment threatens the self-image which the patient cherishes. It may force a re-evaluation of the self which is hard for the patient to accept. (p. 469)

Reviews of suicide risk in the psychiatric epidemiological literature also show the importance of economic losses in suicide. Resnik (7) cites high risk of suicide associated with loss of, among other things, status or job, while Vorkoper and Petty (8) indicate that a high suicide risk occurs in severe reaction to losses, including money and status, and when resources, including employment, are not available or exhausted.

Sociological studies of the population distribution of suicide similarly point to the importance of economic loss. Maris and Lazerwitz (9) find unemployment, blocked aspirations (especially for males), and dissatisfaction with life accomplishments associated with suicide; and Breed (10) identifies downward mobility, decreasing income, and, for males, being out of work.

The psychiatric epidemiology of and sociological findings on suicide are corroborated by studies of the role of stressful life events in depressive illness. Paykel (11), reporting on his and several other studies of United States populations, has demonstrated the importance of undesirable life events including demotion, major financial problems, unemployment, business failure, and being fired. Brown (12), reviewing studies in London by himself and colleagues, states that it is the current environment that most powerfully influences the risk of depression, particularly the loss of self-esteem, of which one cause is the lack of employment.

At the national level, Henry and Short (13) showed that suicide tended to increase in relation to the recession phase of business cycle activity. After the publication of *Mental Illness and the Economy* by this author in 1973 (14), research at aggregate levels of analysis began to shift more specifically toward employment loss and damage to job status as precipitating factors in mental disorders, and especially in clinical depression.

In *Mental Illness and the Economy* it was established that declines in employment rates were associated with increased first admissions under age 65 to New York State mental hospitals, annually, for 1914–1967. In addition, it was found that economic recession was related to increased mental hospitalization over the period 1841–1909.

These findings were found consistent during the 20th century for: both sexes; all marital status groups; 34 ethnic groups; 47 population subdivisions by nationality of first- and second-generation Americans; 22 counties of residence (for males); principal functional psychoses by diagnosis; level of educational attainment; economic status; intellectual level; and hospital readmissions. In this work it was further demonstrated that the hospitalization of higher socioeconomic groups was more sensitive to economic recession in terms of speed and intensity of increase. However, the overall impact with respect to the general volume of increased admissions was greater among lower socioeconomic groups. Thus, higher socioeconomic groups react more quickly when loss occurs, but a relatively small proportion of the population affected by loss is of high socioeconomic status.

This basic relationship has been replicated for mental hospitalization (15–18) and for suicide in the United States (15, 18, 19), as well as for other countries, including Canada, England, Wales, Scotland, France, West Germany, Denmark, and Sweden (20). Mixed results have been obtained with other less specific indices of mental disorder and economic change (21).

COMPETING HYPOTHESES AND POTENTIAL INTEGRATION

In order to investigate the significance of economic loss as a potential explanatory factor in the suicide rate, it is necessary to take into account other factors which might plausibly account for some portion of variance in the suicide rate. Failure to do so can result in serious underestimation or overestimation of the importance of economic changes alone.

In fact, the theoretical and research literature appear to assign the greatest risk of suicide to factors which involve interpersonal sources of separation, apart from economic losses (or threatened or anticipated losses). The classical psychoanalytic framework has been a principal research influence and, with Freud, interprets depression as a mourning experience. Social isolation or, put in reverse terms, the lack of social integration, is also central to Durkheim's sociological view of the source of population variance in the suicide rate.

Psychiatric epidemiology of suicide identifies living alone as a crucial factor. Single persons show twice the rate of suicide as married. Separated, divorced, and widowed persons who live alone have four to five times the rate for married persons (7). Maris and Lazerwitz (9) also find that "in the last year before a suicide attempt or death, suicide completers have fewer close friends than natural deaths, who in turn, have fewer close friends than nonfatal suicide attempters" (p. 298).

These findings on suicide are consistent with research results of the influence of stressful life events on depressive illness. Paykel (5) reports that, in general, these life event studies indicate that recent separations play an important role in the genesis of depression.

Beyond the issue of separation from persons is the importance of severe, usually chronic, and debilitating physical illnesses. These are clearly identified as principal risk factors in suicide (7, 8, 9). Further, with respect to the depressions which occur in the wake of medical diseases, a summary (22) indicates:

> Often each emotional reaction, which the medical profession has tended to ignore, may dominate the symptoms of devastating diseases that threaten the life pattern and independence of the patient. Medical catastrophes such as heart disease, cancer, multiple sclerosis, Parkinson's disease and cerebrovascular accidents are almost always followed by a reactive depression. (p. 1889)

Alcoholism and alcohol abuse are still another major risk in suicide (7, 8). It is estimated that 15% of alcoholics commit suicide, which accounts for between 25% and 35% of all United States suicide (23, 24). In general, heavy alcohol consumption greatly increases the risk of suicide, especially in persons with mental disorders (25).

It is clear then that living alone, divorce, widowhood, severe illness, and heavy alcohol use are important risks to suicide. In order to take these diverse factors into account in a study which focuses on the role of economic change in suicide rates, an integrative framework is required. Such a framework, under development over a 15-year period, is available for this purpose. Referred to as the Economic Change Model of Pathology, it has been used in the analysis, over time, of many different causes of mortality (especially cardiovascular) and mental hospitalization (15, 19). I now turn to a summary of that model and its application to the suicide rate.

THE ECONOMIC CHANGE MODEL OF PATHOLOGY

Economic Growth

The first element of the economic change model of pathology, long-term economic growth, is taken to be the underpinning of social well-being and increases in the life span. This element is responsible for increased resources of wealth per capita, by which society is better able to manage the natural and human environments. The relation between growth and mortality derives from the basic definition that economic growth produces higher levels of resources within a population. Resources can be allocated to: 1) improvements in the standard of living; and 2) investments in the applications of existing knowledge including medical care and education of the population. Economic growth is also the basis for improved working conditions (including health and safety measures), leisure and social insurance (e.g., unemployment, health, and aid to the disabled, elderly, and those in poverty).

Over the long run, the *net* effects are the result of both beneficial and adverse factors made possible by growth. Beneficial factors include the potential of social investment in the development of new knowledge. The application of that knowledge may result in a higher standard of living; good nutrition; climate control via housing; clothing and the use of fuel; parasite control; education; comfortable working conditions; adequate monetary and social renumeration for work; and the provision and utilization of primary health services.

A number of risk factors to physical and mental health, made possible by high mass consumption and technological development related to long-term economic growth, have become unusually prominent during the past two decades. Included are the immoderate consumption of alcoholic beverages, tobacco, and animal fats; increased reliance on nonhuman energy sources and the corresponding effects of sedentary life, such as a decline in cardiovascular fitness and overconsumption of calories; and the improper use of medicine and psychotropic drugs.

Economic growth is also related to a decline in strength and stability of primary relationships, especially nuclear family and extended kinship networks, as indicated by high and increasing divorce rates; high proportions of the population living alone; and the prevalence of female-headed households with career and recession-related disruptions to family formation and childbearing. Disruption to career and social integration is also seen in the diversion of manpower to military service, especially under conditions of conscription.

This general, theoretical conception of the effects of economic growth on health and social well-being leads to the following specific hypothesis:

> The suicide rate will tend to decrease in relation to long-term increases in real per capita income.

Long-term economic growth is defined according to a measure of real per capita disposable income (i.e., accounting for the rate of inflation). The "pure" trend element of economic growth tends to have an exponential form.

I, therefore, fit an exponential trend to the real per capita income, thus eliminating the "cyclical" component, which is measured by the variables to be discussed in the section on economic instability. The relation between an increase in economic growth and the decrease in the overall and specific mortality rates will continue to hold under statistical controls for trends in detrimental factors historically associated with economic growth, such as cigarette smoking, very heavy consumption of alcoholic beverages and animal fats, and measures of social isolation.

Economic Instability

Economic instability is the generic term for recessional and structural economic changes that are damaging to particular subsections of the society. In market economies, downturn in the business cycle, indicated by a rising unemployment rate, high rates of business failures, and declines in labor force participation (among other changes), is known as recession. In both planned and market economies, a disturbance to economic activity involves recession in economic growth, which then proceeds at a slower rate, stalls, or actually declines. As a result, the population fails to gain benefits that it would have received had growth continued at a previous rate. The loss, or interruption of gain, in benefits is not evenly distributed. Persons with little or obsolete skills, workers in declining industries, older workers, and persons living in economically declining areas are likely to lose status permanently.

Under these conditions, certain groups in the population experience downward mobility or the process whereby socioeconomic position is lost or seriously damaged. In the population that is downwardly mobile, the greatest psychological hardships occur when hope of reestablishing their former position is lost. Among the mechanisms involved which lead to psychological harm are fear of loss of social identity; loss of basic economic resources; loss of primary social relationships; forced migration; and fear of the inability — and intensive striving — to reestablish socioeconomic position.

It is also assumed that the effects of recession will adversely affect those who work, as well as those who lose their jobs. A secondary set of mechanisms affects employees who remain at work. These include a lack of promotion and poor or competitive relations among staff, emphasis on high productivity, work overload caused by critical shortages of employees, and an atmosphere of anxiety and tension. Such conditions may generate for much of the population a series of stresses nearly equivalent to employment loss.

In countries with market economic systems, the unemployment rate tends to be the principal indicator of recessional economic loss. At the macro or population level of analysis, increase in the unemployment rate is an indicator of the extent of recession and/or structural, economic decline. These forms of economic distress reflect for some a loss of the work role, loss of income, downward social mobility, increased stress, and possible increases in poverty levels. At this level of analysis, one can identify relations between the aggregate unemployment rate, acting as an indicator of several sources of social distress, and measures of mental health.

Thus, one can derive the following general hypothesis from the theoretical conceptions on the effects of economic instability on morbidity and mortality:

> Economic instability relates to a higher incidence of psychiatric morbidity and suicide.

The industrial failure rate is another prominent recessional indicator and is important in the age group over 45, and especially over 65, for the service, manufacturing, and agricultural worker and manager. As in the case of leaving the labor force, this indicator tends to reflect a period of chronic anxiety and struggle to keep the economic organization from economic destruction prior to failure, as well as a major change in social status and way of life.

Hypotheses which use additional indicators of recessional damage as experienced in countries with market economies are as follows:

> The increased failure rate of economic organizations is related to increases in psychiatric illness and the suicide rate.

> Decreases in labor force participation rates for experienced workers are related to increases in the suicide rate.

> Short-term declines in production or wage rate are related to increases in total and chronic disease mortality rates.

Economic Inequality

Economic inequality relates to the distribution of the product of economic development. For reasons which usually depend on structural changes in the economy, specific populations may not gain—or may actually experience loss—while the majority of the population takes part in the process of economic growth. For example, youth, the elderly, women, and ethnic minorities frequently experience this situation.

Economic inequality has an even greater adverse impact which is compounded during periods of economic growth, when the majority of society is earning at least moderate incomes and is not experiencing very high unemployment. This is occasionally the condition of a significant proportion of youth of lower socioeconomic status and especially of minority ethnic backgrounds. This description also extends to many of the elderly who may be in chronic economic difficulty and to a significant number of female heads of households. Finally, these problems of structural economic deprivation (as opposed to the short-term losses of recessionary periods) and low income have, in the last decade, been extended to former workers in several of the durable goods industries, which have suffered structural declines in employment in the United States.

In periods of economic instability, the economic loss and downward mobility typically associated with a recession lead to further expansion of socioeconomic differentials. Thus, the effects of recession become an even greater burden, proportionally, on the downwardly mobile. Economic inequality becomes even more acute when the general population is moving out of a recession. While some individuals gain, a portion of the population has lost income and never recovers. This group subsequently exhibits lower socioeconomic status and higher mortality rates.

The model allows for the impact of economic inequality on the two preceding relationships by developing hypotheses for specific populations:

> In countries with market economic systems, increases in the unemployment *ratio* for all ages and both sexes are related to pathological indices including the suicide rate.

The reason is that each of the age/sex-specific unemployment rates does not correspond exactly to the fluctuations of the overall unemployment rate, and it would be helpful additionally to identify the relation of each age/sex group's unemployment rate to this pathological pattern. This can be done by using the ratio of age/sex specific unemployment rates to the total unemployment rate.

The unemployment rate and age/sex-specific unemployment ratios measure much of the effect of recessional losses and anxieties, but they actually indicate only the extent to which members of the population are looking for work. Substantial proportions of those who look for work, however, do not find it and are, therefore, "discouraged workers" and leave the labor force entirely. This is especially true of males over age 45 during the past two decades. Since there is likely to have been a span of one or two years of unemployment prior to leaving the labor force, one expects decreases in labor force participation for experienced workers to lead to increased pathology within two years.

Adaptational Error

Adaptational error associated with economic growth refers to the pathological results of specific patterns of consumption and production. Pathological results occur either because of ignorance, difficulty in changing habitual behaviors, or potential damage to economic interests, if changes were to significantly decrease consumption or production of specific items. Examples are immoderate alcohol consumption and abuse of prescription or illicit drugs. Another adaptational problem associated with economic growth pertains to disrupted social relations such as social isolation due to divorce or solitary living arrangements.

Two sets of hypotheses emerge, one to address those adaptational errors resulting from increased mass consumption, and the other to explain the family disorganization that is associated with economic development.

Although moderate levels of drinking may be protective with respect to some illnesses (especially ischemic heart disease), prevalence of *heavy* consumption of alcoholic beverages is expected to show a positive relation to general mortality, depression, and suicide. In the case of relatively short lags (0–5 years), one is concentrating on the already chronically morbid population, as well as on changes in cognitive ability and mood:

> An increase in the heavy consumption of alcoholic beverages is related to high mortality rates, including suicide.

Divorce is one of two prime indicators of potential lack of social integration or social support. It is a standard finding in psychiatric epidemiology and recent studies of morbidity that the divorced population is at considerably greater risk of mortality:

> The divorced population is at considerably greater risk of mortality and mental health problems including suicide.

The number of persons living alone and an increase in the proportion of female heads of households are additional indicators of the potential lack of social support. They are meant to reflect recent findings on the importance of social contact as a negative influence on morbidity, as well as the classic sociological literature on the malintegrative aspects of advanced urban living conditions:

> Persons living alone are at greater risk of mortality and mental health problems.

Random Shock

An additional set of facts, "random shocks" to the population, needs to be taken into account in order to use this elaborated economic change model for detailed explanation or prediction. These factors include: 1) extremely disruptive phenomena, e.g., climatic irregularities such as severe winters; 2) minor epidemics; 3) events which damage the economy and the population in ways that go beyond usual economic predictions, e.g., natural disasters, political or international economic crises; and 4) important demographic changes such as were brought about by sharp increases in the birth rate.

DATA

Validity of the Data

The data on suicide rates are drawn from the annual volumes of the United States *Vital Statistics*. One of the more important criticisms of the use of officially recorded suicide data is that they tend to understate the actual number of deaths by suicide. It is argued that some deaths attributed to accidents, for example, are in fact suicides. In the context of the present analysis, three factors tend to mitigate this problem. First, while the overall level of suicide may be somewhat underenumerated, there is no evidence to suggest that the trends and fluctuations in the suicide rate are *systematically* and regularly influenced by misclassification. Second, even if systematic error did occur in the suicide rate over time, this would not necessarily harm the present analysis; one would simply account for less variance in the suicide rate despite using the relevant epidemiological risk factors. Each risk factor, e.g., economic loss, would nevertheless retain its own integrity and its place in the explanatory process.

The third factor to be considered is that, in principle, if the accident rate (for example) accounts for some of the suicide rate, then one should control for the accident rate in the analysis of suicide. However, one only needs to control for the accident rate if the factors influencing it are substantially different from those which influence the official suicide rate. The literature on stress, on the other hand, tends to indicate that many of the same factors influence both rates — economic and interpersonal losses, heavy alcohol use (often in combination with psychoactive drugs), and social isolation.

Analysis

Time-series regression analysis was used to investigate changes in the U.S. suicide rate, by age and sex, over 1950–1978 (the last year for which data were available).

Stress in Health and Disease

The following explanatory factors were tested for their relationship to the suicide rates.

Economic (over 0-3 years)

Unemployment rate

Unemployment rate, age-specific in ratio to total population rate

Decline in labor force participation rate, ages 25-74 for males and 25-44 for females, indicating inability to obtain employment

Increased labor force participation rate, age over 45, for females, indicating new entry into the labor force probably due to financial necessity (including illness, death, unemployment of spouse, or marital termination), with related decline in social and economic status

Separation — Social isolation (over 0-3 years)

Living alone (proportion of single person households)

Divorce rate

Death of spouse: indicated by increased overall mortality in opposite sex of same age group

Illness

Major physical illness (and subsequent social and economic status losses), indicated by increased mortality in the same age/sex group within previous three years

Severe mental depression, indicated by increased suicide rate in same age/sex group within previous year

Alcohol consumption (over 0-3 years)

Per capita consumption
  Total alcohol (in pure ethanol)
  Spirits
  Wine
  Shift towards heavy alcohol consumption (i.e., of high ethanol beverage) measured by increased spirits consumption in ratio to total alcohol consumption
  Shift toward mild-moderate alcohol consumption (i.e., of low etha-

nol beverage), measured by increased beer consumption in ratio to total alcohol consumption

FINDINGS*

Economic Change Over 0-3 Years and Suicide Rates

Economic changes dominate the explanation of variance, over time, in the male suicide rate. In particular, the national unemployment rate is the outstanding source of explanation. Economic changes, including the unemployment rate as well as the business failure rate, are also highly significant factors in explaining changes in the female suicide rate.

The two-shock (or three-stage) hypothesis of the effects of economic loss is strongly supported in the case of male suicide. Thus, the unemployment rate is related to the male suicide rate at lags of both zero (i.e., within one year of increased unemployment) and two years. These relations are seen for males at ages 15–24, 25–34, 35–44, 45–54, 55–64, and over 75.

In the retirement ages of 65–74 years, only one shock-effect relation is seen, i.e., a somewhat delayed initial relation found at a one-year lag. It is possible that, since retirement is "usual" in the 65–74 age group, the initial shock is not experienced as rapidly, and the second shock may not be experienced because it is not expected that the pre-recession situation will be reestablished. Only the effects of the second shock of increased unemployment, at a two-year lag, are observed for females in the age groups 25–34, 35–44, 45–54, and over 75. In 65–74-year-old female suicides, as in their male counterparts, only one shock relation is observed, and it is at a one-year lag.

Business failures, which normally involve persons of somewhat higher socioeconomic background than is the case with unemployment, are significantly related to male suicide at ages 15–24, 45–54, and 55–64. Female suicides show relations to business failures at ages 25–34, 35–44, and 45–54 at a three-year lag. Interestingly, 35–44-year-old females show the hypothesized double shock relationship at lags zero and three years with respect to business failures.

Decline in labor force participation (the discouraged worker problem) is significantly related to increased suicide in 45–54-year-old males and 35–44-year-old females. Over the age of 45 for females, *increased* labor force participation is known to be associated with financial necessity and separation from (or illness of) spouse. In this study, increased labor force par-

---

*See Figures 1 and 2, and Tables 1 and 2.

Stress in Health and Disease

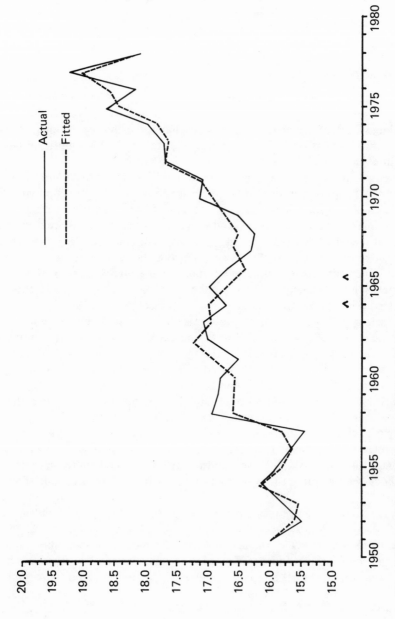

FIGURE 1. Age-adjusted suicide rate, male, United States.

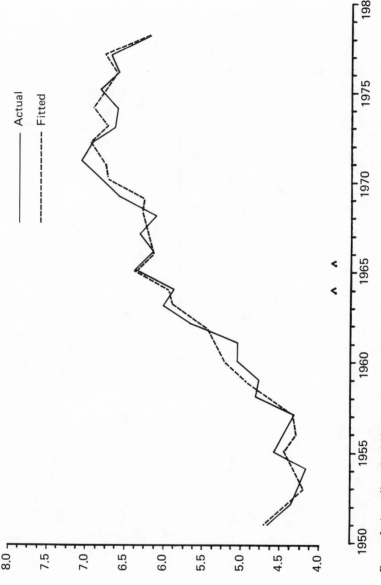

FIGURE 2. Age-adjusted suicide rate, female, United States.

TABLE 1
Multiple Regression Variables for Suicide,
Male, 1951–1978
(Numbers Show Lag in Years)

	Total Age-Adjusted	5–14	15–24	25–34	35–44	45–54	55–64	65–74	75+
Economic									
Per Capita Income		(–)0*				(–)0	(–)0	(–)0	(–)0
Unemployment	0,1	2	0,2*	0*,2	0*,2	0,2*	1*,2	1*	0,2
Unemployment-Ratio			3*				3		1
Business Failures						2	3		
Labor Force Participation					(–)1	1			
Social Isolation									
Divorce				2*		1*	2*	2	
Live Alone	1		0	0,1			3*	1*	

Mortality (opposite sex)									0*
Alcohol Consumption									
Total Consumed		0	3						
Spirits								1*	
Ratio: Spirits/Total					0	0			
Illness									
Physical (total mortality rate/age)	1				1	2*	3*	0	
Depression (Lagged endogenous variable)			1	1					
$\bar{R}^2$	.99	.81	.999	.983	.992	.997	.986	.95	.93
DW	2.34	1.93	2.37	1.92	1.93	2.56	1.96	1.70	2.13
F	1155.5	39.5	2893.8	339.5	732.3	903.6	203.7	68.9	67.3

*Data in Annual changes.
(−) Indicates inverse relation.

TABLE 2
Multiple Regression Variables for Suicide,
Female, 1951–1978
(Numbers Show Lag in Years)

	Total Age-Adjusted	5–14	15–24	25–34	35–44	45–54	55–64	65–74	75+
Economic									
Per Capita Income		(−)0*							
Unemployment	2*			2*	2*	2*	2*	1*	2*
Unemployment-Ratio									
Business Failures	2			3	0,3	3			
Labor Force Participation					(−)3		0	0*	
AFDC		0							
Social Isolation									
Divorce	2*			2*		2*			
Live Alone	3		0		3				0*,2*

	1	2	3	4	5	6	7	8	9
Mortality (opposite sex)									3
Birth Rate							(−)0		
Alcohol Consumption									
Total Consumed		0	0						
Spirits	0			0	0	0	0*		
Wine								0*	
Ratio: Beer/Total							(−)1	(−)2	
Illness									
Physical (total mortality rate/age)	2								
Depression (Lagged endogenous variable)	1			1	1			0*	0*
R̄²	.97	.95	.96	.96	.97	.85	.96	.81	.54
DW	2.0	2.14	1.81	1.93	1.87	1.90	2.01	1.56	2.02
F	97.5	119.6	339.3	122.5	80.8	34.5	103.0	22.1	7.9

*: Data in Annual changes.
(−): Indicates inverse relation.

ticipation is related to increased female suicide rates at ages 55-64 and 65-74.

Increased age-specific unemployment ratios, holding constant the total unemployment rate (a measure of technological, rather than recession-related unemployment) is related to increased suicide of males aged 45-54 and 55-64.

The upward exponential trend in real per capita income, which is a measure of long-term economic growth, is strongly related to declines in suicide for males in the age groups 45-54, 55-64, 65-74, and over 75.

Short-term (i.e., annual) decreases in real per capita (family) income are related to increased suicide in the very young — five-14 years of age — in both sexes. In addition, a measure of family poverty, aid to families with dependent children (AFDC), is related to increased suicide rates in five-14-year-old females.

Separation Over 0-3 Years and Suicide Rates

The proportion of the population living alone (i.e., in single-person households, according to the census definition) is strongly related to suicide rates of males in the younger age groups of 15-24 and 25-34, reflecting the status of being both single and living alone. The female suicide rate at ages 15-24 and 35-44 is also related to increases in living alone, probably for reasons paralleling the relation in younger males. The relation of living alone to suicide does not reappear until later in the life cycle and is found in males 65-74 and females over 75.

The divorce rate shows an acute relation to increased suicide within two years for males and females at ages 25-34, a situation which apparently reflects early marriage crisis for both sexes. This relation reappears only in later middle age where suicide of both sexes shows sensitivity to increased divorce at 45-54 and 55-64. In male suicides this relation to divorce continues into ages 65-74.

Death of spouse, as indicated by increased mortality in the opposite sex of the same age group as the suicide rate, is most clearly related to suicide in the elderly. Male suicide over age 75 increases during the same year in which female overall mortality (i.e., from all causes) over age 75 has increased. Female suicide rates tend to increase on the average of three years following increases in the male mortality rate over 75. In addition, male suicide rates at ages 45-54 and 55-64 increase at an average of two to three years following increases in female overall mortality within the same 10-year age groups. Also, male suicide rates at 65-74 increase within the year of increase of the overall female death rate for the same age group.

Severe Illness Over 0-3 Years and Suicide Rate

The rate of increase in severe illnesses in a specific age/sex group is measured by an increased overall death rate within the past three years in that age/sex group. The relation of an increased overall death rate to the suicide rate could be found only in males, and in the groups 45–54, 55–64, and 65–74. Thus, for males in these age groups, the suicide rate is partly related to mortality of spouses and partly, by inference, to their own severe physical illness.

The potential implications for suicide of severe depressive illness in the previous year was investigated by using the previous year's suicide rate as an indicator of severe depression. This relation (technically referred to as based on a lagged endogenous variable) was found to be significant only for males at ages 15–24 and 35–44. For females the relation is found at 25–34 and 35–44. A possible reason that this relation is not seen later in life is that at over age 45, the physical illnesses, especially heart disease, cancer, and stroke, become important etiological sources of depression which overshadow factors that operate earlier.

Alcohol Consumption Over 0-3 Years and Suicide Rates

The rate of total alcohol consumption (in pure ethanol) irrespective of beverage type was related to increased suicide rates in both sexes in the age groups 5–14 and 15–24. These relationships appear to influence the entire trend of suicide in those age/sex groups. It is possible that the relations are also interactive with drug abuse, but that issue is not investigated in the present study.

The relation of spirits consumption per capita and the suicide rate is clearly seen in female suicides of ages 25–34, 35–44, and 45–54 with lag of under one year. The relation can also be observed in males 65–74 within one year's lag. A more complex relation is found for males at ages 35–44 and 55–64. It appears that in those cases the relation involves a shift in alcohol consumption patterns toward an increase specifically in spirits consumption (measured by the ratio of spirits consumption rates to total consumption rates). This shift toward spirits, the highest ethanol beverage, is seen as a sequence away from moderate and toward heavy alcohol consumption.

Increased wine consumption per capita is associated with an increase in female suicides at the ages of 55–64 and 65–74. At the same time, in these female age groups, a shift toward beer consumption (measured by the ratio of beer consumption rates to total consumption rates) is related to *decreased* suicide rates. It is assumed that a shift toward beer, the alcoholic beverage of lowest ethanol content, indicates a movement toward moderate consumption.

SEQUENCE OF THE LOSS-DEPRESSION RELATIONSHIP

Depression is understood to be the principal psychiatric condition of which suicide is the potential outcome. At the same time, empirical research and theoretical developments indicate increasing awareness of the possible adaptive role of depression as protection against exhaustion and life-threatening conditions (29).

This suggests two stages, one at which agitated seeking for a lost object may in extreme cases lead to hopelessness and suicidal risk if the lost object is of overwhelming significance, and a second which involves a withdrawal period associated with the conservation of energy and resources, and minimization of stimuli, so as to maximize recovery (and minimize vulnerability to additional shocks).

A third stage is proposed by the present author in which, if the loss has involved a *fundamental* and *continuing* concern of life (such as work role and socioeconomic position), then following the conservation-withdrawal period there will be attempts to replace the lost "object." If such attempts fail (i.e., no suitable replacement can be found), then the potential for hopelessness increases along with the renewed risk of suicide.

The third stage proposed above is consistent with Schmale's and Engel's formulations of the role of depression as a mediating factor in somatic illness (26, 27). In a "giving-up given-up" complex, they describe the separate reactions of helplessness and hopelessness to apparently irretrievable loss. The three-stage process is not identical to, but entirely consistent with, the three stages in Selye's General Adaptation Syndrome (alarm, adaptation, exhaustion), based on a continuing stress situation (30). Indeed, the loss-reintegration process for the permanently downward mobile can be seen as an instance of Selye's formulation involving a condition of cumulative stress. Given the isolation and relative infrequency (in society in general) of downward mobility, this condition also leads to considerable self-blame, since the economic system appears to behave in a benign manner with respect to the population majority during economic recovery and expansion. The technical sociological descriptions of this condition would include relative deprivation and "status inconsistency," or lack of "status integration." In the economics lexicon, this condition would be described as involving maximum economic inequality.

In helplessness, the feeling is that the environment is responsible for the loss and the potential for replacing it. In hopelessness, it is felt that personal inadequacies are responsible for the loss, and the environment cannot be expected to provide replacement. Schmale's and Engel's conception relates especially well to Bibring's (28) emphasis on feelings of helplessness and powerlessness in the face of damage to self-esteem as crucial in depression.

The third stage is very much a problem with the downward mobility (i.e., loss of socioeconomic status) that accompanies economic recessions for many individuals. In that case the initial loss of job or (substantial) income is followed by attempts by the subject to become reintegrated at a similar level of socioeconomic status.

Reintegration involves a lower socioeconomic status (lower wage level and job status or permanent exclusion from the labor force), in other words, a second set of losses, as well as changed interpersonal relations. These require a giving up of the career potential (as a vision or "dream" of the future) and friendship patterns related to the old (higher) status position, as well as the symbolic, interpersonal, and material attributes of that position. The crucial question in the reintegration phase is whether substitute goals of life, symbolic and material rewards, and new interpersonal relations can replace those that have had to be relinquished.

The problem of reintegration in stage three is further compounded as a secondary result of recession, because the social environment does not remain constant. Specifically, in the recovery period following economic recession, socioeconomic reintegration of the downward mobile is more likely. However, it is precisely during economic recovery that the population majority, who has not lost status during the recession, now begins to experience socioeconomic advancement as they did prior to the recession. Thus, at the very time that the downward mobile are reintegrated at lower socioeconomic levels, the population majority — including many of the (present and former) associates of the downward mobile — are advancing further. This situation makes it less likely that reestablishment of ties with former associates (at the previous status level) will occur.

The process of reintegration for the downward mobile is therefore associated with loss of self-esteem and social relationships. Since, to those involved, this process appears to take an inexorable course beyond their control (which, in reality, is largely correct), the likelihood of feelings of hopelessness and helplessness is greatly increased.

The period which intervenes between the initial loss of status and the attempted reintegration process involves mixed emotions. On the beneficial side, there is some hope that the previously held socioeconomic status can be restored. Also, the individual who has suffered such loss is likely to receive sympathy and social support from family and friends — especially if there is also evidence of sadness and/or physical illness. The "sick role" in the sociological literature has been seen as an important method of coping with stress (31). At the same time, this intervening phase may involve a continuing erosion of resources — especially financial — and increasing anxiety over whether reintegration will take place, and at what level.

One can estimate that with respect to severe economic loss, it takes two to three years following recession for economic recovery to be completed. Thus, for example, it usually requires two to three years following the business cycle peak of unemployment for the unemployment rate to return (as far as it finally does*) to pre-recession levels (19). The period of two to three years following recession, then, is the time of problematic social and economic reintegration, including renewed loss of status and self-esteem, social isolation, self-blame, and maximum relative deprivation.

Thus, one would expect that it is this period, in addition to the one that involves initial economic loss, that is productive of hopelessness and, therefore, of suicide, for the permanently downward mobile.

The stress of socioeconomic loss is felt by families as well as by those individuals directly subject to the loss. Additional important stresses within the family result from withdrawal and/or aggression by the socially injured household head which, in turn, damages supportive relations among family members (and other close associates).

Nevertheless, the initial and primary loss is to the head of household (traditionally male) and especially at that period of the life cycle where the social role is most exclusively concerned with maintenance and advancement of family socioeconomic status.

Derived losses by family members other than the household head would be more likely to result in hopelessness at the peak of cumulative stress to downward mobility when attempts at social and economic reintegration were taking place.

Economic Loss and the Causal Sequence to Suicide

There are five important causal sequences or pathways leading from economic loss to suicide, each of which affects a proportion of the suicidal population. The first is relatively direct and simple: Loss leads to depression in which suicide is the fatal outcome.

---

*The return of unemployment rates to pre-recession levels within two to three years refers to "normal" recessions. In the recessions since 1970, however, the unemployment rate has never fully returned to its pre-recession level.

The second sequence is indirect but also causally simple. In this sequence economic loss brings about *a* maladaptive behavioral reaction, e.g., heavy alcohol consumption, marital destruction (through separation or divorce), loss of social contacts (especially related to employment), illness, or death (especially of spouse), which, in turn, causes the suicide.

The third sequence is causally direct but cumulative. As in the second sequence, economic loss causes maladaptive behavioral manifestations — but in this case they are *multiple* reactions occurring in the same individual. The multiple reactions are experienced as stresses in themselves and are cumulative. Thus, we have a classic pattern of cumulative life stresses which results in potential suicide.

The fourth sequence is indirect as in the second sequence, but causally complex. This sequence involves at least two intervening factors which are causally related to each other. For example, economic loss will cause, in certain populations, family breakdown. The family breakdown, in turn, will stimulate heavy alcohol intake which may exacerbate depression and provoke suicide. In another example, economic loss will exacerbate physical illness which may lead to isolation of confined persons, in turn provoking depression and suicidal behavior.

The fifth sequence is both causally complex and cumulative. This is a lengthy causal sequence in which stresses (originally stimulated by economic loss) engender one another's existence and thereby bring about a clustering of life problems which induce depressive and suicidal behavior.

The causal sequences in which stresses in an individual's life give rise to other stresses, whereupon the effect is cumulative, have been described as involving a pattern of *stress acceleration* (32). Those sequences in which one person's stressful situation brings about stress in related individuals (i.e., as a result of economic or social-emotional dependencies) are identified as reflecting a pattern of *stress multiplication* (32). These accelerator and multiplier effects are the mechanisms whereby the stressful impact of a comparatively small amount of economic instability is dispersed to a relatively large segment of the population.

Suicide and depression represent only one group of stress outcomes involved in these causal sequences. In principle, other stress-related illnesses — involving responses of the central nervous system (e.g., aggression, neurosis, psychosis), cardiovascular system, metabolic system, immune system, and locomotor system — react in the same way. Thus, we find that mortality due to homicide, heart disease, cardiovascular disease, cirrhosis, and accidents increases in relation to recession within specific lag periods (19).

CONCLUSIONS

Classical, theoretical, and modern research literature indicates that, on the individual level, economic losses are important risk factors to suicide and depressive illness. This position is examined for its ability to account for changes in the suicide rate since 1950 by age and sex. Other prominent risk factors are controlled in the explanatory model. It is concluded that economic losses, especially through unemployment, business failure, and income loss are important explanatory factors. Others are interpersonal separations, severe physical illness, and heavy alcohol use. This integrated, explanatory formulation based on the economic change model of pathology is found to provide an excellent fit to the actual changes in the suicide rate.

The relation between recession and suicide rates occurs in two shock waves. The first increase in suicide is found during the same year as unemployment increases. The second increase in suicide occurs two years later. These empirical findings support a three-stage theory of cumulative stress response for depression, in which the second stage is based on conservation-withdrawal, or at least partial recovery.

REFERENCES

1. Durkheim, E.: *Suicide* (trans. J. A. Spaulding and G. Simpson). Glencoe, IL: The Free Press, 1951.
2. Merton, R. K.: *Social Theory and Social Structure*, Glencoe, IL: The Free Press, 1957.
3. Mendelson, M.: *Psychoanalytic Concepts of Depression*. Philadelphia: The University of Pennsylvania and The Institute of the Pennsylvania Hospital, 1974.
4. Group for the Advancement of Psychiatry. Committee of Psychiatry in Industry: *Job Loss—A Psychiatric Perspective*. New York: Mental Health Materials Center, 1982.
5. Paykel, E. S.: Environmental variables in the etiology of depression. In: F. F. Flach and S. C. Draghi (Eds.), *The Nature and Treatment of Depression*. New York and London: John Wiley, 1975.
6. Arieti, S.: Affective disorders: Manic-depressive psychosis and psychotic depression—Manifest symptomatology, psychodynamics, sociological factors and psychotherapy. In: S. Arieti and G. B. Brody (Eds.), *American Handbook of Psychiatry*. New York: Basic Books, 1974.
7. Resnik, H. L. P.: Suicide. In: H. S. Kaplan, A. M. Freeman, and B. J. Sadock (Eds.), *Comprehensive Textbook of Psychiatry/III*. Baltimore/London: Williams & Wilkins, 1980.
8. Vorkoper, C. F., and Petty, C. S.: Suicide investigation. In: W. J. Curran, A. L. McGarry, and C. S. Petty (Eds.), *Modern Legal Medicine, Psychiatry, and Forensic Science*. Philadelphia: F. A. Davis, 1980.
9. Maris, R., and Lazerwitz, B. M.: *Pathways to Suicide*. Baltimore: The Johns Hopkins University Press, 1981.
10. Breed, W.: Occupational mobility and suicide among white males. *Am. Sociological Rev.*, 28:179–188.
11. Paykel, E. S.: Recent life events in the development of the depressive disorders. In: R. A. Depue (Ed.), *The Psychobiology of the Depressive Disorders: Implications for the Effects of Stress*. New York and London: Academic Press, 1979.

12. Brown, G. W.: The social etiology of depression – London studies. In: R. A. Depue (Ed.), *The Psychobiology of the Depressive Disorders: Implications for the Effects of Stress*. New York and London: Academic Press, 1979.
13. Henry, A. F., and Short, J. F., Jr.: *Suicide and Homicide*. New York: Macmillan, 1954.
14. Brenner, M. H.: *Mental Illness and the Economy*. Cambridge, MA: Harvard University Press, 1973.
15. Brenner, M. H.: *Estimating the Social Costs of National Economic Policy: Implications for Mental and Physical Health and Criminal Aggression*. U.S. Congress, Joint Economic Committee, Washington, D.C., 1976.
16. Draughton, M.: Relationship between economic decline and mental hospital admissions continues to be significant. *Psychol. Rep.,* 36:382, 1975.
17. Marshall, J. R., and Funch, D. P.: Mental illness and the economy: A critique and practical replication. *J. Hlth. Soc. Behav.,* 20:282, 1979.
17a. Sclar, E. D., and Messeri, P.: Estimating the long-term impact of economic stagnation upon the mental health of a local community. Paper presented at the annual meeting of the American Sociological Association, 1981.
18. Stokes, G., and Cochrane, R.: The relationship between national levels of unemployment and the rate of admission to mental hospitals in England and Wales, 1950–1976. Unpublished manuscript. Department of Psychology, University of Birmingham, England.
19. Brenner, M. H.: *Estimating the Effects of Economic Change on National Health and Social Well-Being*. U.S. Congress, Joint Economic Committee, Washington, D.C., 1984.
20. Brenner, M. H.: Economic change in mortality by cause in selected European countries. Paper prepared for WHO Workshop on Health Policy in Relation to Unemployment in the Community, 1982, (WHO, 1984, forthcoming).
21. Catalano, R., and Dooley, C. D.: Economic predictors of depressed mood and stressful life events in a metropolitan community. *J. Hlth. Soc. Behav.,* 18:292, 1977.
22. Reich, P., and Kelly, M. J.: The neuroses. In: M. M. Wintrobe, R. D. Adams, E. Braunwald, K. Isselbacher, R. Petersdorf, and G. W. Thorne (Eds.), *Principles of Internal Medicine*. New York: McGraw-Hill, 1975.
23. Miles, C. P.: Conditions predisposing to suicide. A Review. *J. Nerv. Ment. Dis.,* 164:231–246, 1977.
24. Murphy, G. E.: Suicide and attempted suicide. *Hosp. Pract.,* 12 (11):73–81, 1977.
25. Ritson, B.: Alcoholism and suicide. In: G. Edwards and M. Grant (Eds.), *Alcoholism: New Knowledge and New Responses*. London: Croom Helm, 1977.
26. Schmale, A. H.: Relationship of separation and depression to disease: I: A report on a hospitalized medical population. *Psycosom. Med.,* 20:259–275, 1958.
27. Engel, G. L.: A psychological setting of somatic disease: The "giving-up given-up" complex. *Proc. Roy. Soc. Med.,* 60:553–555, 1967.
28. Bibring, E.: The mechanism of depression. In: P. Greenacre (Ed.), *Affective Disorders*. New York: International Universities Press, 1953, pp. 13–48.
29. Schmale, A. H.: Adaptive role of depression in health and disease. In: J. P. Scott and E. C. Senay (Eds.), *Separation and Depression*. Washington, D.C.: American Association for the Advancement of Science, 1973.
30. Selye, H.: Toward an animal model of depression. *Psychiatr. Res.,* 4:65–71, 1966.
31. Vlasak, G. J.: Medical sociology. In: S. Perlin (Ed.), *A Handbook for the Study of Suicide*. New York and London: Oxford University Press, 1975.
32. Brenner, M. H.: Influence of the social environment on psychopathology: The historical perspective. In: T. E. Barrett, R. M. Rose, and G. L. Klerman (Eds.), *Stress and Mental Disorder*. New York: Raven Press, 1979.

Part IV

STRESS MANAGEMENT AND THE ROLE OF PSYCHIATRY

8

Short-Term Therapeutic Interventions in Stress-Related Disorders

Mardi J. Horowitz, M.D.

Psychological responses to serious life events are composed of at least five components. These are: 1) universal psychological stress-response tendencies, those found in most human beings; 2) typological psychological stress-response tendencies, those found in persons with a given personality style; 3) habitual but individual stylistic responses to a given type of stress or event; 4) individual responses contoured because of the nature of the current social and physical environment (including the nature of the event); and 5) psychological responses as dictated by current neurobiological capacity. The treatment of an individual with a stress disorder will depend on formulation of these parameters. In my exploration I shall focus on a more limited domain in order to concentrate on brief dynamic psychotherapy for stress-response syndromes. That is, I shall assume that the individual has sustained a recent serious life event that is now over as an external stimulus, that he has universal, typological, and individual responses contributing to symptom formation, and that his current environmental and biological circumstances are not particularly curtailed.

This type of situation is in many ways ideal for brief psychotherapy. The person presumably has had a better level of pre-event functioning than found in the period of symptoms formed after the serious life event. There may be good reason to hope that he can rapidly return to this premorbid level of good functioning with the assistance provided by the relationship and communication with a therapist. Preexisting personality features that have been caught up with the meaning of the serious life event may also be in an especially flexible form, one which may allow some change processes to take place in a short treatment. The increased need for close human relationships found under circumstances of stress may also allow for a more than usually rapid formation of a therapeutic alliance and a motivation to overcome the usual resistances to self-exposure in psychotherapy.

BACKGROUND

One of the first paradigms in forming psychoanalytic theory consisted of the concept that overwhelming life events led to subsequent symptoms, such as compulsive repetitions. The traumatic life events were thought to produce excessive stimulation by breach of a stimulus barrier. The excess energy and the memory were then contained within the mind, like some type of foreign body, that had to be worked out at some later time. Reliving the traumatic event in therapy was thought to lead to useful change by means of two processes called abreaction and catharsis (1).

In the abreaction process traumatic events are recalled in complete and vivid detail. The individual during abreaction may be self-reflectively "present" in a way that he was not at the time of the traumatic event. At the traumatic event the individual may have instead entered into an altered state of consciousness. This was called a "hypnoid state" after the French schools of thought of both Mesmerism and hypnosis (2). The hypnoid state, it was believed, was induced by the overwhelming implications and emotional excitations of the moment. During an abreaction, the therapist worked in collaboration with the patient and the traumatic memories were related to the corpus of other memories and self-organizing experiences.

At the same time, the vivid reliving of a traumatic memory was thought to produce an opportunity for the process of catharsis. Catharsis was viewed as a discharge of the pent-up emotions and motoric associations triggered originally by the event but then warded off by subsequent defensive reactions. By such catharsis, a necessary cycle of responses was thought to be completed, allowing the configuration persistent in the form of intrusive and repetitive reenactments or recollections to cease.

During the study of combat reactions during World War II, a third therapeutic component was added to abreaction and catharsis — this was the process of socialization. The traumatized person could report to other people the ideas and feelings subjectively experienced during the serious life event. These concepts would then be found not to be as terrible as they seemed when they were kept as a secret memory. Later, especially in the Korean war, the concept of early treatment was added.

Lindemann (3) and Caplan (4) viewed the serious life event as precipatory of a syndrome that itself might be time-limited. The extremities of the syndrome might be mediated by having professional help as a short sustainment when crucially needed. The specific brevity of the treatment was thought to prevent dependency that might otherwise take place as a response to personal injury and loss. A review of these approaches to the treatment of stress disorders is provided elsewhere (5). In that review an important factor seemed present but insufficiently highlighted: the phases of response after a serious life event.

These phases of response, a general human response tendency but not one necessarily found in every individual, are shown in Figure 1. Figure 1 also indicates some of the differences between normal stress-response states and pathological states of mind that may be intensifications or deflections from these stress responses. The important feature is to distinguish what may be happening in denial phases from what may be happening in intrusive phases.

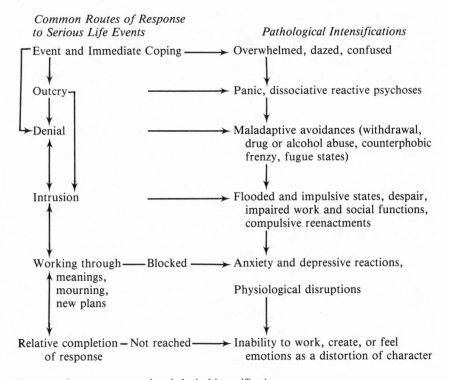

Common Routes of Response to Serious Life Events

Pathological Intensifications

Event and Immediate Coping ⟶ Overwhelmed, dazed, confused

Outcry ⟶ Panic, dissociative reactive psychoses

Denial ⟶ Maladaptive avoidances (withdrawal, drug or alcohol abuse, counterphobic frenzy, fugue states)

Intrusion ⟶ Flooded and impulsive states, despair, impaired work and social functions, compulsive reenactments

Working through — Blocked ⟶ Anxiety and depressive reactions,
meanings, mourning, new plans

Physiological disruptions

Relative completion — Not reached ⟶ Inability to work, create, or feel
of response

emotions as a distortion of character

FIGURE 1. Stress response and pathological intensification.

In denial phases, the individual's regulatory efforts are often in relative predominance over expressive tendencies. In the intrusive phases of a response to a serious life event, the expressive tendencies are relatively strong, and the experiences are intrusive because they represent defensive breakthroughs. That is why the experiences of denial phases seem opposite to the experiences of intrusive phases, as summarized in Tables 1 and 2.

As earlier written material about the treatment of stress disorders was reviewed, it seemed that many of the variety of interventions recommended by diverse authors could be grouped according to the phase of response in which they might be more or less useful. That is synopsized in Table 3. It might then be possible to relate different phases of treatment to different states of mind in the patient. That overall concept is summarized in Table 4.

To recapitulate, accumulated clinical theory has indicated that there are general stress-response tendencies, leading to particular phases of response to serious life events. If pathological intensification or distortion occurs during these phases of response, then a relatively short therapeutic intervention, one aimed at facilitating normal working-through processes such as mourning, may have a good hope of success. During such an effort, generally useful techniques may be modified or selectively used according to the typological and individual characteristics of the specific patient. Guidance for such a working-through process needs to be based on some type of theoretical formulation of what is involved in assimilating and accommodating to a life change or

TABLE 1

Symptoms and Signs During Denial Phases

Daze

Selective inattention

Inability to appreciate significance of stimuli

Amnesia (complete or partial)

Disavowal of meanings of stimuli

Constriction and inflexibility of thought

Presence of fantasies to counteract reality

A sense of numbness or unreality

Over-controlled states of mind

Sleep disturbances (e.g., too little or too much)

Tension-inhibition responses of the autonomic nervous system, with felt sensations such as bowel symptoms, fatigue, headache

Frantic overactivity to jam attention with stimuli

Withdrawal from ordinary life activities

TABLE 2

Symptoms and Signs During Intrusive Phases

Hypervigilance

Startle reactions

Illusions or pseudohallucinations

Intrusive-repetitive thoughts, images, emotions, and behaviors

Overgeneralization of associations

Inability to concentrate on other topics, because of preoccupation with event-related themes

Confusion or thought disruption when thinking about event-related themes

Labile or "explosive" entry into intensely emotional and undermodulated states of mind

Sleep and dream disturbances

Sensations or symptoms of flight or flight readiness (or of exhaustion from chronic arousal) including tremor, nausea, diarrhea, sweating (adrenergic, noradrenergic, or histaminic arousals)

Search for lost persons or situations, compulsive repetitions

---

major threat. That will be discussed next, followed by a return to issues of therapeutic technique.

THEORY OF THE WORKING-THROUGH PROCESS IN RESPONSE TO A SERIOUS LIFE EVENT

Traumatic events involve large amounts of new information that are incongruent with preexisting inner schematizations or mental models (5, 6, 7). Serious life events are by definition those that will eventually change cognitive maps of how the self articulates with the world. The processing of information that leads to such integrated change is slow, and having time to review implications of the news inherent in stressor life events is essential. The mind continues to process the new information until reality and inner models are brought into some type of accord. This tendency to persist in information processing until new external conditions match with internal models can be called a completion tendency.

THE COMPLETION TENDENCY AND ACTIVE MEMORY STORAGE

Until a traumatic event can be integrated, the memories are stored in an active form. These active memory contents tend toward repeated mental representation in some form (images, words, bodily changes). Each representa-

Stress in Health and Disease

Treatments for Stress-Response Syndromes

STATES

Denial — Numbing Phase	*Intrusive — Repetitive Phase*
Reduce controls — interpret defenses, attitudes that make controls necessary — suggestion of recollection	Supply controls externally — structure time and events for patient when essential — organize information Reduce external demands and stimulus levels Rest Provide identification models, group membership, good leadership, orienting values Permit temporary idealization, dependency
Encourage abreaction Encourage description — association — speech — use of images rather than just words in recollection and fantasy — conceptual enactments possibly with addition of role playing, art therapy Reconstructions (to prime memory and associations)	Work through and reorganize by clarifying and educative interpretive work Differentiate — reality from fantasy — past from current schemata — self attributes from object attributes Remove environmental reminders and triggers; interpret their meaning and effect Teach "dosing," e.g., attention on and away from stress-related information
Encourage catharsis Explore emotional aspects of relationships and experiences of self during event Supply support and encourage emotional relationships (to counteract numbness)	Support Evoke other emotions; e.g., benevolent environment Suppress emotion; e.g., selective use of anti-anxiety agents Desensitization procedures and relaxation

tion sets information-processing in motion once again. Eventually, new meaning structures are established and the process is terminated. That is, as new schematic structures are established, the news becomes a part of long-term memory, and the codifications in active memory decay.

As ideas associated with a stressful event are represented, there is a comparison of this information with varied enduring beliefs. There will be a dis-

TABLE 4
Priorities of Treatment

Priority Patient's Current State	*Treatment Goal*
1. Under continuing impact of external stress event	− Terminate external event or remove patient from continuity with it − Provide temporary relationship − Help with decisions, plans, or working through
2. Swings to intolerable levels: − Ideational-emotional attacks − Paralyzing denial and numbness	− Reduce amplitude of oscillations down to swings of tolerable intensity of ideation and emotion − Continue emotional and ideational support − Selection of techniques cited for states of intrusion in Table 2
3. Frozen in overcontrol state of denial and numbness with or without intrusive repetitions	− Help patient "dose" reexperience of event and implications that help to remember for a time, put out of mind for a time, remember for a time, and so on. Selection of denial techniques from Table 2. − During periods of recollection, help patient organize as well as express experience. Increase sense of safety in therapeutic relationship so patient can allow resumption of processing the event.
4. Able to experience and tolerate episodes of ideation and waves of emotion	− Help patient work through associations: the conceptual, emotional, object-relations, and self-image implications of the stress event − Help patient relate this stress event with prior threats, relationship models, and self-concepts, as well as future plans − Work through loss of therapeutic relationship
5. Able to work through ideas and emotions on his own	− Terminate treatment

crepancy, because stressful experiences are by definition beyond the customary forms or automatic response capacities of our lives. This discrepancy feeds forward into emotional responses.

The consequences of a given train of thought are assessed unconsciously in terms of the kind of emotional arousal that is likely to happen if conscious contemplation or action on that line of thought were to take place. The consequence of this unconscious decision-making process – signal anxiety – affects regulatory processes. Defenses and coping strategies are formed out of the operation of the resulting controls of thought, feeling, and action.

The first processing of the news of the serious life event consists of rapid appraisal of how best to cope with it (8). The low level of inhibitory regulation leads to excitation of emotional systems and the outcry response. The amount of information requiring change in mental schemata is so great that complete processing and integration are not possible. The emotional implications are too overwhelming, and so inhibiting regulatory efforts are eventually added in order that the stressful information can be more gradually assimilated, in a dose-by-dose manner.

Excessively prolonged inhibitory controls may interrupt the assimilation and accommodation process. This high level of control, relative to the tendency of active memory toward repeated representation, leads to avoidant- or denial-type states of mind. Failures of control lead either to a continuation of outcry, as in prolonged panic states, or to the intrusive states that may occur after a latency phase of relative denial.

Optimally, adaptive controls reduce ideational and emotional processing to tolerable levels. In working through, which may include oscillating periods of intrusion and denial, the person learns to make new decisions and to record new intentions and beliefs as future plans. These conditions lead toward the relative completion of phases of response as noted in Figure 1.

Biological and social factors may be involved in these sequences. A theory, not yet adequately tested experimentally or empirically, is that the processing of psychological meanings of traumatic perceptions will activate certain neural or neuro-hormonal networks in unusual ways. For example, with continued strain of processing, there might be exhaustion in certain neurotransmitter systems, disposing the person toward depressive states. Conversely, excessive arousal of certain neurotransmitter systems, such as the noradrenergic system, could lead to perpetuation of anxious states of mind. Once certain biological systems are hyperaroused or depleted in terms of capacity, other metabolic functions may be set in motion that have their own necessary course toward an eventually reestablished equilibrium. During some states along this course it may be difficult for a person to adaptively process psychological meanings. For example, a person may become so depleted and unable to function that, initially, supportive treatment would be indicated.

A BRIEF DYNAMIC PSYCHOTHERAPY FOR STRESS-RESPONSE SYNDROMES

Based on the type of theoretical formulation presented above, one can design a general rationale for a brief, psychodynamic, psychotherapeutic approach. Once again, this approach would be used when there is a relatively recent event and the overall characterological picture is not unduly complex. If the patient has a very disturbed personality, an extremely complex social situation, and is reacting to many previous traumatizations, a time-limited therapy is probably not indicated. Instead, a long-term psychotherapy, or at least one in which there is no time limit, might be preferable.

After a serious life event some patients, because of their distress, will be more than usually likely to establish a therapeutic alliance. Some patients, however, perhaps because of the nature of the event, may have unusual difficulty in establishing trust and open communication. When this is so, the opening phase of treatment becomes a combination of work to establish a therapeutic alliance and efforts to accomplish sufficient working-through of the traumatic event, so that the patient is reassured enough to allow the development of a working relationship. Establishment of a therapeutic alliance tends in and of itself to alter the status of the patient's controls. That is, within increased safety it is not as necessary to impose repressive or distorting defenses. The warded-off contents of active memory may then be examined. To this nonspecific property of psychotherapy the therapist then adds various intervention strategies, most of which further alter the status of the patient's controls.

In our Center, partly for research as well as clinical purposes, we imposed a time limit of 12 sessions on our brief therapy process, following the reasoning presented by Mann (9). At a frequency of once a week, a 12-hour therapy is completed in one season, three months. This is usually much less than the mourning period after a personal loss, but the goal of these treatments is not to have patients past all distressing states of mind precipitated by the serious life event, but to have helped them sufficiently so that they can go through the necessary processes of working through on their own. Because we establish a time limit at the beginning, periodic reminders and review of the time-limit issue take place midway through the therapy. If it seems inappropriate for a given patient to end at the time limit, then that is thoroughly discussed, and the time limit may be set aside.

As shown in Table 5, it is possible to give a general format for a prototypical 12-session therapy (see individual case presentations [5, 6, 7]). The patient often begins by telling the story of the serious life event. The therapist's main activity, at this point, is to discuss the preliminary focus, which often includes the linkages between the serious life event and fundamental meanings involved in the patient's self-organization. The now-past serious life event will have deranged present and future aims, purposes, and values in life, and these internal meaning structures will need to be evaluated. Work on the story of the event often involves the presentation to the therapist of ideas and emotions that have been withheld from other persons, even the clos-

TABLE 5

Sample Twelve-Session Dynamic Therapy for Stress Disorders

Session	Relationship Issues	Patient Activity	Therapist Activity
1	Initial positive feeling for helper	Patient tells story of event	Preliminary focus discussed
2	Lull as sense of pressure is reduced	Event related to previous life	Takes psychiatric history. Gives patient realistic appraisal of his syndrome
3	Patient tests therapist for various relationship possibilities	Patient adds associations to indicate expanded meaning of event	Realignment of focus; interpretation of resistances to contemplating stress-related themes
4	Therapeutic alliance deepened	Contemplation of implications of event in the present	Further interpretation of defenses and warded-off contents with linking of latter to stress event and responses
5		Work on themes that have been avoided	Encouragement of active confrontation with feared topics and reengagement in feared activities
6		Contemplation of the future	Time of termination discussed
7–11	Transference reactions interpreted and linked to other configurations	Continued working-through of central conflicts and issues of termination as related to the life event and reactions to it	Clarification and interpretation related to central conflicts and termination; clarification of unfinished issues and recommendations
	Acknowledgment of pending separation		
12	Saying goodbye	Realization of work to be continued on own	Acknowledgment of real gains and summary of future work for patient to do on his own
		Telling hopeful plans for the future	

est persons in the patient's life. A sense of pressure because of fear of revealing certain aspects or reactions to the event, or of the event itself, is reduced as the therapist maintains a stance of concerned but noncritical supportiveness.

Telling the story, establishing a preliminary focus, and adding often warded-off components to some degree is often completed within the first two or three sessions of the psychotherapy. At this point the patient begins to add associations, but also to test the therapist to see if warded-off aspects of this serious life event, and responses to it, can be accepted by the therapist. There are also tests to see if there are possibilities or dangers of certain transference reactions; or there may be fantasies of social relationships with the therapist, if these are needed in the patient's life even though they are inappropriate within the therapeutic contract. During this period, the middle phase of therapy, there may be a realignment of focuses after the therapist knows more about what is going on. The therapist may begin to interpret resistances to contemplating certain ideas and feelings or themes connected with the serious life event. Further interpretations gradually link up different features in the patient's past, current, and future life.

As the patient is willing to work on what has been avoided, and begins to work through some deeper but more problematic meaning in reaction to the serious life event, the issue of termination may also be discussed. Termination itself is a loss of what now has become a meaningful relationship. Deeper meanings of response to the losses involved in the serious life event may be examined as the issues concerning loss of the therapist are actively contemplated.

In this context it is likely that incipient transference reactions will manifest themselves with more intensity than earlier in the therapy. Interpretations of transference reactions that link patterns found in the present to patterns of response to the serious life event are probably useful if the patient can perform the kind of parallel processing necessary to assimilate such interpretations (6). This issue will be discussed in more detail later. Work on reactions to termination continue through the ending phase of the therapy as shown in Table 5.

ILLUSTRATIVE CASE

While such brief therapies vary, a case vignette will clarify some of the sequences generalized in the prototype of Table 5.

The patient was a young woman in her mid-twenties. She sought help because of feelings of confusion, intense sadness, and loss of initiative six weeks after the sudden, unexpected death of her father. Her first aim was to regain a sense of self-control. This was accomplished within a few sessions, because she found a substitute for the idealized, positive relationship with her father in the relationship with the therapist and experienced a realistic hope that she could understand and master her changed life circumstances.

As she regained control, and could feel pangs of sadness without entering flooded, overwhelmed, or dazed states, she began to wonder what she might further accomplish in the therapy and if therapy was worthwhile. The focus gradually shifted from recounting the story of his death and her responses, to understanding her past and current inner relationship with her father. The focus of therapy became her vulnerability to entering stages governed by defective, weak, and evil self-concepts. These self-concepts related to feelings that her father had scorned her in recent years because she had not lived up to his ideals.

This image of herself as bad and defective was matched by a complementary image of him as scornful of her. She felt ashamed of herself and angry at him for not confirming her as worthwhile. In this role-relationship model, she held him to be strong, even omnipotent, and in a magical way saw his death as his deliberate desertion of her. These ideas had been warded off because of the intense humiliation and rage that would occur when they were clearly represented, but contemplation of such ideas in therapy allowed her to review and reappraise them, revising her view of herself and of him.

Every person has multiple self-images and role-relationship models. In this patient, an additional important self-image was of herself as a person too weak to tolerate the loss of a strong father. As is common, no life event occurs in isolation from other life changes, but is almost invariably part of a cluster of events and effects. As she returned from the funeral for her father, she turned to her lover for consolation and sympathy. She had selected a lover who, like her father, displayed himself as superior, cool, and remote.When she needed compassionate attention, he was unable to provide it, and they separated. Establishment of a therapeutic alliance provided much-needed support, but termination threatened her once again with loss of a sustaining figure. In the mid-phase of therapy, it was necessary to focus on these weak self-images in order to test them against her real capability for independence.

To recapitulate, early in therapy this patient rapidly established a therapeutic alliance around a working focus to relieve her of the acute distress of the intrusive phase of a stress-response syndrome, in this case an Adjustment Disorder. This alliance led to rapid attenuation of the problematic states of mind. With this symptom reduction, the focus shifted to the aim of working through various aspects of her relationship to her father. In addition to the primary meanings around grief, that is, the loss of a continued relationship with her father and hope for working further changes in it, she had to work through several additional themes: herself as scorned by her father; herself as too weak to survive without her father; and herself as evil and partly responsible for his death.

These important self-images, present before the death, were worked with during the mid-phase of therapy. They were related to not only her father, but other past figures (mother and siblings), current social relationships, and transference themes. As she could contemplate and work with these themes, the focus expanded from past and current versions of these constellations to include future issues. Were she to continue with these self-images and views of role relationships, she might either reject men altogether or continue with a neurotic repetition of efforts to regain her father and convert him to the ideal figure she remembered from early adolescence. This prospective work also included examination of her reaction to separation from the therapist, and how she would in the future interpret that relationship.

CONTROLS

An important aspect of the middle phase of treatment involves dealing with the patient's control operations. That is, patients will continue to defend against certain aspects of reaction to the serious life event that they unconsciously believe will lead to overwhelmingly unpleasant states of mind. While these are often individually varied, certain typological commonalities have been found. These are described in terms of case examples in more detail elsewhere (7, 10), and are synopsized in Table 6, 7, and 8.

CHANGES AND CHANGE PROCESSES

A time-limited dynamic psychotherapy for stress-response syndromes is not one that is aimed at major characterological revision. However, the reaction to an external stress event, such as pathological grief after the death of a loved one, inevitably combines both the consequences of examining the meanings of the life event and preexisting personality forms. In a well-focused therapy it may be possible to effect some changes in the preexisting forms as well as a working-through of the stressful experience. One important aspect of such a therapy is a review of the sequences of events that have triggered entry into states of mind characterized by symptoms. Very frequently these states of mind have an additional quality: They are experienced by the patient as out of control. Part of the review process consists of learning to feel

TABLE 6

Some "Defects" of Hysterical Style and Their Counteractants in Therapy

Function	Style as "Defect"	Therapeutic Counter
Perception	Global or selective inattention	Ask for details
Representation	Impressionistic rather than accurate	"Abreaction" and reconstruction
Translation of images and enactions to words	Limited	Encourage talk Provide verbal labels
Associations	Limited by inhibitions Misinterpretation based on schematic stereotypes, deflected from reality to wishes and fears	Encourage production Repetition Clarification
Problem-solving	Short circuit to rapid but often erroneous conclusions Avoidance of topic when emotions are unbearable	Keep subject open Interpretations Support

TABLE 7

Some "Defects" of Obsessional Style and Their Counteractants in Therapy

Function	Style as "Defect"	Therapeutic Counter
Perception	Detailed and factual	Ask for overall impressions and statements about emotional experiences
Representation	Isolation of ideas from emotions	Link emotional meanings to ideational meanings
Translation of images and enactions to words	Misses emotional meaning in a rapid transition to partial word meanings	Focus attention on images and felt reactions to them
Associations	Shifts sets of meanings back and forth	Holding operations Interpretation of defense and of warded-off meanings
Problem-solving	Endless rumination without reaching decisions	Interpretation of reasons for warding off clear decisions

TABLE 8

Some "Defects" of Narcissistic Style and Their Counteractants in Therapy

Function	Style as "Defect"	Therapeutic Counter
Perception	Focused on praise and blame	Avoid being provoked into either praising or blaming
	Denial of "wounding" information	Tactful timing and wording to counteract denials
Representation	Dislocates attributes as to whether of the self or another person	Clarify who is who in terms of attributes
Translation of images and enactions to words	Slides meanings of images to words	Consistently define and evaluate meanings
Associations	Overbalanced in terms of finding routes to self-enhancement	Cautious deflation of grandiose meanings
Problem-solving	Distortion of reality to maintain self-esteem, obtain illusory gratifications, forgive selves too easily	Tactfully point out corruptions, encourage reality-fidelity
		Support of self-esteem during period of surrender of illusory gratification
		Help develop appropriate sense of responsibility

in control when having the emotions that color such states of mind. For example, as a consequence of a previous serious life event, it may be appropriate to feel angry, remorseful, or frightened when reconsidering the present and future implications. The patient may learn for the first time how to experience such intense affects without having simultaneously a sense that something bad is happening by virtue of having such feelings. After grieving a loss for the first time, a person may have a new ability, the ability to enter and tolerate states of mourning. It may then be possible to tolerate mourning for other past events as well as current changes in life, ones that must be accepted, such as personal aging and the departure of children from the home.

Very often the reduced symptoms as a consequence of a brief therapy for stress-response syndrome are due to a shift from less competent to more competent self-concepts. This is called a shift because the relatively more competent self-concepts were present before the injury or loss that constituted the serious life event. In response to the event there was a shift to earlier, latent, and now reactivated self-concepts of less competence, ones perhaps with untoward qualities such as viewing the self as damaged, defective, bad, or extremely vulnerable. The task for the therapist in aiding a patient to again shift to the more competent self-concepts is in some ways easier than in treating a person with characterological difficulties in which competent self-concepts and realistic views of adult relationships with others have never been developed. To develop new structure seems to require long-term work; to shift from a regressive to a progressive position that has already been obtained at some time in the past may be a matter that can be readily accomplished. The activation of latent self-concepts as a consequence of stressful experiences, especially in bereavement, has been described in more detail (11, 12).

While the majority of symptomatic improvement in the brief therapy for a stress reaction will be found in a progression out of a regressive state, for some patients there will be the gaining of a new recognition of having the strength to master a traumatic experience. This is the type of gain that provides at least some small compensation for the pain and suffering induced by the life event.

In the working-through process one often encounters irrational ideas that have endured from early developmental periods. These range from ideas about the omnipotence and invulnerability of the self to ideas about the nature of interpersonal relationships and the relation of the individual to fate, destiny, or the spiritual world. Contemplation of the themes activated by the stressful life event involves conscious recognition that one has these often magical or illusionary beliefs, which now seem startlingly out of accord with the new realities. This conscious contemplation often can lead to revision of attitudes, which is why some people describe stressful life experiences as "eye openers."

SUMMARY

This chapter has dealt with some of the generalities concerning the brief therapeutic approach to persons who develop pathological reactions to serious life events. The general, nearly universal response tendencies of phases of intrusive- and denial-type states of mind have been delineated and related to certain therapeutic approaches. Beyond these relatively universal tendencies, and their pathological intensifications, there are various typological variations, especially in how the person attempts to cope with or defend against the reactions activated by the stressful experience. These, too, play a role in therapy, and lead to a variation in the general technique of helping a patient to work through and master the serious life events. Beyond typological variations, there are many individual concerns that involve the unique history of that person. The task for the psychotherapist is to understand the range of universal, typological, and individual variations in the person's unique social and biological context, bringing to bear a clear rationale of what therapeutic interventions to use.

REFERENCES

1. Breuer, J., and Freud, S.: Studies in hysteria (1895). *Standard Edition*, 2:1–310. London: Hogarth Press, 1955.
2. Ellenberger, H. F.: *Discovery of the Unconscious*. New York: Basic Books, 1964.
3. Lindemann, E.: Symptomatology and management of acute grief. *Amer. J. Psychiat.*, 101: 141–148, 1944.
4. Caplan, E.: *Principles of Preventive Psychiatry*. New York: Basic Books, 1964.
5. Horowitz, M.: *Stress-Response Syndromes*. New York: Jason Aronson, 1976.
6. Horowitz, M.: *States of Mind*. New York: Plenum, 1979.
7. Horowitz, M., Marmar, C., Krupnick, J., Wilner, N., Kaltreider, N., and Wallerstein, R.: *Personality Styles and Brief Psychotherapy*. New York: Basic Books, 1984.
8. Lazarus, R.: *Psychological Stress and the Coping Process*. New York: McGraw-Hill, 1966.
9. Mann, J.: *Time-limited Psychotherapy*. Cambridge, MA: Harvard University Press, 1973.
10. Horowitz, M.: *Stress-Response Syndromes*. New York: Aronson, 1976.
11. Horowitz, M., Wilner, N., Marmar, C., and Krupnick, J.: Pathological grief and the activation of latent self-images. *Am. J. Psychiat.*, 137:1157–1162, 1980.
12. Kaltreider, N., Becker, T., and Horowitz, M.: Relationship testing after parental bereavement. *Am. J. Psychiat.*, 141:243–246, 1984.

9

Type A Behavior Pattern: Its Relationship to Coronary Heart Disease and Its Modification by Behavioral and Pharmacological Approaches

Ray H. Rosenman, M.D.,
and Margaret A. Chesney, Ph.D.

INTRODUCTION

An indiscriminate increase in coronary heart disease began occurring in middle-aged and younger males with the start of the 20th century and has mainly been associated with urbanization and industrialization (1, 2). This increase cannot be ascribed merely to improved diagnostic methods, an older population at risk, or any sudden change in genetic predisposition (2). Additionally, studies (3) indicating environmental factors—such as diet and physical inactivity (14–16)—or risk factors—such as cigarette smoking, elevated serum lipid levels, and high blood pressure (4, 5)—have failed to provide a full explanation.

For instance, it has become clear, whether one considers individuals in the population at large or in prospective studies, that those who suffer coronary heart disease (CHD) are not found to have exhibited prior differences in dietary fats or level of physical activity when compared to those who remained free of clinical disease (7, 8). Although the risk factors are without a doubt associated with a higher incidence of CHD in prospective studies, even when

206

combined, they account numerically for only about one-third of the CHD incidence in such longitudinal studies (10, 13). These same risk factors also fail to identify future victims of CHD with any individual specificity (6), and they fail to predict the rate of progression of basic coronary atherosclerosis (6a). Finally, various risk factors exist at high levels in several populations that still enjoy low rates of CHD (9).

The failure of risk factors to account for more than a fraction of CHD incidence is further demonstrated by examining their prevalence in different cultural settings (4, 11, 12). For example, in comparative prospective studies, Framingham males suffer about twice the CHD rate as do European males at equivalent levels of the risk factors (10). After statistical adjustment for differences of the risk factors, Framingham males are shown to suffer even greater differences of CHD incidence when compared to those male subjects followed in prospective studies in Honolulu, Puerto Rico (11), and Yugoslavia (12). Despite a prevailing and remarkable faith in the roles of the diet, physical activity, and the risk factors in CHD, their alteration or elimination have had extremely limited success in diminishing the rates of either primary or secondary CHD morbidity (17–22, 22a).

It is therefore not surprising that critical reviews of epidemiological data conclude that while much has been learned about precursors of CHD, these classical contributing factors do not provide the total explanation for its increased incidence in the 20th century or the occurrence of CHD in specific individuals (17–19, 23–25). Consequently, an ongoing search for other contributing factors has occurred (11, 18), and in view of the association of CHD with urbanization and industrialization, it is only to be expected that this search would extend into the realm of various psychosocial factors.

ASSOCIATION OF CHD WITH PSYCHOLOGICAL AND PSYCHOSOCIAL FACTORS

A wide variety of demographic, social, psychological, and emotional factors have been studied in relationship to CHD. These include social class and status; education level; religious affiliation; ethnic origin; marital status; occupational factors; work over- and underload; social and geographic mobility; status incongruities; anxiety; neuroticism and other emotional factors; life events and changes; life satisfactions and dissatisfactions; emotional deprivation and loss; and others. The results of many such studies have then been critically examined (26–40) and comprehensively reviewed (24, 41). Unfortunately, a number have used retrospective data or are flawed in other ways (41a), but, overall, these data still suggest there are several psychological and psychosocial factors which put subjects at an increased risk for CHD (41, 42).

The most consistent evidence relates certain personality characteristics and behaviors to the incidence of CHD and to its occurrence in specific individuals. As early as 1868, von Dusch observed that persons exhibiting loud vocal stylistics in association with excessive work involvement were predisposed to CHD (43). At the end of the 19th century, Osler (44) strongly implicated hard-driving behavior in the pathogenesis of CHD. He wrote, "I believe that the high pressure at which men live, and the habit of working the machine to its maximum capacity are responsible for [arterial degeneration] rather than excesses in eating and drinking." He described his own typical patient with CHD as "not the delicate, neurotic person . . . but the robust, the vigorous in mind and body, the keen and ambitious man, the indicator of whose engine is always set at full speed ahead."

It was not until 1936 that patients with CHD came under the scrutiny of psychiatrists. At that time, the Menningers noted the strongly aggressive tendencies of these patients (45). Dunbar found them to be hard-driving and goal-directed (46), and Kemple perceived them to be ambitious and compulsively striving to achieve goals that incorporated power and prestige (47). Arlow (48) and Gildea (49) also noted their ambitious and hard-driving behaviors, while Stewart, in England, correlated newer types of stress in the industrialized world with the increased rate of CHD (50).

In general, the observations of these early psychiatrists portrayed a behavioral façade similar to characteristics currently observed in patients with CHD, the difference being—except for Stewart—they failed to consider the role of the environmental milieu in either inducing or interacting with such observed behaviors. Stewart, on the other hand, recognized the unique aspects of milieu stress associated with urbanization and industrialization, and that they coincided with the rapid 20th-century increase of CHD (51).

TYPE A BEHAVIOR PATTERN

More than two decades ago, Friedman and Rosenman (52, 53) described a complex of characteristics, including excessive competitive drive and an habitual sense of time urgency, which they designated Type A Behavior Pattern (TAB). TAB appeared to be a rather specific action-emotion complex exhibited by most patients with CHD, and particularly those who suffered CHD prior to 60 years of age. TAB is exemplified by persons engaged in a habitual and excessive struggle to conquer environmental challenges, despite a chronic lack of appropriate time and the frequent opposition of other things and persons in the same environment. Although Type A persons are in a chronic struggle to achieve more, and in habitual conflict with other persons and time, they rarely fear losing the struggle, regardless of its intensity or duration. In this way, TAB differs from states of anxiety where individuals withdraw or seek counsel when they believe challenges or afflictions to be overwhelming. Instead, Type As prefer to grapple with the challenges that people with anxiety and other neuroses are most likely to retreat from.

The 20th-century Western milieu has probably increased the prevalence of TAB, if only by offering special rewards to those who can perform more competitively, aggressively, and rapidly than others. The urbanization and technology of Western society also offer unique stresses: densification of population and an increased need for finely timed synchronization of interdependent human services, stimulating competitiveness and frustration that lead to hostility and anger. These are stresses not experienced by earlier generations or by contemporary populations not characterized by dense urbanization and industrialized pace.

Although TAB may stem largely from personality attributes, it is most likely to occur when added environmental challenges elicit the particular cluster of Type A behaviors in predisposed individuals. In fact, if the challenges are severe enough and of chronic nature, almost any individual may respond with TAB, regardless of basic personality. It is believed by some that TAB is a characteristic style of response used to maintain a person's control over the environment. Indeed, Type As often exhibit high drive and pace with a vocational devotion that neglects other aspects of life in favor of an impatience to achieve goals that are often poorly defined.

TAB is a life-style as well as an overt behavioral syndrome characterized by enhanced competitiveness and leading to aggressive and ambitious achievement-orientation. It is associated with hyper-alertness, muscular tension, explosive speech stylistics, restlessness, and a chronic sense of time urgency that underlies habitual acceleration of the pace of most activities and thought. A prominent outcome of this orientation is frustration and associated irritability that is manifested by enhanced hostility, although this often is covert. An individual without such chronic behaviors was originally conceptualized as exhibiting the converse Type B behavior pattern. Type B persons are generally far more relaxed, easy-going and easily satisfied, rarely being self-harassed to obtain extravagances from their environment or to participate in an excessive number of events without adequate time. Subsequently, Type B behavior has been shown to be not merely an absence of TAB, but also characteristic of persons who do not often respond to environmental demands and stresses by perceiving a need to either accelerate the pace of acitivity or exhibit impatience and hostility.

Thus, TAB is not so much a simple response to stress, but rather a style of overt behaviors with which Type A persons confront their surroundings when they perceive a challenge to be relevant. Underlying this behavior pattern is a characteristic set of values, thoughts, and approaches to interpersonal relationships manifested in characteristic gestures, taut facial expressions, respiratory patterns, increased motor activity and pace, and emphatic and explosive speech stylistics. Indeed, TAB is readily recognized by the behavioral façade that was originally observed (52–57) and later confirmed (41, 42, 58, 59) and described in detail (60).

Many psychologists have provided strong construct validity to this façade, finding such persons to be, among other things, orderly and well-planned (61); self-controlled (62); self-confident (63); preferring to work alone when challenged (64) and not easily distracted from performance of tasks (65); outgoing (65); hyper-alert (65, 67); fast-paced (60–69); competitive (63, 70, 71); tense and unrelaxed (72); impatient (73); aggressive (74, 75, 86–88); time-conscious (73, 75–77); involved with vocation and unable to relax away from work (62, 72, 78); excessively striving and exhibiting hostility which is often suppressed and becomes more overt when perceiving a sense of frustration (75, 77, 78). Type As tend to deny fatigue (65, 84, 85) and failure (84), to suppress symptoms (65), and to deny illness, including CHD (85). Their desire to control the environment (59, 87) leads to greater occupational conflicts and dissatisfactions (63, 88–91). They are self-involved and achievement-oriented (79–83, 92).

ASSESSMENT OF TAB

A challenge-type Structured Interview designed to assess TAB (60, 93) is based on the elicitation of characteristic Type A verbal reports, voice stylistics, and psychomotor and other nonverbal behaviors during the challenge. It is necessary to use such an interview because Type A persons often do not respond with TAB to an environment that fails to present salient challenges. The 10–15 minute Structured Interview has been found to have high rates of inter-observer agreement (94–97) and stability over time (93). The validity of the emphasis given to the speech stylistics of the subject during the interview (60, 93) for the assessment of the respective A/B behavior patterns has been confirmed by independent studies (98, 99). Less attention has been given to the content of answers to the questions in the structured interview because many persons have inadequate insight into their own behaviors.

We (and others) have studied the use of a variety of psychological questionnaries to assess A/B behavior patterns, including the Adjective Checklist of Gough and Heilbrun, the Thurstone Temperament Schedule, Eyesenck

Personality Inventory, Symptom Distress Checklist, State-Trait Anxiety Inventory (STAI), Work Environment Scale, California Psychological Inventory, MMPI, Cattell 16-Personality Factors Test, and Barrett Impulsiveness Scale. However, the absence of suitable challenge and the relative lack of insight and accurate self-appraisal, particularly by Type A persons, often leads to gross inaccuracy of responses, and such questionnaires appear to have a very limited ability to assess TAB (66, 100–105). Nevertheless, consistency of findings for Type A and B subjects on psychological items and scales from these questionnaires (107) is of great interest.

Several questionnaires have been developed specifically to duplicate the Structured Interview. Bortner's scale correctly classified 70% (100) to 75% of subjects (67), but most other scales appear to be less valid. The most widely used questionnaire is the Jenkins Activity Survey (JAS) (109, 109a), which has been found to be significantly related to the prevalence (59, 110–113) and incidence of CHD (110, 114, 115), and in some (116) but not all studies (117, 118), it is also related to the severity of basic coronary atherosclerosis. Compared to the Structured Interview, it is a much weaker predictor of CHD incidence (119), severity of basic coronary atherosclerosis (117), and challenge-induced physiological arousal that characterizes TAB (96, 105, 118). The Structured Interview is based upon actual observation of elicited Type A behaviors (60, 93), while the JAS and other questionnaires are based upon the answers to questions (50, 93). In fact, the JAS probably measures an individual's attitudes rather than behaviors and thus only provides an inadequate overlap with TAB.

RELATIONSHIPS OF TAB TO CORONARY HEART DISEASE

Prevalence Studies

TAB was initially found to be related to the *prevalence* of CHD in both sexes (52, 53), and this association was confirmed in a large number of studies, whether TAB was assessed by the Structured Interview (120–122), the JAS (59, 110–113, 120, 123–126), the Bortner Type A Rating Scale (67), the Framingham Type A Questionnaire (128), other TAB scales (129), or the major facets of TAB (41, 42, 58, 88, 91, 112, 129–139). In view of the influence of response bias and sample selection in case-control studies, these replications become more significant because random phenomena rarely replicate; they include a variety of populations rather than narrowly-defined and selected subjects, and epidemiological studies often find that replicated associations based on prevalence data are prospectively related as well (140).

The relationship of TAB to the prevalence of CHD may help to explain population differences in CHD that are not ascribable to differences of standard risk factors. For example, the A/B relationships to CHD may help to explain: 1) the much higher rates of CHD in the densely populated and industrialized regions of the U.S. and United Kingdom (17, 141, 142) when compared to farm belts that are often characterized by high habitual consumption of dairy products and other saturated fats; 2) the apparently low rates of CHD in closely knit religious groups (208); 3) the generally higher rates of CHD in the U.S. compared to Europe (4, 10); 4) the higher CHD rates in the more, versus less, industrialized countries in Europe (4); and 5) the striking differences in CHD rates found in Framingham males compared to those in Hawaii and Puerto Rico (11) and in Yugoslavia (12), areas where much lower prevalence of TAB was found (126).

Incidence Studies

Considering the prevalence of CHD, TAB has been found to relate strongly to the incidence of CHD in *prospective* studies. This was initially observed in the Western Collaborative Group Study (93, 143–147). The findings were also generally confirmed for both sexes in the Framingham Study (105, 106, 128, 148), the Japanese-American Study (155), and the Belgian-French Collaborative Study (155a). In the Western Collaborative Group Study, the TAB/CHD relationship was found to prevail for new cases of symptomatic or silent myocardial infarction as well as for angina pectoris (143–147, 151, 158), and also prevailed for the risk of recurring and fatal CHD events (115, 149, 149a). These relationships were found to be independent of other risk factors (144–147) and appeared to indicate a synergistic pattern in CHD risk in which TAB operated with a nearly constant multiplicative effect that applied to whatever background level resulted from other risk factors. TAB was found to double the risk of CHD at all levels of other risk factors (146, 147) in a relationship that could not be explained by chance fluctuations (150).

In the Western Collaborative Study, CHD incidence was also significantly related to the standard risk factors, as were HDL cholesterol levels, corneal arcus (153), and reported family history of CHD (154) in younger subjects. As in most prospective studies, the systolic blood pressure was found to be a stronger predictor of CHD than was the diastolic pressure (152), an important finding in view of its primarily noradrenergic mechanism. The subject's diet in this study, as at Framingham (7), did not predict either the levels of serum lipids or the risk of CHD.

In the Japanese-American Study (155), only 15% of the Japanese males in Hawaii were found to exhibit TAB. Japanese men in Hawaii who had undergone westernized cultural change were found to be more prone to CHD than those who had not. However, men who were both culturally mobile and who exhibited TAB were found to have two to three times the risk of CHD during follow-up compared to men without either of these attributes. Indeed, the former exhibited a CHD risk similar to that of Caucasians (113, 125, 150). These findings support the original conceptualization of TAB as an interplay of specific personality attributes and behaviors combined with an environmental setting that elicits TAB in susceptible persons.

Subjects who score high on the Activity Scale of the Thurstone Temperament Schedule enjoy a rapid psychomotor pace for most daily activities, even when they do not have to function at this accelerated pace. This attribute correlates well with TAB (102–105). It is therefore significant that in the Minnesota study of businessmen, a positive association was found between the incidence of CHD at follow-up, the scores on the Activity Scale (68), and the adrenergic response that occurred during the Cold Pressor Test administered at intake (157).

RELATIONSHIP OF SPECIFIC COMPONENTS OF TAB TO CHD

The Structured Interview was designed to assess not only the global Type A/B behavior patterns but also the various components of TAB that include ambitiousness, aggressive drive, competitiveness, hostility/anger, achievement-orientation, impatience, pace of activity, and sense of time urgency (93). Similarly, analysis of data from the Western Collaborative Group Study indicates that the incidence of CHD was particularly related to such behaviors as competitive drive, impatience, and the potential for hostility (158), rather than to hard-driving, achievement-oriented behavior (113, 156). Indeed, the Japanese have exhibited a successful adaptation to the American standard of success without individual competitiveness (156), resulting in their rapid industrialization not yet being associated with an increased incidence of CHD, even in Type A subjects, unless cultural mobility has occurred in association with enhanced competitiveness and hostility (126, 156). This particular association between Type A competitive hostility and CHD has also been found to prevail for the severity of basic coronary atherosclerosis in both sexes (159), as well as for an enhanced adrenergic response to challenge tasks in the laboratory setting (96).

RELATIONSHIP OF TAB TO CORONARY ATHEROSCLEROSIS AND
PRECIPITATION OF CORONARY EVENTS

In large part, the clinical manifestations of CHD are complications of underlying coronary atherosclerosis. It now appears that TAB is associated with not only the prevalence and incidence of clinical CHD, but also the severity of basic coronary atherosclerosis. An increased severity of coronary atherosclerosis in Type A compared to Type B subjects has been observed at autopsy in men in the Western Collaborative Group Study (176) who died during follow-up, and in both sexes in most studies that used coronary angiography to determine the severity of basic atherosclerosis (116, 117, 174, 175).

In part, TAB may relate to CHD incidence by way of an increased precipitation of fatal coronary events. The role of psychological stress in the precipitation of fatal ventricular fibrillation is well known (160, 161). The mechanism appears to be sympathetic nervous system discharge (151), and Type A subjects exhibit increased adrenergic secretion (162). Their enhanced response to the Cold Pressor Test (163) may have accounted for their exaggerated response to this test being a strong predictor of the CHD incidence observed in the Minnesota study of businessmen (157). In this study, high scores on the Activity Scale of the Thurstone Temperament Schedule also proved to be an independent predictor of CHD.

It is significant that TAB has been found to be associated with enhanced catecholamine secretion in response to the daily milieu (164), as well as during specific psychological (83, 96, 165) and physical challenges (166). TAB has been found to be associated with fatal CHD events (149) and to sudden coronary death (167). The potential of Type As to respond with increased adrenergic secretion is shown by their heightened physiological arousal during various challenge tests (59, 83, 96). Such important Type A behaviors as hostility and anger are associated with augmented secretion of norepinephrine (168), increased prevalence and incidence of CHD (128, 148, 158), and increased severity of coronary atherosclerosis (159). Nixon (168) has well conceptualized the sequential mechanisms that are capable of triggering coronary events that include sudden coronary death.

Another mechanism that may relate TAB to the incidence of CHD is that which increases the risk of coronary thrombosis. The precipitation of myocardial infarction by psychological stress is well recognized (86, 88, 89, 130, 138, 139, 168–171), and the association of such stress with increased blood clotting and platelet aggregation is also well known (172). It is significant that TAB is also associated with accelerated blood clotting time (177) as well as with increased platelet aggregation (165, 173).

RELATIONSHIP OF TAB TO DEMOGRAPHIC AND SOCIOECONOMIC VARIABLES

There is inadequate knowledge about the relationship of TAB to demographic and socioeconomic variables. TAB appears to be more prevalent, as might be expected, in densely populated and industrialized urban areas. Lower prevalence is observed in European communities as compared to the U.S.A., but even in the latter it varies in different population groups (178, 179). For example, it is apparently quite low in the more relaxed Hawaiian ambience (126), which may, in part, account for this group's lower association of CHD with other risk factors as compared to the associations observed to occur in Framingham (11).

No particular association of TAB with age has been noted (93, 178-180), although it appears to be less prevalent in younger age groups (112, 181). A modest correlation of TAB with higher social class and level of education has been found (66, 93, 112, 178, 181-183), and this may, in part, underlie reported associations of TAB with occupational status (93, 112, 178, 181-183) and with career advancement and achievement (59, 63, 181, 183). Higher prevalence of TAB has generally been found in white collar rather than blue collar workers (112, 128, 184) and is less prevalent in black than in white populations (112).

TAB has not been correlated with anxiety, somatic symptoms, or behavioral correlates of stress (59, 66, 104, 185). Despite a correlation of TAB with stressful life events and current level of tension (185), it has not been found to correlate with standard psychological stress tests (104) or psychopathology.

HEREDITARY AND DEVELOPMENTAL ANTECEDENTS OF TAB

Although there is little evidence for any genetic component of TAB (187), a modest genetic variance has been found for certain Type A personality traits, such as drive, competitiveness, compulsiveness, dominance, sociability, and impulsiveness (102, 103, 188-190). Reported family history of CHD is related to the incidence of CHD at younger ages (154, 224), doubtless in part related to familial aggregation of risk factors in addition to family habits of diet, weight, smoking, exercise and other behaviors (154, 186). The existence of TAB in such familial aggregations has not been clarified, however, since it is difficult to separate genetic influences from learned behaviors. Parental attitudes can influence the attitudes of their offspring, with teachers and environmental standards playing an additional role in engendering such Type A behaviors as competitiveness and achievement-striving (81, 191). For example, a familial correlation of TAB in children and parents (187-196) has been found and associated with adult modeling and conditioning processes that affect offspring behaviors (193–195). It is therefore not surprising to find more TAB in children of parents with higher levels of education and occupational status (196), in children living in urban compared to rural areas (197), in males compared to females (191), and also to find that TAB in children closely resembles that in adults (191, 196, 198). TAB probably has origins in childhood, but environmental factors appear to play a greater role than genetic factors in the emergence of TAB in adulthood (102). The important role of cultural factors in the development of TAB (113, 126, 156) was also shown in several large studies by its lower prevalence in areas such as Belgium (108), Hawaii (113, 156), and in generally less industrialized populations.

There is a different mixture of personality attributes and learned behaviors in the TAB exhibited by different individuals. Hence, the classifications provided by the Structured Interview (93, 160) or by scores on the JAS (108) cannot be taken to represent a true continuum. A lower prevalence of TAB in younger individuals (192), for instance, is probably due to the absence of occupational competitiveness, lighter work load, fewer conflicting demands, fewer responsibilities, and fewer socioeconomic factors experienced at the outset of vocational careers (63, 122) and marriage (197). This relationship of TAB to the work setting has previously been reviewed (199).

RELATIONSHIP OF TAB TO OTHER RISK FACTORS AND BIOCHEMICAL FINDINGS

TAB shows only small correlations with other risk factors for CHD (93, 150) and operates independently in its relationship to CHD (146, 150), although Type As are more likely to be heavier cigarette smokers (117, 122, 182, 200, 201). Also, an increase in serum cholesterol, not ascribable to dietary influences (58, 117, 207, 295) can occur in some individuals at times of occupational stress and deadlines (177, 202–213) or during annoyance over life events (58, 177, 203–213). Type A subjects tend to exhibit higher levels of serum cholesterol (52, 53, 59, 60, 112, 117, 122, 214–218) and higher fasting and postprandial triglycerides (218–220) than Type B individuals. This higher triglyceride level is accompanied by postprandial sludging of red blood cells after intake of either saturated or unsaturated fats (210, 220). The association of psychological traits with serum lipid levels has previously been reviewed (217, 221, 222).

There are no Type A/B differences of plasma uric acid or glucose, although Type As may exhibit a hyperinsulinemic response to glucose (57, 223, 224). Plasma thyroxine and cortisol also do not differ (164); Type As appear to excrete less 17-hydroxycorticoids than do Type Bs when challenged with corticotropin (22), and Type As exhibit higher plasma corticotropin levels during waking hours (225). The elevation of serum triglycerides in Type A subjects can be temporarily abolished by the administration of corticotropin, but not hydrocortisone (226, 227). Type As also exhibit lower plasma growth hormone levels (223), and their growth hormone response to an infusion of arginine is less than in Type Bs (228). Growth hormone is essential for maintenance of plasma cholesterol, and its administration to Type A men induces a prompt, albeit temporary, fall in serum cholesterol (229, 230).

Catecholamines probably play a mediating role between TAB and CHD. The increase of CHD in the 20th century appears to be associated with the recent industrialized pace (1, 2, 51) and its associated pressures and demands (113). Raab early emphasized a role of catecholamines in 20th century life and recognized that adrenergic responses were increased in individuals with Type A behaviors (231, 232). Levi (233, 234) later pointed out that the stress responses which evolved in primitive man have not changed through time, with the result that "modern man is constantly poised for flight or fight, but without the civilized possibility of either aggressive fight or fleeing." It is probably important to note that patients with CHD exhibit enhanced catecholamine secretion during physical exertion and emotional stress (162, 235, 236), that such enhanced secretion is associated with aggression, competitive drive, anger, and time urgency (215, 237–239)—the attributes of coronary-prone Type A behavior which lead to performance at maximum capacity (248) and hyperreactiveness to actual or perceived threats (59), and that Type A subjects exhibit increased noradrenergic secretion within the working milieu (164) and competitive activities (83, 96, 98, 165, 166, 240).

There are no apparent Type A/B differences of resting heart rate or blood pressure (93, 112, 122), but consistent differences occur during challenge stressors. Because enhanced secretion of norepinephrine occurs when specific challenges require rapid and competitive responses (164, 165, 245, 246), it is not surprising that Type As, compared to paired Type Bs, exhibit significantly greater increases in heart rate and blood pressure during Cold Pressor testing (98, 241), and greater catecholamine secretion and cardiovascular responses during administration of the challenge-type Structured Interview, reaction time tasks, cognitive puzzle-solving, psychomotor performance tests, exposure to noise and other uncontrollable averse situations, and other similar challenges (82, 83, 95, 105, 185, 214–247). The response is greater in males than females (244, 246, 248), and also when the challenges are of high rather than low levels. The greatest responses are found to occur in Type A subjects who manifest the higher levels of competitiveness, impatience, and hostility, in other words, the specific Type A behaviors which correlate with the incidence of CHD (148, 158) as well as the severity of coronary atherosclerosis (159).

Relationships of TAB to other relevant factors have not been well studied, but it may be important that Type A subjects exhibit shorter blood-clotting time in response to occupational stress, as well as enhanced platelet aggregation (156, 173, 177).

The National Heart, Lung, and Blood Institute of the NIH recently assembled a panel of eminent scientists, representing a variety of biomedical and behavioral specialties, in order to critically examine the existing evidence for an association between TAB and CHD. In its final report (268), it was stated that

> the Review Panel accepts the available body of scientific evidence as demonstrating that Type A behavior (as defined by the Structured Interview, JAS, and Framingham Scale) is associated with an increased risk of clinically apparent CHD in employed, middle-aged U.S. citizens. This increased risk is over and above that imposed by age, systolic blood pressure, serum cholesterol, and smoking, and appears to be of the same order of magnitude as the relative risk associated with any of these factors.

INTERVENTION ON TAB

The data that have accumulated over a period of 25 years appear to fully justify discussion of the modification of coronary-prone Type A behaviors, both for primary and secondary prevention of CHD. The need appears to be more relevant in view of the lack of evidence of significant CHD prevention from programs that have altered diet (8, 22a) and habits of physical activity (15), reduced serum cholesterol or blood pressure (17, 18, 24, 25, 184, 221, 249), or even eliminated cigarette smoking (20–22). There are now valid reasons to believe that to improve results may require the modification of coronary-prone behaviors as well (25).

TAB is multidimensional, and its coronary-prone behaviors have cognitive, behavioral, psychological, and environmental components that interact in a complex manner. Interventions by methodologies such as typical stress management training in relaxation, biofeedback, and guided imagery, autogenic training, and similar approaches cannot be expected to provide sustained modification of TAB. Coronary-prone Type A individuals are compulsive strivers, overly ambitious and aggressive, time-pressured, and competitively hostile, and they often enjoy such behaviors. They report more self-esteem at work, and greater job involvement and satisfaction. This increases their resistance to change, particularly because they tend to be field-independent persons who use autonomous functioning to process environmental stimuli. It has become clear that a face-to-face approach, alone or in groups, is required for effective modification (250–272). The concept of intervention on TAB is a new area (267, 269–273), and the difficulties encountered in modification of long-standing habits of diet, smoking, alcohol, and physical activity are perhaps greater when these are associated with Type A behaviors that are deeply rooted in life-style, which neither the individual nor urbanized society considers to be adverse. It is difficult to conceive of easily changing the societal values and work environments characterized by accelerated pace and competitiveness. Behavior change methods developed for disorders of self-control are less useful for TAB itself. Moreover, management of hostility/anger dimensions is difficult, and the arousal occurring in Type As is far more likely to be associated with such responses than with fear, guilt, sadness, joy, or exhilaration.

The theoretical risk of CHD should be diminished if it were possible to reduce the frequency, intensity, and duration of excessive Type A neuro-hormonal and associated cardiovascular responses (23, 146, 147, 151). There now is evidence that such benefit accrues from behavioral modification of TAB through the reduction of recurring myocardial infarction and other secondary CHD events (258, 277, 278). Before discussing a behavioral approach to modification of coronary-prone Type A behaviors, however, the possibilities of pharmacological intervention will be reviewed.

Pharmacological Modification of TAB

The concept of using beta-adrenergic blockade for improving long-term survival after acute myocardial infarction was initiated in the mid-1960s. Evidence has accrued to support this hypothesis as well for reduction of secondary CHD events. The belief that enhanced sympathetic nervous system arousal may also play a role in the pathogenesis of basic coronary atherosclerosis, and in its clinical complications, has long been considered (231, 232), resulting in the hypothesis that noradrenergic inhibition or blockade should be considered for primary prevention of CHD (24, 273). Indeed, enhanced noradrenergic secretion may operate as a common denominator for at least some of the adverse effects of many risk factors for CHD, including cigarette smoking, physical inactivity, diabetes, obesity, excess alcohol ingestion, stress, hypertension, caffeine consumption, serum lipids, gender, urbanization (with its associated noise, crowding, competitiveness, and rushed pace), anger/hostility dimensions, and coronary-prone Type A behaviors.

Soon after the introduction of beta-adrenergic blocking drugs for various cardiovascular disorders, beta-adrenergic blockade was found to have beneficial effects on reduction of anxiety (276, 279, 284, 288-290, 292). Beta-adrenergic stimulation produces cardiovascular symptoms of arousal in persons with anxiety and produces anxiety symptoms and attacks in individuals with anxiety neurosis and panicogenic syndromes (279). Excess catecholamine secretion or hypersensitivity induces a hypermetabolic state such as that in hyperthyroid patients, which is associated with behavioral dysfunctions. These dysfunctions cease after return to a euthyroid state, but even before this occurs, the behavioral dysfunctions can be rapidly stopped by administration of beta-adrenergic blocking drugs. Because beta-adrenergic blocking drugs are particularly effective in blocking situational anxiety (290), their effects are generally ascribed to a reduction of somatic symptoms, which is achieved by blocking peripheral effects of epinephrine (276). This interpretation is supported by the finding that persons who exhibit mainly somatic manifestations of anxiety benefit more by beta-adrenergic blockade than those with anxiety associated primarily with cognitive mechanisms (291).

Whereas beta-adrenergic blockade immediately relieves somatic manifestations of anxiety, experience has shown that after a few weeks of therapy, psychologic anxiety also is relieved (279). There are several possible explanations for this. One is that the lipophilic beta-blockers penetrate the central nervous system (CNS), and it is known that they do affect psychomotor performance (287). Moreover, beta-blockers that penetrate the CNS are more effective in relieving psychological feelings of anxiety than are hydrophilic drugs with far less CNS penetration (279). Nevertheless, hydrophilic beta-blockers still impair certain (274), if not all, tests of psychomotor function (283).

The fact that beta-adrenergic agonists produce not only somatic but also psychological manifestations of anxiety is probably due to the presence of active beta-receptors on the surface of brain cells, as well as in the heart and cardiovascular system. Stimulation of these receptors thus simultaneously induces emotional and cardiovascular symptoms. This is certainly manifest in the hyperbeta-adrenergic state associated on the one hand with panicogenic syndromes (279), and on the other, with mitral valve prolapse.

Penetration into the CNS may not prove to be the primary mechanism by which beta-adrenergic blockade reduces anxiety, and it may instead reside in its peripheral actions (288, 292, 293). The somatic experience of anxiety may be an end result of a sequence of events beginning with sympathetic stimulation that induces somatic cardiovascular symptoms and tremor, and it is the perception of these responses that acts to reinforce the psychological elements of anxiety (294). Thus, beta-blockers may inhibit this feedback and reduce anxiety by interrupting the somatic-psychic interaction.

This sequence may be relevant for TAB. Type As generally exhibit enhanced noradrenergic response to salient environmental stressors. However, the same enhanced response has been observed to occur even under general anesthesia (285, 286). This suggests that Type A subjects may have an underlying psychobiological basis for coronary-prone behaviors (295), with a constitutional basis for their enhanced noradrenergic responses to salient stressors that underlies their impatience, hostility, and characteristic speech stylistics. Another factor in their cardiovascular responses concerns epinephrine, which can be accumulated from the circulation in sympathetic nerve endings where its release may enhance norepinephrine release through activation of the local modulatory system mediated by presynaptic beta-adrenoreceptors (275, 280).

Regardless of the mechanism, experience over a period of many years has shown that perceptive individuals taking drugs, which either inhibit central secretion or block peripheral effects of noradrenergic stimulation, report feeling calmer, in conjunction with improved well-being, decreased irritability and anger over work interruptions, reduced involvement with emotional upsets, and even improved productivity. When Type A individuals are taking such medications, their spouses tend to report improved levels of communication.

Behavioral Modification of TAB

As TAB became recognized as a risk factor for CHD, interest in its modification has increased. Due to the lack of definitive knowledge on mechanisms by which TAB increases CHD risk, intervention with TAB has involved varied approaches. There are, however, common themes in these approaches. Reflecting the definition of TAB as a behavioral response distinct from stress and anxiety, these intervention strategies are not psychiatric or psychotherapeutic in their emphasis, i.e., they do not seek to identify and resolve underlying conflicts or fears. Instead, these approaches emphasize behavior change strategies such as self-observation and contracting. Although the TAB treatment programs are more directive and structured than traditional psychotherapy, TAB modification strategies are conveyed in a supportive environment by a therapist, nurse, or clinician, in either individual or group settings.

There have been over 16 published reports of studies focusing on either primary or secondary prevention of CHD through TAB change. Selected examples drawn from the research literature will be briefly described. For a complete review of these studies, the reader is referred to comprehensive papers written by Suinn (296) and Razin (297).

An example of primary prevention research in the area of TAB modification is the controlled intervention study conducted by Levenkron and his associates (298) with 38 healthy male subjects. A comprehensive behavior therapy procedure focusing on self-control strategies was evaluated in this project. Subjects assigned to this treatment met in eight consecutive weekly group meetings with a therapist. These subjects were taught to identify situations that elicit TAB and to apply to these situations various behavior change strategies to avoid TAB responses. The specific strategies included modifying situations so that they no longer elicited TAB and purposely responding to situations with more adaptive coping behaviors such as relaxation. Subjects were also taught, using cognitive restructuring (299), to alter their perceptions and "internal self-verbalizations" in situations where TAB emerged. Finally, subjects were given relaxation training in a manner similar to systematic desensitization and led through exercises during which they practiced rehearsing relaxation while imagining situations previously selected for their ability to elicit each individual's TAB.

The comprehensive behavior therapy group was compared to two other treatment conditions. One of these, group support, was included to control for therapist contact and was designed to follow the group therapy treatments employed with post-myocardial infarction patients by increasing awareness of TAB and inducing change through nonspecific support from group members and the therapist. The support group met for eight weekly sessions, but, unlike the behavior therapy group, no explicit behavioral techniques for altering TAB were presented.

The second comparison condition consisted of a two-hour brief information session during which subjects were urged to reduce TAB and given a prepared handout on stress and TAB, and practical suggestions for habit change.

Changes in TAB were assessed using questionnaires, and changes in physiological responses to stress were evaluated using a stressful mental task. After the eight-week treatment phase, the subjects in the comprehensive behavior therapy group showed the greatest significant pre- to post-test improvement on all of the Type A measures employed. The group support subjects also showed significant improvement in some, but not all, of the Type A measures. All subjects, including those in the brief information group, showed a significant reduction in blood pressure responses to the stressful task, suggesting habituation to the task. However, the behavior therapy subjects showed significantly greater reductions in plasma free fatty acids in response to the stressful task than the subjects in either the group support or brief information groups.

The authors concluded that group treatment provided to healthy men appears to initiate change in TAB. Moreover, teaching subjects specific, behavioral change strategies seems to be the most effective approach. However, the phenomena of group support also led to significant changes in self-report of TAB on questionnaires, as had been noted in previous studies (see [296] and [297] for reviews).

The largest Type A intervention study to date is the Recurrent Coronary Prevention Project (RCPP), a large-scale trial designed to determine the degree to which TAB can be modified in post-infarction patients and to what extent recurrent rates of coronary events can be reduced in those patients whose TAB has been significantly modified (278). In the RCPP, approximately 900 men and women under age 65 were randomly assigned to one of two experimental sections, and another 150 patients served as controls. Both experimental sections were further divided into therapy groups of 10 to 15 patients each.

In one of the two experimental conditions, approximately 300 patients received extensive medical information about CHD and learned about specific, medically-approved steps they could take to reduce reinfarction risk. These subjects met in small groups bi-monthly with cardiologists as their group leaders.

In the second of the two experimental conditions, approximately 600 patients learned to modify their TAB in addition to receiving the medical advice just described. The subjects in this condition met in small groups with specially-trained therapists. During the first two months of treatment, these groups met monthly. Then, during months three through six, groups met bi-weekly. For the remainder of the five-year program, the groups met on a bi-monthly basis. During these sessions, patients were taught the importance of controlling physiological variables that could increase reinfarction risk and were instructed in the regular use of relaxation exercises. As in the previously discussed behavior therapy interventions, an emphasis was placed on increasing the patient's awareness of specific Type A behaviors and the conditions under which these behaviors occur. The patients were then instructed to practice daily "drills" to reduce key coronary-prone behaviors, including hostility, impatience, and time urgency. The treatment also encouraged patients to change those aspects of their environment that provoked Type A responses. In addition to changing the external environment, subjects were taught to examine their internal cognitive appraisals of the world around them. Patients learned to examine closely those thoughts, beliefs, and expectations that led to hostility and impatience (300). Although the final report of this five-year trial has not been published, preliminary findings have been reported (277) to show a significantly reduced rate of recurrence for patients in the behavioral change group compared to those in the other experimental conditions. These significantly lower recurrence rates are accompanied by data indicating that patients in the behavioral change program are also modifying their TAB, as measured by self-report questionnaires and by ratings of videotaped interviews.

The results of the RCPP are anxiously awaited by the field of TAB intervention. The majority of the other treatment studies lacks the large number of subjects and the established clinical endpoints that make this project so unique. Without outcome variables such as CHD incidence or recurrence, the other primary and secondary prevention studies have examined changes in risk factor levels and have reported inconsistent results with a number of studies reporting reductions (255, 256) and others reporting increased or mixed findings (252, 253, 298). While the results of such intervention studies assessing changes in CHD risk factors are mixed and underscore the need for further research in this area, the findings of the RCPP appear to be promising and suggest an important role of Type A intervention in CHD prevention.

Recommendations for TAB Modification

Interventions to modify TAB, such as those discussed in the previous section, include a focus on one or more of three interacting factors: the environment; the individual's responses, both behavioral and cognitive, to the environment; and the physiological concomitants of TAB.

Western industrial society provides an environment that elicits and reinforces TAB. There are a number of alternative strategies to counteract the environmental situations that often "trigger" TAB. In every case these strategies include teaching the patient to identify the environmental situations that elicit his TAB and to place limits on the amount of time spent in such settings. For example, Type As who observe that traffic is an environmental "trigger" might select less congested, more pleasant routes for commuting to work, or might consider mass transit or car pooling. Interruptions constitute another common environmental condition that frequently evokes TAB. The Type A patient observing this to be true would be trained to modify the environment to reduce the impact of such interruptions, perhaps by arranging for time without interruptions by using a telephone answering device.

Although the environment plays a significant role in eliciting TAB, it is only rarely that the environment can be altered sufficiently to reduce the frequency and severity of TAB responses. Therefore, in addition to changing the environment, it is usually necessary to train Type As to alter their characteristic ways of responding. This training process involves self-observation, i.e., teaching Type As to witness their own actions in daily living and to relate these actions to the appropriate environmental cues. Observation of TAB will promote awareness but not necessarily change. For modification of Type A responses, self-contracting is employed. This involves the selection of a target — either overt behavior or covert thought — to be changed, setting a goal, and designating a plan to achieve the goal.

In selecting the targets for TAB change, an emphasis is placed on those components of TAB that are thought to be particularly coronary-prone. Thus, the focus of Type A intervention is on impatience, competitive drive, and hostility rather than on fast-paced, achievement-oriented behavior. With the increasing evidence that the competitive-hostility characteristic of TAB is particularly coronary-prone, TAB modification is shifting to an emphasis on reducing anger and hostile responses to environmental challenge.

Strategies for reducing the extent of Type A hostility involve training Type As to identify the provocative or frustrating situations that elicit irritation, creating environments that minimize these situations, and developing new, more effective alternatives for responding to those situations that are unavoidable. When provocative situations cannot be avoided, a two-stage approach is typically emphasized in TAB modification. The first stage involves evaluating whether a situation needs to be taken so seriously. The manner in which an event is experienced is largely determined by the person's cognitive assessment of it, rather than any objective feature of the event itself. Type As tend to assign major importance to most of their responsibilities and environmental challenges, and they thus respond with heightened arousal, even to tasks others might designate as being of relatively minor significance. To modify these responses, Type As are trained to identify and question their cognitive appraisals, to recognize the association between these appraisals and the anger, hostility, and increased physiological arousal they experience, and to develop new, less arousing cognitions that are more appropriate for the situation and their long-range goal of reduced TAB.

The second stage in reducing Type A hostility involves practicing new cognitive appraisals and behavioral responses in the very situations that typically elicit irritation. Specifically, Type As are instructed to place themselves in those situations that they have identified as typically provoking anger and hostility and to practice more effective coping with the situation.

Three major avenues for changing Type A behaviors were outlined earlier in this section. The first involved changing the environment and the second changing behavioral responses to the environment. Recently, with the increased knowledge about the adrenergic hyperresponsivity of many Type As, there is growing interest in a third approach: reducing the enhanced physiologic responses associated with TAB. In addition to the pharmacologic approaches discussed in some detail earlier, physiologic interventions have also included training Type As in the use of progressive relaxation and biofeedback. The rationale is that, once trained in these procedures, Type As will have available a physiological coping skill they can use to reduce or manage their physiological hyperresponsiveness to environmental challenge. Initial findings indicate that Type As do show reduced cardiovascular arousal after such training (296); however, further research is required to examine the extent to which these effects are sustained in the natural environment.

SUMMARY

There has been a dramatic increase in CHD during the 20th century. In this chapter, the ongoing search for factors that may contribute to the pathogenesis and prevention of CHD has been discussed. Among these are psychosocial factors, including Type A Behavior or TAB. The methods of TAB assessment were presented and the relationship of TAB to CHD was described, including recent evidence indicating that certain Type A characteristics such as hostility are particularly coronary-prone. Although the risk associated with TAB has been established in prospective and retrospective studies, considerable research is needed in the areas of genetic and developmental factors, socioeconomic correlates, and, most important, underlying physiological mechanisms. Despite these research needs, the risk associated with TAB has motivated investigators and clinicians to proceed with intervention studies and trials of pharmacological and behavioral approaches to TAB modification. The evidence to date, though admittedly tentative, suggests that such interventions may have a role to play in the prevention and treatment of CHD.

REFERENCES

1. Michaels, L.: Etiology of coronary artery disease: An historical approach. *Brit. Heart J.*, 28:258–264, 1966.
2. White, P. D.: The historical background of angina pectoris. *Mod. Concepts Cardiovasc. Dis.*, 43:109–112, 1974.
3. Epstein, F. H.: The epidemiology of coronary heart disease: A review. *J. Chron. Dis.*, 18:735–774, 1965.
4. Keys, A.: Coronary heart disease in seven countries. *Circulation*, 41: Supplement 1, 1970.
5. Truett, J., Cornfield, J., and Kannel, W.: A multivariate analysis of the risk of coronary heart disease in Framingham. *J. Chron. Dis.*, 20:511–524, 1967.
6. Gordon, T., and Verter, J.: Serum cholesterol, systolic blood pressure and Framingham relative weight as discriminators of cardiovascular disease. The Framingham Study: An epidemiological investigation of cardiovascular disease. Section 23. Washington, D.C.: Government Printing Office, 1969.

6a. Kramer, J. R., Kitazume, H., Proudfit, W., Matsuda, Y., Williams, G. W., and Sones, F. M., Jr.: Progression and regression of coronary atherosclerosis: Relation to risk factors. *Am. Heart J.*, 105:134–144, 1943.

7. Kannel, W. B.: The Framingham Study — An epidemiological investigation of cardiovascular disease. Section 24 — The Framingham diet study: Diet and the regulation of serum cholesterol. National Heart and Lung Institute, DHEW, 1970.

8. Mann, G. V.: Diet-heart: End of an era. *New Engl. J. Med.*, 297:644–650, 1977.

9. Bruhn, J. G., and Wolf, S.: Studies reporting "low rates" of ischemic heart disease: A critical review. *Am. J. Public Health*, 60:1477–1495, 1970.

10. Keys, A., Aravanis, C., Blackburn, H., Vanbuchem, F. S. P., Buzina, R., Djordjenic, B. S., Fidanza, F., Karvonen, M. J., Menotti, A., Puddu, V., and Taylor, H. L.: Probability of middle-aged men developing coronary heart disease in 5 years. *Circulation*, 45: 815–828, 1972.

11. Gordon, T., Garcia-Palmieri, M. R., Kagan, A., Kannel, W. B., and Schiffman, J.: Differences in coronary heart disease in Framingham, Honolulu and Puerto Rico. *J. Chron. Dis.*, 27:329–337, 1974.

12. Kozarevic, D., Pirc, B., Ravic, Z., Dawber, T. R., Gordon, T., and Zukel, W. J.: The Yugoslavia cardiovascular disease study — II. Factors in the incidence of coronary heart disease. *Am. J. Epidemiol.*, 104:133–140, 1976.

13. Keys, A.: Paper presented at Annual Conference on CV Disease Epidemiology of the American Heart Association, Tampa, Florida, February 28, 1972. *Epidemiology Council Newsletter,* 1972.

14. Yudkin, J.: Diet and coronary thrombosis, hypothesis and fact. *Lancet*, 2:155–162, 1957.

15. Trulson, F. F.: The American diet: Past and present. *Am. J. Clin. Nutr.*, 7:91–97, 1959.

16. Froelicher, V. F., Longo, M. R., and McIver, R. G.: The effects of chronic exercise on the heart and on coronary atherosclerotic heart disease: A literature survey. USAF School of Aerospace Med. Report *SAM-TR-76-6*, Brooks Air Force Base, Texas, 1976.

17. Can I avoid a heart attack? Editorial. *Lancet*, 1:605–607, 1974.

18. Corday, E., and Corday, S. R.: Prevention of heart disease by control of risk factors: The time has come to face the facts. Editorial. *Am. J. Cardiol.*, 35:330–333, 1975.

19. Werko, L.: Risk factors and coronary heart disease — Fact or fancy? *Am. Heart J.*, 91:87–98, 1976.

20. Sparrow, D., Dawber, T. R., and Colton, T.: The influence of cigarette smoking on prognosis after a first myocardial infarction: A report from the Framingham Study. *J. Chron. Dis.*, 31:425–433, 1978.

21. Gordon, T., Kannel, W. B., and McGee, D.: Death and coronary attacks in men after giving up cigarette smoking — A report from the Framingham Study. *Lancet*, 2:1345–1348, 1974.

22. Seltzer, C.: Smoking and coronary heart disease. *New Engl. J. Med.*, 228:1186, 1977. Stopping smoking and CHD. *Lancet*, p. 420, Feb. 19, 1977.

22a. Multiple risk factor intervention trial: Risk factor changes and mortality results. *J.A.M.A.*, 248:1465–1477, 1982.

23. Rosenman, R. H., and Friedman, M.: The possible role of behavior patterns in proneness and immunity to coronary heart disease. In: H. I. Russek and B. L. Zohman (Eds.), *Coronary Heart Disease.* Philadelphia: J. B. Lippincott, 1971.

24. Rosenman, R. H.: The role of the Type A behavior pattern in ischemic heart disease: Modification of its effects by beta-blocking agents. *Brit. J. Clin. Practice*, 32 (Suppl. 1): 58–65, 1978.

25. Rosenman, R. H.: The heart you save may be your own. In: J. Chacko (Ed.), *Health Handbook*. Amsterdam: North-Holland Publishing Co., 1979.
26. Morris, J. N., and Gardner, M. J.: Epidemiology of ischemic heart disease. *Am. J. Med.*, 46:674–683, 1969.
27. Simborg, D. W.: The status of risk factors and coronary heart disease. *J. Chron. Dis.*, 22:515–552, 1970.
28. Fisher, S. H.: Psychological factors and heart disease. *Circulation*, 27:113–117, 1963.
29. Keith, R. A.: Personality and coronary heart disease: A review. *J. Chron. Dis.*, 19: 1231–1243, 1966.
30. Minc, S.: Psychological factors in coronary heart disease. *Geriatrics*, 20:747–755, 1965.
31. Myocardial infarct and other psychosomatic disturbances. *Psychother. Psychosom*, 16: 189–292, 1968.
32. Mordkoff, A. M., and Parsons, O. A.: The coronary personality: A critique. *Psychosom. Med.*, 29:1–14, 1967.
33. Mordkoff, A. M., and Parsons, O. A.: The coronary personality: A critique. *Int. J. Psychiat.*, 5:413–426, 1968.
34. Syme, S. I.: Psychological factors and coronary heart disease. *Int. J. Psychiat.*, 5:429–433, 1968.
35. Social stress and cardiovascular disease. *Milbank Mem. Fund Quart.*, *45*(2):1–192, Part 2, 1967.
36. Lehman, E. W.: Social class and coronary heart disease: A sociological assessment of the medical literature. *J. Chron. Dis.*, 20:381–391, 1967.
37. Antonovsky, A.: Social class and the major cardiovascular diseases. *J. Chron. Dis.*, 21:65–106, 1968.
38. Mai, F. M. M.: Personality and stress in coronary heart disease. *J. Psychosom. Res.*, 12: 275–287, 1968.
39. Christian, P.: Interdependenz von Umwelt und Person am Beispiel des Herzinfarktes. *Psychother. Psychosom.*, 16:210–223, 1968.
40. Mertens, C., and Segers, M. J.: L'Influence des facteurs psychologiques dans la genèse des affections coronariennes. I. Données bibiographiques. *Bull. Acad. R. Med. Belg.*, 11:155–199, 201–221, 1971.
41. Jenkins, C. D.: Psychological and social precursors of coronary disease. *New Engl. J. Med.*, 284: 244–255, 307–317, 1971.
41a. Kasl, S. V.: Pursuing the link between stressful life experiences and disease. In: C. L. Cooper (Ed.), *Stress Research: Issues for the Eighties*. Chichester and New York: John Wiley, 1983.
42. Jenkins, C. D.: Recent evidence supporting psychologic and social risk factors for coronary disease. *New Engl. J. Med.*, 294:987–994, 1033–1038, 1976.
43. von Dusch, T.: *Lehrbuch der Herzkrankheiten*. Leipzig: Verlag Von Wilhelm Engelman, 1868.
44. Osler, W.: The Lumleian Lectures on angina pectoris. *Lancet*, 1:839–844, 1910.
45. Menninger, K. A., and Menninger, W. C.: Psychoanalytic observations in cardiac disorders. *Am. Heart J.*, 11:10–26, 1936.
46. Dunbar, H. F.: *Psychosomatic Diagnosis*. New York: Paul B. Hoeber, 1943.
47. Kemple, C.: Rorschach method and psychosomatic diagnosis: Personality traits of patients with rheumatic disease, hypertension, cardiovascular disease, coronary occlusion, and fracture. *Psychosom. Med.*, 7:85–89, 1945.
48. Arlow, J. A.: Identification of mechanisms in coronary occlusion. *Psychosom. Med.*, 7: 195–209, 1945.

49. Gildea, E.: Special features of personality which are common to certain psychosomatic disorders. *Psychosom. Med.*, 11:273-277, 1949.
50. Stewart, I. M. G.: Coronary disease and modern stress. *Lancet*, 2:867-878, 1950.
51. Toynbee, A.: *A Study of History* (Vol. 12). London: Oxford University Press, 1961, p. 603.
52. Friedman, M., and Rosenman, R. H.: Association of specific overt behavior pattern with blood and cardiovascular findings. *J.A.M.A.*, 169:1286-1296, 1959.
53. Rosenman, R. H., and Friedman, M.: Association of specific behavior pattern in women with blood and cardiovascular findings. *J.A.M.A.*, 24:1173-1184, 1961.
54. Rosenman, R. H., and Friedman, M.: The possible relationship of the emotions to clinical coronary heart disease. In: G. Pincus (Ed.), *Hormones and Atherosclerosis*. New York: Academic Press, 1959.
55. Rosenman, R. H., and Friedman, M.: The role of a specific overt behavior pattern in the occurrence of ischemic heart disease. *Cardiol. Practica*, 13:42-53, 1962.
56. Rosenman, R. H.: The role of a specific overt behavior pattern in the genesis of coronary heart disease. In: W. Raab (Ed.), *Preventive Cardiology*. Springfield, IL: Charles C Thomas, 1967.
57. Rosenman, R. H., and Friedman, M.: The central nervous system and coronary heart disease. In: E. Braunwald (Ed.), *The Myocardium: Failure and Infarction*. New York: H. P. Publishing, 1974.
58. Jenkins, C. D.: Behavioral risk factors in coronary artery disease. *Ann. Rev. Med.*, 29:543-562, 1978.
59. Glass, D. C.: *Behavior Patterns, Stress and Coronary Disease*. Hillsdale, NJ: Lawrence Erlbaum, 1977.
60. Rosenman, R. H.: The interview method of assessment of the coronary prone behavior pattern. In: T. M. Dembroski, S. M. Weiss, J. L. Shields, et al. (Eds.), *Coronary-Prone Behavior*. New York: Springer-Verlag, 1978.
61. Barry, A. J.: Physical activity and psychic stress/strain. *Canad. Med. Ass. J.*, 96:848-853, 1967.
62. Russek, H. I.: Role of emotional stress in the etiology of clinical coronary heart disease. *Dis. Chest.*, 52:1-9, 1967.
63. Howard, J. H., Cunningham, D. A., and Rechnitzer, P. A.: Work patterns associated with Type A behavior. A managerial population. *Hum. Relations*, 30:825-836, 1977.
64. Dembroski, T. M., and MacDougall, J. M.: Stress effects on affiliation preferences among subjects possessing the Type A coronary-prone behavior pattern. *J. Personal. Soc. Psychol.*, 36:23-33, 1978.
65. Mathews, K. A., and Bronson, B. I.: Allocation of attention and the Type A coronary-prone behavior pattern. *J. Personal. Soc. Psychol.*, 37:2081-2090, 1979.
66. Caffrey, B.: Reliability and validity of personality and behavioral measures in a study of coronary heart disease. *J. Chron. Dis.*, 21:191-204, 1968.
67. Bortner, R. W., and Rosenman, R. H.: The measurement of Pattern A behavior. *J. Chron. Dis.*, 20:525-533, 1967.
68. Brozek, J., Keys, A., and Blackburn, H.: Personality differences between potential coronary and noncoronary subjects. *Ann. N.Y. Acad. Sci.*, 134:1057-1064, 1966.
69. Abrahams, J. P., and Birren, J. E.: Reaction time as a function of age and behavioral predisposition to coronary heart disease. *J. Gerontol.*, 28:471-478, 1973.
70. Brown, R. C., and Ritzmann, L.: Some factors associated with absence of coronary heart disease in persons aged 65 or older. *J. Amer. Geriat. Soc.*, 15:239-250, 1967.
71. Van Egeren, L. F.: Social interactions, communications, and the coronary-prone behavior pattern: A psychophysiological study. *Psychosom. Med.*, 41:2-19, 1979.

72. Lovell, R. R. H., and Verghese, A.: Personality traits associated with different chest pains after myocardial infarction. *Brit. Med. J.*, 3:327-330, 1967.
73. Burnam, M. A., Pennebaker, J. W., and Glass, D. C.: Time consciousness, achievement striving, and the Type A coronary-prone behavior pattern. *Abnormal Psychol.*, 84:76-79, 1975.
74. Van der Valk, J. M., and Groen, J. J.: Personality structure and conflict situations in patients with myocardial infarction. *J. Psychosom. Res.*, 11:41-46, 1967.
75. Carver, C. S., and Glass, D. C.: Coronary-prone behavior pattern and interpersonal aggression. *J. Personal. Soc. Psychol.*, 36:361-366, 1978.
76. Cohen, S., and Parsons, O. A.: The perception of time in patients with coronary artery disease. *Psychosom. Res.*, 8:1-7, 1964.
77. Glass, D. C., Snyder, M. L., and Hollis, J. F.: Time urgency and the Type A coronary-prone behavior pattern. *Applied Soc. Psychol.*, 4:125-140, 1974.
78. Wendkos, M. D., and Wolff, K.: Emotional correlates of angina pectoris. *J. Am. Geriat. Soc.*, 16:845-858, 1968.
79. Dreyfuss, F., Shanan, J., and Sharon, M.: Some personality characteristics of middle-aged men with coronary artery disease. *Psychother. Psychosom.*, 14:1-16, 1966.
80. Snow, B.: Level of aspiration in coronary prone and noncoronary prone adults. *Personal. Soc. Psychol. Bull.*, 4:416-419, 1978.
81. Mathews, K. A., and Saal, F. E.: The relationship of the Type A coronary prone behavior pattern to achievement, power, and affiliation motives. *Psychosom. Med.*, 40:631-636, 1978.
82. Zoleman, T. M., Thomas, G., Olewine, P. A., et al.: Coronary-prone behavior patterns: Relationship to alpha and self-concept. *Personal. Soc. Psychol. Bull.*, 36:350-356, 1978.
83. Scherwitz, L., Berton, K., and Leventhal, H.: Type A behavior, self-involvement and cardiovascular response. *Psychosom. Med.*, 40:593-609, 1978.
84. Weidner, G., and Mathews, K. A.: Reported physical symptoms elicited by unpredictable events and the Type A coronary-prone behavior pattern. *J. Personal. Soc. Psychol.*, 36: 1213-1220, 1978.
85. Pittner, M. S., and Houston, B. K.: Response to stress, cognitive coping strategies and the Type A behavior pattern. *J. Personal. Soc. Psychol.*, 39:147-157, 1980.
86. Greene, W. A., Moss, A. J., and Goldstein, S.: Delay, denial and death in coronary heart disease. In: R. S. Eliot (Ed.), *Stress and the Heart*. New York: Futura, 1974.
87. Krantz, D. S., Glass, D. C., and Snyder, M. L.: Helplessness, stress level, and the coronary-prone behavior pattern. *J. Exper. Soc. Psychol.*, 10:284-300, 1974.
88. Theorell, T., and Rahe, R. H.: Psychosocial factors and myocardial infarction. I. An inpatient study in Sweden. *J. Psychosom. Res.*, 15:25-31, 1971.
89. Kavanagh, T., and Shephard, R. J.: The immediate antecedents of myocardial infarction in active men. *Canad. Med. Assoc. J.*, 109:19-22, 1973.
90. Sales, S. M., and House, J.: Job dissatisfaction as a possible risk factor in coronary heart disease. *J. Chronic. Dis.*, 23:861-873, 1971.
91. Groen, J. J., Dreyfuss, F., and Guttman, L.: Epidemiological, nutritional, and sociological studies of atherosclerotic (coronary) heart disease among different ethnic groups in Israel. In: C. J. Miras, A. N. Howard, and R. Paoletti (Eds.), *Recent Advances in Atherosclerosis*. New York: S. Karger, 1968.
92. Freidman, M., and Rosenman, R. H.: The key cause — Type A behavior pattern. In: A. Monat and K. S. Lazarus (Eds.), *Stress and Coping: An Anthology*. New York: Columbia University Press, 1977.

93. Rosenman, R. H., Freidman, M., Straus, R., Wurm, M., Kositchek, R., Hahn, W., and Werthessen, N. T.: A predictive study of coronary heart disease. The Western Collaborative Group Study. *J.A.M.A.*, 189:15-22, 1964.

94. Jenkins, C. D., Rosenman, R. H., and Freidman, M.: Replicability of rating the coronary-prone behavior pattern. *Brit. J. Prevent. Soc. Med.*, 22:16-22, 1968.

95. Caffrey, B.: Reliability and validity of personality and behavioral measures in a study of coronary heart disease. *J. Chron. Dis.*, 21:191-204, 1968.

96. Dembroski, T. M., MacDougall, J. M., Shields, J. L., et al.: Components of Type A coronary-prone behavior pattern and cardiovascular responses to psychomotor performance challenge. *J. Behav. Med.*, 1:159-176, 1978.

97. National Institute of Health: The MRFIT behavior pattern study—I. Study design, procedures, and reproducibility of behavior pattern judgments. *J. Chron. Dis.*, 32:293-305, 1979.

98. Scherwitz, L., Berton, K., and Leventhal, H.: Type A assessment and interaction in the behavior pattern interview. *Psychosom. Med.*, 39:229-240, 1977.

99. Schucker, B., and Jacobs, D. R.: Assessment of behavioral risks for coronary disease by voice characteristics. *Psychosom. Med.*, 39:219-228, 1977.

100. Bortner, R. W.: A short rating scale as a potential measure of Pattern A Behavior. *J. Chron. Dis.*, 22:87-91, 1969.

101. Wardwell, W. I., and Bahnson, C. B.: Behavioral variables and myocardial infarction in the Southeastern Connecticut Heart Study. *J. Chron. Dis.*, 26:447-461, 1973.

102. Rosenman, R. H., Rahe, R. H., Borhani, N. O., and Feinlieb M.: Heritability of personality and behavior. (Proceedings of the First International Congress of Twin Studies, Rome, Italy, November, 1974.) *Acta. Genet. Med. Gemellol.*, 25:221-224, 1976.

103. Rahe, R. H., Hervig, L., and Rosenman, R. H.: Heritability of Type A behavior. *Psychosom. Med.*, 40:478-486, 1978.

104. Chesney, M. A., Black, F. W., Chadwick, J. H., and Rosenman, R. H.: Psychological correlates of the coronary-prone behavior pattern. *J. Behav. Med.*, 4:217-220, 1981.

105. MacDougall, J. M., Dembroski, T. M., and Musante, L.: The structured interview and questionnaire methods of assessing coronary-prone behavior in male and female college students. *J. Behav. Med.*, 2:71-83, 1979.

106. Haynes, S. B., Levine, S., Scotch, N. A., et al.: The relationship of psychological factors to coronary heart disease in the Framingham Study: I. Methods and risk factors. *Am. J. Epidemiol.*, 107:362-383, 1978.

107. Rosenman, R. H.: Assessment of Type A Behavior Pattern. Paper presented at Annual Meeting of the American Psychological Association, Toronto, Canada, August, 1978.

108. Rustin, R. M., Dramaiz, M., Kittle, F., Degre, C., Kornitzer, M. Thilly, C., and de Backer, G.: Validation de techniques d'evaluation du profil comportemental "A" utilizées dans le "Projet Belge de Prevention d'affections cardiovasculaires" (P. B. S.). *Rev. Epidem. Sante Publ.*, 24: 497-507, 1976.

109. Jenkins, C. D., Rosenman, R. H., and Friedman, M.: Development of an objective psychological test for the determination of the coronary-prone behavior pattern in employed men. *J. Chron. Dis.*, 20:371-379, 1967.

109a. Jenkins, C. D., Rosenman, R. H., and Zyzanski, S. J.: *Jenkins Activity Survey.* New York: The Psychological Corp., 1979.

110. Jenkins, C. D., Zyzanski, S. J., Rosenman, R. H., and Cleveland, G. L.: Association of coronary-prone behavior pattern scores with recurrence of coronary heart disease. *J. Chron. Dis.*, 24:601-611, 1971.

111. Kenigsberg, D., Zyzanski, S. J., Jenkins, C. D., Wardwell, W. I., and Licciardello, A. T.: The coronary-prone behavior pattern in hospitalized patients with and without coronary heart disease. *Psychosom. Med.*, 36:344–351, 1974.
112. Shekelle, R. B., Schoenberger, J. A., and Stamler, J.: Correlates of the JAS Type A behavior score. *J. Chron. Dis.*, 29:381–394, 1976.
113. Cohen, J. B.: Sociocultural change and behavior patterns in disease etiology: An epidemiologic study of coronary disease among Japanese Americans. Unpublished doctoral dissertation, University of California at Berkeley, 1974.
114. Jenkins, C. D., Rosenman, R. H., and Zyzanski, S. J.: Prediction of clinical coronary heart disease by a test for the coronary-prone behavioral pattern. *New Eng. J. Med.*, 290:1271–1275, 1974.
115. Jenkins, C. D., Zyzanski, S. J., and Rosenman, R. H.: Risk of new myocardial infarction in middle-aged men with manifest coronary heart disease. *Circulation*, 53: 342–347, 1976.
116. Zyzanski, S. J., Jenkins, C. D., Ryan, T. J., et. al.: Psychological correlates of coronary angiographic findings. *Arch. Int. Med.*, 136:1234–1237, 1976.
117. Blumenthal, J. A., Williams, R., Kong, Y., et al.: Type A behavior and angiographically documented coronary disease. *Circulation*, 58:634–639, 1978.
118. Dimsdale, J. E., Hackett, T. P., Hutter, A. M., Jr., Block, P. C., and Catanzo, D.: Type A personality and extent of coronary atherosclerosis. *Am. J. Cardiol.*, 42:583–586, 1978.
119. Brand, R. J., Rosenman, R. H., Jenkins, C. D., et al.: Comparison of coronary heart disease prediction in the Western Collaborative Group Study using the structured interview and the Jenkins Activity Survey assessments of the coronary-prone Type A behavior pattern. In press.
120. Caffrey, B.: Behavior patterns and personality characteristics related to prevalence rates of coronary heart disease in American monks. *J. Chron. Dis.*, 22:93–103, 1969.
121. Keith, R. A., Lown, B., and Stare, F. J.: Coronary heart disease and behavior patterns: An examination of method. *Psychosom. Med.*, 27:424–434, 1965. See also Cassel, J. C. Letter to the editor. *Psychosom. Med.*, 28:282–284, 1966.
122. Howard, J. H., Cunningham, D. A., and Rechnitzer, P. A.: Health patterns associated with Type A behavior: A managerial population. *Human Stress*, 24–32, 1976.
123. Kittel, F., Kornitzer, M., Zyzanski, S. J., Jenkins, C. D., Rustin, R. M., and Degre, C.: Two methods of assessing the Type A coronary-prone behavior pattern in Belgium. *J. Chron. Dis.*, 31:147–155, 1978.
124. Appels, A., Jenkins, C. D., Rosenman, R. H., and Esterman, A.: A cross validation of coronary-prone behavior pattern as measured by the JAS in Holland. *J. Behav. Med.*, 5:83–90, 1982.
125. Orth-Gomer, K., Ahlbom, A., and Theorell, T. Impact of pattern A behavior on ischemic heart disease when controlling for conventional risk factors. In: *Studies on Ischemic Heart Disease*. Stockholm: Karolinska Institute, 1979.
126. Cohen, J. B.: The influence of culture on coronary prone behavior. In: T. M. Dembroski, S. M. Weiss, J. L. Shield et al. (Eds.), *Coronary-Prone Behavior*. New York: Springer-Verlag, 1978.
127. Heller, R. F.: Type A behavior and coronary heart disease. *Brit. Med. J.*, 2:368, 1979.
128. Haynes, S., Feinlieb, M., Levine, S., et. al.: The relationship of psychosocial factors to coronary heart disease in the Framingham study: Prevalence of coronary heart disease. *Am. J. Epidemiol.*, 107: 384–402, 1978.
129. Wardwell, W. I., Hyman, M., and Bahnson, C. B.: Socio-environmental antecedents to coronary heart disease in 87 white males. *Soc. Sci. Med.*, 2:165–183, 1968.

130. Wardwell, W. I., Hyman, M., and Bahnson, C. B.: Stress and coronary heart disease in three field studies. *J. Chron. Dis.*, 17:73–84, 1964.

131. Russek, H. I.: Stress, tobacco and coronary disease in North American professional groups. *J.A.M.A.*, 192:189–194, 1965.

132. Ganelina, I. E., and Kraevskij, J. M.: Premorbid personality traits in patients with cardiac ischemia. *Cardiologia* (Moscow), 2:40–45, 1971.

133. Goulet, C., Allard, C., and Poirier, R.: Etude epidémiologique d'une population urbine Canadienne-Française: Facteurs associés au profile coronarien. *L'Union Med. du Canada*, 97:1104–1109, 1968.

134. Orth-Gomer, K.: Ischemic heart disease and psychological stress in Stockholm and New York. *J. Psychosom. Res.*, 23:165–173, 1979.

135. Theorell, T., Lind, E., and Floderus, B.: The relationship of disturbing life-changes and emotions to the early development of myocardial infarction and other serious illnesses. *Int. J. Epidemiol*, 4:281–293, 1975.

136. Theorell, T., and Rahe, R. H.: Behavior and life satisfactions characteristic of Swedish subjects with myocardial infarction. *J. Chron. Dis.*, 25:139–147, 1972.

137. Romo, M., Siltanen, P., Theorell, T., and Rahe, R. H.: Work behavior time urgency and life dissatisfactions in subjects with myocardial infarction — A cross-cultural study. *J. Psychosom. Res.*, 18:1–6, 1974.

138. Rahe, R. H., Romo, M., Bennett, L., and Siltanen, P.: Recent life changes: Myocardial infarction and abrupt coronary death. *Arch. Int. Med.*, 133:221–227, 1974.

139. Thiel, H. G., Parker, D., and Burce, T. A.: Stress factors and the risk of myocardial infarction. *J. Psychosom. Res.*, 17:43, 1973.

140. Feinlieb, M., Brand, R. J., Remington, R., and Zyzanski, S. J.: Association of the coronary-prone behavior pattern and coronary heart disease. In: T. M. Dembroski, S. M. Weiss, J. L. Shield et al. (Eds.), *Coronary-Prone Behavior*. New York: Springer-Verlag, 1978.

141. Sigler, L. H.: The mortality form arteriosclerotic and hypertensive heart diseases in the United States. I. Possible relation to distribution of population and economic status. *Am. J. Cardiol.*, 1:605, 1959.

142. Enterline, P. E., and Stewart, W. H.: Geographic patterns in deaths from coronary disease. *Pub. Health Rep.*, 71:849, 1959.

143. Rosenman, R. H., Friedman, M., Straus, R., Wurm, M., Jenkins, C. D., and Messinger, H. B.: Coronary heart disease in the Western Collaborative Group Study: A follow-up experience of 2 years. *J.A.M.A.*, 195:86–92, 1966.

144. Rosenman, R. H., Friedman, M., Straus, R., Jenkins, C. D., Zyzanski, S. J., and Wurm, M.: Coronary heart disease in the Western Collaborative Group Study: A follow-up experience of 4½ years. *J. Chron. Dis.*, 23:173–190, 1970.

145. Rosenman, R. H., Brand, R. J., Jenkins, C. D., Friedman, M., Straus, R., and Wurm, M.: Coronary heart disease in the Western Collaborative Group Study: Final follow-up of 8½ years. *J.A.M.A.*, 233:872–877, 1975.

146. Rosenman, R. H., Brand, R. J., Sholtz, R. I., and Friedman, M.: Multivariate prediction of coronary heart disease during 8.5 year follow-up in the Western Collaborative Group Study. *Am. J. Cardiol.*, 37:903–910, 1976.

147. Brand, R. J., Rosenman, R. H., Sholtz, R. I., and Friedman, M.: Multivariate prediction of coronary heart disease in the Western Collaborative Group Study compared to the findings of the Framingham study. *Circulation*, 53:348–355, 1976.

148. Haynes, S. G., Feinlieb, M., and Kannel, W. B.: The relationship of psychosocial factors to coronary heart disease in the Framingham study. III. 8-year incidence of CHD. *Am. J. Epidemiol.*, 111:37–58, 1980.

149. Rosenman, R. H., Friedman, M., Jenkins, C. D., et al.: Recurring and fatal myocardial infarction in the Western Collaborative Group Study. *Am. J. Cardiol.*, 19:771-775, 1967.
149a. Rosenman, R. H., Friedman, M., Jenkins, C. D., et al.: Clinically unrecognized myocardial infarction in the Western Collaborative Group Study. *Am. J. Cardiol.*, 19:776-782, 1967.
150. Brand, R. J.: Coronary-prone behavior as an independent risk factor for coronary heart disease. In: T. M. Dembroski, S. M. Weiss, J. L. Shields et al. (Eds.), *Coronary-Prone Behavior*. New York: Springer-Verlag, 1978.
151. Rosenman, R. H., Friedman, M., Jenkins, C. D., Straus, R., Wurm, M., and Kositchek, R.: The prediction of immunity to coronary heart disease. *J.A.M.A.*, 198:1159-1162, 1966.
152. Rosenman, R. H., Sholtz, R. I., and Brand, R. J.: A study of comparative blood pressure measures in predicting risk of CHD. *Circulation*, 54:51-58, 1976.
153. Rosenman, R. H., Brand, R. J., Sholtz, R. I., and Jenkins, C. D.: The relationship of corneal arcus to cardiovascular risk factors and the incidence of coronary heart disease. *New Engl. J. Med.*, 291:1322-1323, 1974.
154. Sholtz, R. I., Rosenman, R. H., and Brand, R. J.: The relationship of reported parental history to the incidence of CHD in the Western Collaborative Group Study. *Am. J. Epidemiol.*, 102:350-356, 1975.
155. Kagan, A., Harris, B. R., Winkelstein, W., et al.: Epidemiologic studies of CHD and stroke in Japanese men living in Japan, Hawaii and California. *J. Chron. Dis.*, 27:354-564, 1974.
155a. French-Belgian Collaborative Group: Ischemic heart disease and psychological patterns. Prevalence and incidence studies in Belgium and France. In: H. Denolin (Ed.), *Psychological Problems Before and After Myocardial Infarction*. Basel, Munich: S. Karger, 1982.
156. Cohen, J. B., Syme, S. L., Jenkins, C. D., et al.: The cultural context of Type A behavior and the risk of CHD. *Am. J. Epidemiol.*, 102:434, 1975.
157. Keys, A., Taylor, H. L., Blackburn, H., Brozek, J., and Anderson, J. T.: Mortality and coronary heart disease among men studied for 23 years. *Ann. Int. Med.*, 128:201-205, 1971.
158. Matthews, K. A., Glass, D. C., Rosenman, R. H., and Bortner, R. W.: Competitive drive, pattern A, and coronary heart disease: A further analysis of some data from the Western Collaborative Group Study. *J. Chron. Dis.*, 30:489-498, 1977.
159. Williams, R. B., Haney, T. L., Lee, K. L., Yong, Y., Blumenthal, J. A., and Whalen, R. E.: Type A behavior, hostility, and coronary atherosclerosis. *Psychosom. Med.*, 42:539-549, 1980.
160. Lown, B.: Sudden cardiac death. *Am. J. Cardiol.*, 43:313-328, 1979.
161. Lown, B., and Verrier, R. L.: Neural activity and ventricular fibrillation. *N. Engl. J. Med.*, 294:1165-1170, 1976.
162. Nestel, P. J., Verghese, A., and Lovell, R. R. H.: Catecholamine secretion and sympathetic nervous responses to emotion in men with and without angina pectoris. *Am. Heart J.*, 73:227-234, 1967.
163. Voudoukis, I. J.: Exaggerated cold-pressor response in patients with atherosclerotic vascular disease. *Angiol.*, 22:57-62, 1971.
164. Friedman, M., St. George, S., and Byers, S. O.: Excretion of catecholamines, 17-ketosteroids, 17-hydroxycorticoids, and 5-hydroxyindole in men exhibiting a particular behavior pattern (A) associated with high incidence of clinical coronary artery disease. *J. Clin. Invest.*, 39:758-764, 1960.
165. Friedman, M., Byers, S. O., Diamant, J., and Rosenman, R. H.: Plasma catecholamine response of coronary-prone subjects (Type A) to a specific challenge. *Metab.*, 4:205-210, 1975.

166. Simpson, M. T., Olewine, D. A., Jenkins, C. D., Ramsey, F. H., Zyzanski, S. J., Thomas, G., and James, C. G.: Exercise-induced catecholamines and platelet aggregation in the coronary-prone behavior pattern. *Psychosom. Med.*, 36:476–487, 1974.
167. Friedman, M., Manwaring, J. H., Rosenman, R. H., et al.: Instantaneous and sudden death: Clinical and pathological differentiation in coronary artery disease. *J.A.M.A.*, 225:1319–1328, 1973.
168. Nixon, P. G. F.: The human function curve, with special reference to cardiovascular disorders. *The Practitioner*, 275:765–935, 1976.
169. Engel, G. L.: Psychologic stress, vasodepressor syncope and sudden death. *Ann. Int. Med.*, 89:403–412, 1978.
170. Bruhn, J. G., McCrady, K. E., and du Plessis, A.: Evidence of emotional drain preceding death from myocardial infarction. *Psychiat. Dig.*, 29:34–40, 1968.
171. Wolf, S.: The end of the rope: The role of the brain in cardiac death. *Canad. Med. Ass. J.*, 97:1022–1025, 1967.
172. Haft, J. I., and Fani, K.: Intravascular platelet aggregation in the heart induced by stress. *Circulation*, 47:353, 1973.
173. Jenkins, C. C., Thomas, G., Olewine, D., et al.: Blood platelet aggregation and personality traits. *J. Hum. Stress*, 1:34–46, 1975.
174. Frank, K. A., Meller, S. S., Kornfield, D. S., et al.: Type A behavior and coronary heart disease: Angiographic confirmation. *J.A.M.A.*, 240:761–763, 1978.
175. Krantz, D. S., Sanmarco, M. I., Selvester, R. H., and Mathers, K. A.: Psychological correlates of progression of atherosclerosis in man. *Psychosom. Med.*, 41:467–475, 1979.
176. Friedman, M., Rosenman, R. H., Straus, R., et al.: The relationship of behavior pattern A to the state of the coronary vasculature: A study of fifty-one autopsy subjects. *Amer. J. Med.*, 44:525–537, 1968.
177. Friedman, M., Rosenman, R. H., and Carroll, V.: Changes in the serum cholesterol and blood-clotting time in men subjected to cyclic variation of occupational stress. *Circulation*, 17:852–861, 1958.
178. Zyzanski, S. J.: Associations of the coronary-prone behavior pattern. In: T. M. Dembroski, S. M. Weiss, J. L. Shields et al. (Eds.), *Coronary-Prone Behavior*. New York: Springer-Verlag, 1978.
179. Rose, R. M., Jenkins, C. D., and Hurst, M. W.: *Air Traffic Controller Health Change Study: A Prospective Investigation of Physical, Psychological and Work-Related Changes.* University of Texas, Galveston. Published by the authors, 1978.
180. Zyzanski, S. J., Wrzesniewski, K., and Jenkins, C. D.: Cross-cultural validation of the coronary-prone behavior pattern. *Soc. Sci. Med.*, 13A:405–412, 1979.
181. Mettlin, C.: Occupational careers and the prevention of coronary-prone behavior. *Soc. Sci. Med.*, 10:367–372, 1976.
182. Waldron, I., Zyzanski, S., Shekelle, R. B., Jenkins, C. D., and Tennebaum, S.: The coronary-prone behavior pattern in employed men and women. *J. Human Stress*, 3:2–18, 1977.
183. Waldron, I.: The coronary-prone behavior pattern, blood pressure, employment and socioeconomic status in women. *J. Psychosom. Res.*, 22:79–87, 1978.
184. Rosenman, R. H., Bawol, R. D., and Oscherwitz, M.: A 4-year prospective study of the relationship of different habitual vocational physical activity to risk and incidence of ischemic heart disease in volunteer male Federal employees. In P. Milvy (Ed.), *The Marathon: Physiological, Medical, Epidemiological, and Psychological Studies.* New York: New York Academy of Sciences, 1977.

185. Caplan, R. D., and Jones, K. W.: Effects of work load, role ambiguity, and Type A personality on anxiety, depression, and heart rate. *J. Applied Psychol.*, 60:713-719, 1975.
186. Report of the Inter-Society Commission for Heart Disease Resources: Primary preventions of the atherosclerotic diseases. *Circulation*, 41:A55-A95, 1970.
187. Bortner, R. W., Rosenman, R. H., and Friedman, M.: Familial similarity in pattern A behavior: Fathers and sons. *J. Chron. Dis.*, 23:39-43, 1970.
188. Horn, J. M., Plomin, R., and Rosenman, R.: Heritability of personality traits in adult male twins. *Behav. Genet.*, 6:17-30, 1976.
189. Mathews, K. A., and Krantz, D. S.: Resemblances of twins and their parents in Pattern A behavior. *Psychosom. Med.*, 28:140-144, 1976.
190. Plomin, R., DeFries, J. C., Rowe, D. C., Horn, J. M., and Rosenman, R. H.: Genetic and environmental influences on human behavior: Multivariate analysis. Unpublished manuscript. University of Colorado, 1978.
191. Mathews, K. A.: Assessment and developmental antecedents of the coronary-prone behavior pattern in children. In: T. M. Dembroski, J. M. Weiss, J. L. Shields et al. (Eds.), *Coronary-Prone Behavior*. New York: Springer-Verlag, 1978.
192. Matthews, K. A.: Caregiver – child interactions and the Type A coronary-prone behavior pattern. *Child Devel.*, 48:1752-1756, 1977.
193. Bandura, A., and Walters, R. H.: *Adolescent Aggression*. New York: Ronald, 1959.
194. McClelland, D.: *The Achieving Society*. New York: Free Press, 1961.
195. McKinley, D. G.: *Social Class and Family Life*. New York: Free Press of Glencoe, 1964.
196. Howard, J. H., Cunningham, D. A., and Rechnitzer, P. A.: Childhood antecedents of Type A behavior. Unpublished manuscript. University of Western Ontario, Canada, 1976.
197. Howard, J. H., and Anderson, L. B.: Managerial work habits and the marriage partner. Unpublished manuscript. University of Western Ontario, Canada, 1979.
198. Matthews, K. A.: Efforts to control by children and adults with the Type A coronary-prone behavior pattern. *Child Devel.*, 52:842-847, 1981.
199. Chesney, M. A., and Rosenman, R. H.: Type A behavior in the work setting. In: C. Cooper and R. Payne (Eds.), *Current Concerns in Occupational Stress*. New York: John Wiley, 1980.
200. Jenkins, C. D., Rosenman, R. H., and Zyzanski, S. J.: Cigarette smoking: Its relationship to coronary heart disease and related risk factors in the Western Collaborative Group Study. *Circulation*, 38:1140-1155, 1968.
201. Jenkins, C. D., Zyzanski, S. J., and Rosenman, R. H.: Biologic, psychologic and social characteristics of men with different smoking habits. *Health Service Reports*, 88:834-843, 1973.
202. Hammarsten, J. F., Cathey, C. W., Redmond, R. F., and Wolf, S.: Serum cholesterol, diet and stress in patients with coronary artery disease (abstr.). *J. Clin. Invest.*, 36:897, 1957.
203. Wertlake, P. T., Wilcox, A. A., Haley, M. I., and Peterson, J. E.: Relationship of mental and emotional stress to serum cholesterol levels. *Proc. Soc. Exp. Biol. Med.*, 97:163-165, 1968.
204. Thomas, C. B., and Murphey, E. A.: Further studies on cholesterol levels in the Johns Hopkins medical students: The effect of stress at examination. *J. Chron. Dis.*, 8:661-670, 1958.
205. Dreyfuss, F., and Czaczkes, J. W.: Blood cholesterol and uric acid of healthy medical students under the stress of an examination. *Arch. Int. Med.*, 103:708-711, 1959.
206. Grundy, S. M., and Griffin, A. C.: Effects of periodic mental stress on serum cholesterol levels. *Circulation*, 19:496-498, 1959.

207. Wolf, S., McCabe, W. R., Yamamoto, J., Adsett, C. A., and Schottstaedt, W. W.: Changes in serum lipids in relation to emotional stress during rigid controls of diet and exercise. *Trans. Am. Clin. Climatol. Assoc.*, 73:162–175, 1961.
208. Groen, J. J., Tjiong, B., Kamminger, C. E., and Willebrands, A. F.: The influence of nutrition, individuality and some other factors, including various forms of stress on the serum cholesterol: An experiment of nine months duration in 60 normal human volunteers. *Voeding*, 13:556, 1962.
209. Peterson, J. E., Keith, R. A., and Wilcox, A. A.: Hourly changes in serum cholesterol concentration: Effects of the anticipation of stress. *Circulation*, 25:798–803, 1962.
210. Carruthers, M., and Taggart, P.: Endogenous hyperlipidemia induced by emotional stress of racing drivers. *Lancet*, 1:363–366, 1971.
211. Rahe, R. H., Rubin, R. T., and Arthur, R. J.: The three investigators study serum uric acid, cholesterol and cortisol variability during stress of everyday life. *Psychosom. Med.*, 36:258–268, 1974.
212. Rahe, R. H., Rubin, R. T., Gunderson, E. K. E., and Arthur, R. J.: Psychologic correlates of serum cholesterol level in man. *Psychosom. Med.*, 33:399–410, 1971.
213. Clark, D. A., Arnold, E. L., Foulds, E. L., Brown, D. M., Eastmead, D. R., and Parry, E. H.: Serum urate and cholesterol levels in Air Force Academy Cadets. *Aviat. Space. Environ. Med.*, 46:1044, 1975.
214. Lovallo, W. R., and Pishkin, V.: A psychophysiological comparison of Type A and B men exposed to failure and uncontrollable noise. *Psychophysiol.*, in press.
215. Carruthers, M. E.: Aggression and atheroma. *Lancet*, 2:1170, 1969.
216. Sloane, R. B., Davidson, L., Holland, L., and Payne, R. W.: Aggression and effects of upbringing in normal students. *Arch. Gen. Psychiat.*, 7:374–379, 1962.
217. Jenkins, C. D., Hames, C. G., Zyzanski, S. J., Rosenman, R. H., and Friedman, M.: Psychological traits and serum lipids. I. Findings from the California Psychological Inventory. *Psychosom. Med.*, 31:115–128, 1969.
218. Rosenman, R. H., and Friedman, M.: Behavior patterns, blood lipids, and coronary heart disease. *J.A.M.A.*, 184:934–938, 1963.
219. Friedman, M., Rosenman, R. H., and Byers, S. O.: Serum lipids and conjunctival circulation after fat ingestion in men exhibiting Type A behavior pattern. *Circulation*, 29:874–886, 1964.
220. Frideman, M., Byers, S. O., and Rosenman, R. H.: Effect of unsaturated fats upon lipemia and conjunctival circulation. *J.A.M.A.*, 193:882–889, 1965.
221. Harlan, W. R., Oberman, R. E., Mitchell, R. E., and Graybiel, A.: Constitutional and environmental factors related to serum lipid and lipoprotein levels. *Ann. Int. Med.*, 66:540–551, 1967.
222. Hatch, F. R., Reisell, P. K., Poon-King, T. M. W., et al.: A study of coronary heart disease in young men: Characteristics and metabolic studies of patients and comparison with age matched healthy men. *Circulation*, 33:679, 1966.
223. Rosenman, R. H., and Friedman, M.: Neurogenic factors in pathogenesis of coronary heart disease. *Med. Clin. No. Amer.*, 58:269–279, 1974.
224. Friedman, M., Byers, S. O., Rosenman, R. H., and Elevitch, F. R.: Coronary-prone individuals (Type A behavior pattern). Some biochemical characteristics. *J.A.M.A.*, 212:1030–1037, 1970.
225. Friedman, M., Byers, S. O., and Rosenman, R. H.: Plasma ACTH and cortisol concentration of coronary-prone subjects. *Proc. Soc. Exper. Biol. Med.*, 140:681–684, 1972.
226. Friedman, M., Byers, S. O., and Rosenman, R. H.: Effect of corticotropin upon triglyc-

eride levels. Results in coronary-prone subjects and patients with Addison's disease. *J.A.M.A.*, 190:959-964, 1964.

227. Friedman, M., Rosenman, R. H., Byers, S. O., and Eppstein, S.: Hypotriglyceridemic effect of corticotropin in man. *J. Clin. Endocrinol. Metab.*, 27:775-782, 1967.

228. Friedman, M., Byers, S. O., Rosenman, R.H., et al.: Coronary-prone individuals (Type A behavior pattern): Growth hormone responses. *J.A.M.A.*, 217:929-932, 1971.

229. Friedman, M., Byers, S. O., Rosenman, R. H., et al.: Hypocholesterolemic effect of human growth hormone in coronary-prone (Type A) hypercholesterolemic subjects. *Proc. Soc. Exper. Biol. Med.*, 141:76-80, 1972.

230. Friedman, M., Byers, S. O., Rosenman, R. H., Li, C. H., and Newman, R.: The effect of subacute administration of human growth hormone on various serum lipid and hormone levels of hypercholesterolemia and normocholesterolemic subjects. *Metab.*, 23:905-912, 1974.

231. Raab, W. (Ed.): *Prevention of Ischemic Heart Disease.* Springfield, IL: Charles C Thomas, 1966.

232. Raab, W.: *Hormonal and Neurogenic Cardiovascular Disorders.* Baltimore: Wilkins and Wilkins, 1953.

233. Levi, L.: Autosclerosis. *The Magazine of the World Health Organization*, October, 1975.

234. Levi, L., and Anderson, L.: Population, environment, and quality of life. *Eskistics*, 236, 1975.

235. Raab, W., and Gigee, W.: Total urinary catechol excretion in cardiovascular and other diseased conditions. *Circulation*, 9:592, 1954.

236. Gazes, P. C., Richardson, J. A., and Woods, E. F.: Plasma catecholamine content in myocardial infarction and angina pectoris. *Circulation*, 19:657, 1959. Also in *Prog. Cadiovasc. Dis.*, 6:56, 1963.

237. Funkenstein, D. H., King, S. H., and Drolette, M. E.: *Mastery of Stress.* Cambridge, MA: Harvard University Press, 1957.

238. Elmadjian, F., Hope, J. M., and Lamson, E. T.: Excretion of epinephrine and norepinephrine under stress. *Recent Prog. Hormone Res.*, 14:513, 1958.

239. Von Euler, V. S., Gemzell, L. A., Levi, L., and Strom, G.: Cortical and medullary adrenal activity in emotional stress. *Acta Endocrinol. (Kbh)*, 30:567, 1959.

240. Frankel, E.: Coronary disease and personality. *Brit. Med. J.*, 1:382-383, 1969.

241. DeBacker, G., Kornitzer, M., Kiefer, F., Bogaert, M., Van Durme, J., Rustin, R., Degre, C., and DeSchaepdriver, A.: Relation between coronary-prone behavior pattern, excretion of urinary catecholamines, heart rate and rhythm. *Preventive Med.*, 8:14-22, 1979.

242. Dembroski, T. M., MacDougall, J. M., and Shields, J. L.: Physiologic reactions to social challenge in persons evidencing the Type A coronary-prone behavior pattern. *J. Human Stress*, 3:2-9, 1977.

243. Sime, W. E., and Parker, C.: Physiological arousal in male and female students with either Type A or B behavior patterns. *Med. Sci. Sports*, 10:51, 1978.

244. Manuck, S. B., Craft, S. A., and Gold, K. J.: Coronary-prone behavior pattern and cardiovascular response. *Psychophysiol.*, 15:403-411, 1978.

245. Obrist, P. A., Gaebelein, C. J., Teller, E. S., et al.: The relationship among heart rate, cortid dp/dt, and blood pressure in humans as a function of the type of stress. *Psychophysiol.*, 15:102-115, 1978.

246. Dembroski, T. M., and MacDougall, J. M.: Psychosocial factors and coronary heart disease: A biobehavioral model. In: U. Stockmeier (Ed.), *Advances in Stress Research*. Berlin: Springer-Verlag, in press.

247. Lott, C. C., and Gatchel, R. J.: A multi-response analysis of learned heart rate control. *Psychophysiol.*, 15:576-581, 1978.

248. Lazarus, R. S.: Psychological stress and the coping process, New York: McGraw-Hill, 1966.

249. Rosenman, R. H.: Role of Type A behavior pattern in the pathogenesis of ischemic heart disease, and modification for prevention. (Proceedings of PAAVO NURMI Conference, Helsinki, Finland, September, 1977.) *Adv. Cardiol.*, 25:1-12, 1978.

250. Friedman, M., and Rosenman, R. H.: The prudent management of the coronary-prone individual. *Geriat.*, 27:74-79, 1972.

251. Suinn, R. M.: Type A behavior pattern. In: R. B. Williams and W. D. Gentry (Eds.), *Behavioral Approaches to Medical Treatment.* Cambridge, MA: Ballinger, 1979.

252. Suinn, R. M., and Bloom, L. J.: Anxiety management training for pattern A behavior. *J. Behav. Med.*, 1:25-35, 1978.

253. Jenni, M. A., and Wollersheim, J. P.: Cognitive therapy, stress management training and the Type A behavior pattern. *Cog. Ther. Res.*, 3:61-73, 1979.

254. Roskies, E.: Considerations in developing a treatment program for the coronary-prone (Type A) behavior pattern. In: P. Davidson and S. Davidson (Eds.), *Behavioral Medicine: Changing Health Life Styles.* New York: Brunner/Mazel, 1980.

255. Roskies, E., Spevack, M., Surkis, A., Cohen, C., and Gilman, S.: Changing the coronary-prone (type A) behavior pattern in a non clinical population. *J. Behav. Med.*, 1:201-216, 1978.

256. Roskies, E., Kearney, H., Spevack, M., Surkis, A., Cohen, C., and Gilman, S.: Generalizability and durability of treatment effects in an intervention program for coronary-prone (Type A) managers. *J. Behav. Med.*, 2:195-207, 1979.

257. Thompson, P. B.: Effectiveness of relaxation techniques in reducing anxiety and stress factors in Type A, post-myocardial infarction patients. Unpublished doctoral dissertation, University of Massachusetts, 1976.

258. Rahe, R. H., Ward, H. W., and Hayes, V.: Brief group therapy in myocardial infarction rehabilitation: Three- to four-year follow-up of a controlled trial. *Psychosom. Med.*, 41:229-242, 1979.

259. Friedman, M., and Rosenman, R. H.: *Type A Behavior and Your Heart.* New York: Knopf, 1974.

260. Matsumoto, Y. S.: Social stress and coronary heart disease in Japan. A hypothesis. *Milbank Memorial Fund Quarterly*, 48:9-36, 1970.

261. Weiss, S. M.: Effects of coping responses on stress. *J. Comp. Physiol. Psychol.*, 65:251-260, 1968.

262. Lazarus, R. S., Cohen, J. B., Folkman, S., Kanner, A., and Schaefer, C.: Psychological stress and adaptation: Some unresolved issues. In: H. Selye (Ed.), *Guide to Stress Research.* New York: Van Nostrand, 1983.

263. Roskies, E., and Lazarus, R. S.: Coping theory and the teaching of coping skills. In: P. Davidson and S. Davidson (Eds.), *Behavioral Medicine: Changing Health Life Styles.* New York: Brunner/Mazel, 1980.

264. Weiner, H.: Some psychological factors related to cardiovascular responses: A logical and empirical analysis. In: R. Roessler, and W. S. Greenfield (Eds.), *Physiological Correlates of Psychological Disorders*, Madison: University of Wisconsin Press, 1952.

265. Mason, J. W.: A reevaluation of the concept of non-specificity in stress theory. *J. Psychiatr. Res.*, 8:323, 1971.

266. Stoyva, J., and Budzynski, T.: Cultivated low arousal—An anti-stress response. In: L. V. DiCara (Ed.), *Limbic and Autonomic Nervous Systems Research.* New York: Plenum, 1974.

267. Rosenman, R. H., and Friedman, M.: Modifying Type A behavior pattern. *J. Psychosom. Res.*, 21:323–331, 1977.

268. Coronary-prone behavior and coronary heart disease: A critical review. Report of the Coronary-prone Behavior Review Panel. *Circulation*, 13:1199–1215, 1981.

269. Chesney, M. A., and Rosenman, R. H.: Strategies for modifying Type A behavior. *Consultant*, 216–222, June, 1980.

270. Chesney, M. A., and Rosenman, R. H.: Type A behavior: Prescriptions for change. *Colloquy*, 10–12, September, 1981.

271. Chesney, M. A., Eagleston, J. R., and Rosenman, R. H.: Type A behavior: Assessment and intervention. In: C. K. Prokop and L. A. Bradley (Eds.), *Medical Psychology: Contributions to Behavioral Medicine*. New York: Academic Press, 1980.

272. Chesney, M. A., Frautschi, N. M., and Rosenman, R. H.: Modification of Type A behavior. In: J. C. Rosen and L. J. Solomon (Eds.), *Disease Prevention and Health Psychology*. Hanover, NH: University Press of New England, in press.

273. Rosenman, R. H.: Coronary-prone behavior pattern and coronary heart disease. Implications for the use of beta-blockers for primary prevention. In: R. H. Rosenman (Ed.), *Psychosomatic Risk Factors and Coronary Heart Disease: Indications for Specific Preventive Therapy*. Bern, Stuttgart, and Vienna: Hans Huber Publishers, 1983.

274. Salem, S. A., and McDevitt, D. G.: Central effects of beta-adrenoreceptor antagonists. *Clin. Pharmacol. Therap.*, 33:552–557, 1982.

275. Svensson, T. H., Almgren, O., Dahlof, C., Elam, M., Engberg, G., Hallberg, H., and Thoren, P.: Alpha- and beta-adrenoreceptor-mediated control of brain noradrenaline neurons and antihypertensive therapy. *Clin. Sci.*, 59:479s–481s, 1980.

276. Turner, P.: Beta-blockade and the human central nervous system. *Drugs*, 25:262–264, 1983.

277. Thoresen, C. E., Friedman, M., Gill, M., and Ulmer, J. J.: The recurrent coronary prevention project: Some preliminary findings. *Acta Med. Scand.* (Suppl.), 660:172–192, 1982.

278. Friedman, M., Thoresen, C. E., and Gill, M.: Feasibility of altering Type A behavior pattern after myocardial infarction. Recurrent coronary prevention project study: Methods, baseline results, and preliminary findings. *Circulation*, 66:83–92, 1982.

279. Pitts, F. N., Jr., and Allen, R. E.: Beta-adrenergic blockade in the treatment anxiety. In: P. J. Mathews (Ed.), *The Biology of Anxiety*. New York: Brunner/Mazel, 1982.

280. Rand, M. J., Majewski, H., and Tung, L. H.: Activation of prejunctional beta-adrenoreceptors by adrenaline: Acting as a cotransmitter: A possible cause of hypertension. *Drugs*, 25 (Suppl 2): 64–68, 1983.

281. Krantz, D. S., Durel, L. A., Davia, J. E., Shaffer, R. T., Arabian, J. M., Dembroski, T. M., and MacDougall, J. M.: Propranolol medication among coronary patients: Relationship of Type A behavior and cardiovascular response. *J. Human Stress*, 8:4–13, 1982.

282. Schmieder, F. G., Neus, H., Rudel, H., von Eiff, W.: The influence of beta blockers on cardiovascular reactivity and Type A behavior pattern in hypertensives. *Psychosom. Med.*, 45:417–432, 1983.

283. Harms, D., and Pachale, E.: Effect of atenolol on reaction times and concentration. *Drugs*, 25 (Suppl 2): 265–267, 1983.

284. Frishman, W. H., Razin, A., Swencionis, C., and Sonnenblick, E. H.: Beta-adrenoreceptor blockade in anxiety states: A new approach to therapy. *Cardiovasc. Rev. and Reports*, 2: 447–459, 1981.

285. Kahn, J. P., Kornfeld, D. S., Frank, K. A., Heller, S. S., and Hoar, P. F.: Type A behavior and blood pressure during coronary artery bypass surgery. *Psychosom. Med.*, 42:407–414, 1980.

286. Krantz, D. S., Arabian, J. M., Davia, J. E., and Parker, J.: Type A behavior and coronary artery bypass surgery: Intra-operative blood pressure and perioperative complications. *Psychosom. Med.*, 44:373–384, 1982.
287. Landauer, A. A., Jellett, L. B., and Kirk, J.: Propranolol and skilled human performance. *Pharmacol., Biochem. Therap.*, 26:428–432, 1976.
288. Middlemiss, D. N., Buxton, D. A., and Greenwood, D. T.: Beta-adrenocreceptor antagonists in psychiatry and neurology. *Pharmacol. Therap.*, 12:419–437, 1981.
289. Noyes, R.: Beta-blocking drugs and anxiety. *Psychosom.*, 23:155–170, 1982.
290. Patel, L., and Turner, P.: Central actions of beta-adrenoreceptor blocking drugs in man. *Medicinal Res. Rev.*, 1:387–410, 1981.
291. Tyrer, P. J.: The role of bodily feelings in anxiety. London: Oxford University Press, 1976.
292. Tyrer, P. J.: The use of beta-blocking drugs in psychiatry and neurology. *Drugs*, 20:300–308, 1980.
293. Weiner, N.: Drugs that inhibit adrenergic nerves and block adrenergic receptors. In: A. G. Gilman, L. S. Goodman, and A. Gilman (Eds.), *Goodman and Gilman's Pharmacological Basis of Therapeutics* (6th Ed.). New York: MacMillan, 1980.
294. Schachter, S., and Singer, J. E.: Cognitive, social, and physiological determinants of emotional state. *Psychol. Rev.*, 69:379–399, 1962.
295. Rosenman, R. H.: Health consequences of anger and implications for treatment. In: M. A. Chesney, R. H., Rosenman, and W. E. Goldston (Eds.), *Anger and Hostility in Behavioral Medicine*. New York: Hemisphere/McGraw Hill, 1984.
296. Suinn, R. M.: Intervention with Type A behaviors. *J. Consult. Clin. Psychol.*, 50:933–949, 1982.
297. Razin, A. M.: Psychosocial intervention in coronary artery disease: A review. *Psychosom. Med.*, 44:363–387, 1982.
298. Levenkron, J. C., Cohen, J. D., Mueller, H. S., and Fisher, E. B.: Modifying the Type A coronary-prone behavior pattern. *J. Consult. Clin. Psych.*, 51:192–204, 1983.
299. Meichenbaum, D.: *Cognitive-Behavior Modification*. New York: Plenum Press, 1977.
300. Price, V. A.: Assessment and treatment implications of the proposed model of Type A behavior. In: V. A. Price (Ed.), *Type A Behavior Pattern: A Model for Research and Practice*. New York: Academic Press, 1982.

10

The Role of the Psychiatrist in Health Promotion

Robert Michels, M.D.

AESCULAPIUS

In taking the Hippocratic oath, the physician swears not only by Aesculapius, the ancient god of the medical art, but also by his daughters, Hygeia and Panacea, the goddesses of health and healing. These two themes, health and healing, have persisted from ancient times to the present in our understanding of the functions of the medical profession. On the one hand, doctors are concerned with the sick, with comforting, caring, treating, and in modern times even occasionally curing those who are ill. This is the domain of personal medical care, the doctor-patient relationship, that largely provides the popular image of medical practice and describes most of the activities of physicians. On the other hand, medicine is interested in disease prevention and health promotion for all citizens in the community. This has been the traditional domain of public health rather than personal medical care, and it suggests images of the Broad Street pump, sewage systems, filtration plants, vaccinations, and fluoridation. Common notions of preventive medicine are so closely tied to public health that the two have become almost synonymous, and the terms are often linked in the names of textbooks and academic departments.

Psychiatry, like most other medical specialties, has reflected this dual theme with perhaps a particularly heavy emphasis on personal medical care rather than public health, disease prevention, and health promotion. Its particular type of personal care has blended the more humanistic concerns of caring and

242

comforting with the more scientific concerns of treating and curing. This tradition, of which the profession should be quite proud, stems from both the nature of psychiatric disorders with their close relationship to the realm of subjective experience and social relationships and the complex scientific problems that psychiatric disorders present, associated with the somewhat slower development of effective technologies oriented toward treatment and cure. However, this special flavor of psychiatric practice is clearly in the mainstream of medicine with its orientation toward personal medical care for patients who have diseases.

Psychiatry has also developed a less prominent theme of prevention and public health. This has focused on those issues that are seen as relevant to the prevention of psychiatric disorders. Social issues have received the greatest attention, and during the last two decades some leaders of the profession have argued that nuclear war, women's rights, racism, poverty, urban crowding, and a broad range of social engineering projects could all be seen as related to mental health and, therefore, as appropriate arenas for psychiatric intervention. Their arguments have not been refuted, but in recent years many psychiatrists have questioned their approach. The boundaries of psychiatric disorders have been delineated more precisely, and there has been greater interest in differentiating them from other forms of human misery, while the legitimacy of psychiatry's claim of expertise in dealing with those social ills and personal suffering that are not clearly associated with psychiatric disorders has been challenged. Furthermore, the optimism that we could marshal sufficient resources to solve all of our major problems has waned; the efficacy of psychiatry's professional involvement in these issues has been seen as questionable; and many fear that the credibility of the profession's expertise in matters closer to its traditional domain, along with public support for more specifically psychiatric goals, might diminish if psychiatry were to become linked to controversial positions on a large number of those social issues.

One result has been a greater emphasis on social issues that are more closely related to the concerns of psychiatric patients and mental health practitioners — deinstitutionalization, community care, chronic mental patients, the organization and funding of mental health services, reimbursement, etc. A consensus is forming in the profession which argues that all good citizens are concerned with peace, freedom, equality, and prosperity, while psychiatry has a special concern with psychiatric disorders, their prevention and treatment, and certain other activities that require psychiatric knowledge and training (1).

Psychiatrists have been interested in specific stressors or settings that might be relevant to the prevention of psychiatric disease and the promotion of mental health. Bereavement would be one example of such a stress, the workplace of such a setting. Psychiatrists have also attended to educational activities in their disease-preventing and health-promoting activities. Advice in regard to family life, parenting, child guidance, sexual behavior, and almost any other area of human activity has been promoted as relevant to mental health. Some programs in consultation-liaison psychiatry are conceptualized as psychosocial interventions designed to prevent psychiatric complications to medical illness. Genetic counseling, nutritional advice, and programs designed to improve prenatal care or to decrease exposure to environmental lead are psychiatrically relevant aspects of public health.

In most of these psychiatric programs, as in the rest of medicine, the division between personal medical care for the sick and mass public preventive or health-promoting programs endures. However, there are a few exceptions; for example, child guidance and genetic counseling are often delivered in the context of a personal doctor-patient relationship.

Hygeia and Panacea

A new development that is inconsistent with, and at times even contradictory to, this traditional scheme of medical practice has emerged in recent years. It is marked by an interest in disease prevention and health promotion as goals of personal medical care rather than public health, the office practice of Hygeia as well as Panacea. This is related to what has come to be called "behavioral medicine," but the popularity of the latter term has been in part a result of its multiple and ambiguous definitions, so that it might be better to avoid it. There are several factors that have stimulated this development and one extremely powerful factor that has inhibited it.

Experts have long recognized the relatively low correlation between medical care and health. Indeed, this is hardly surprising, since several of the physician's major activities, such as reassuring the fearful or comforting and caring for those who are suffering or dying, have a great deal to do with the human condition and relatively little to do with health. However, the public has generally assumed that doctors and medicine were somehow good for health. In recent years, with growing attention to the economics of medical care, there has been a general discovery that society is paying more and more for something that does not provide the results that many had assumed (2). This cost-benefit analysis of medical care first concerned employers, insurers, HMOs, and others caring for closed populations; however, as costs continued to grow and government involvement increased, it became apparent that the entire nation could be seen as a large HMO, albeit a rather disorganized and ineffective one. Although this recognition of the dissociation between medical care and health has had very little impact on the demand for medical care—most citizens still want to see a doctor when they are sick—it has led to an interest in what doctors might do to prevent disease and promote health. Most of the obvious and politically acceptable public health measures, such as sanitation or the regulation of food production, have been accomplished. That leaves two other avenues of approach: politically unpopular public health measures that require major resources or conflict with other widespread values; and a redirection of the personal medical care system so that it pays more attention to prevention and promotion (3).

At the same time that these social and economic forces led to an interest in new goals for medical care, new knowledge was being accumulated suggesting that we might actually be able to achieve those goals. Medicine has known how to comfort and care for hundreds of years, and something about how to treat and cure for decades, but knowledge relevant to prevention is new and relatively limited. The field had been dominated by folklore (although some of our new data are surprisingly consistent with that folklore). We have learned that everything that grandmother told us, with one glorious exception, is actually true! Epidemiologic and basic science studies have demonstrated that a variety of relatively simple behaviors are correlated with morbidity and mortality (4). A recent editorial in *Science*, by Hamburg (5), summarizes that

> . . . much of the world's burden of illness is behavior-related. . . . About half the mortality from the ten leading causes of death in the United States is strongly linked to long-term patterns of behavior (lifestyle). Such known behavioral risk factors as cigarette smoking, excessive consumption of alcoholic beverages, use of illicit drugs, certain dietary habits, insufficient exercise, reckless driving, noncompliance with medication regimens, and maladaptive responses to stress are involved in the pathogenesis of cardiovascular diseases and cancers as well as accidental disabilities and other disorders. (p. 4627)

Of course, the identification of behaviors that are related to health is necessary but not sufficient for planning a health-promotion program. It is also necessary to develop interventions that will modify those behaviors (but more of this later).

In addition to economic concerns with the benefits of medical care and new knowledge regarding the importance of behavioral determinants for general health, several other factors have contributed to the growth of medical interest in modifying health-related behaviors. There is a long history of interest in the relationship between psychological factors and physical illness, and several decades ago, in the form of psychosomatic medicine and its numerous synonyms, this field represented psychiatry's hope for a rapprochement with medicine. This was well before the current interest in the remedicalization of psychiatry through the emphasis on the medical model for the understanding of psychiatric disorders and biomedical interventions for their treatment.

Unfortunately, the clinical aspects of the psychosomatic strategy have largely failed. Models of psychological functioning, borrowed from studies of psychopathology, generally failed when they were applied to medical illnesses. Physical diseases were seen as "psychophysiologic," or as stemming from psychic conflict, stress responses, or personality patterns, and they were treated in the same way as psychiatric disorders. This approach had the advantage of being ingenious and intellectually intriguing, and of providing a familiar role for psychiatrists — essentially the same role that they had assumed with patients suffering from traditional psychopathology, though with some recognition that patients with psychosomatic disorders were poorly motivated and not psychologically-minded. Unfortunately, the approach also had the disadvantage of not working very well; the treatments were sometimes helpful, but often were not.

Many psychiatrists lost their enthusiasm for the clinical aspects of psychosomatic medicine, but they did not lose their interest in the general subject matter of medically ill patients. The field of consultation-liaison psychiatry emerged in part as an attempt to systematize what the psychiatrist could offer to this group of patients, at least in the hospital setting. It combined several different components: the remains of psychosomatic medicine; the relatively recent advances psychiatry had made in the management of crises and life stress; recognition of the importance of disturbed brain functioning and other psychiatric disorders that either complicate or are complications of medical disorders; recognition of the importance of substance abuse in medical patients; long-standing psychiatric interest in the therapeutic milieu and its impact on the patient; and psychiatry's continuing concern with the humanistic aspects of the doctor-patient relationship.

Each of the ingredients makes sense, but there has been difficulty formulating the appropriate role of the psychiatrist in the process. Is he an educator, a clinical consultant, an institutional consultant, a caretaker, or some combination of these? For the most part, the consultation-liaison concept has flourished only in institutional settings and has had little impact on patients who are not involved with institutional care. Despite strenuous efforts to demonstrate its value, it has not always competed effectively for scarce institutional resources, and, in the absence of strong educational programs or support from a parent psychiatry department, it has tended to be undernourished. The result is that psychiatry's interest in the medically ill, which began with psychosomatics and was sustained by consultation-liaison psychiatry, is still searching for a rationale and justification that would clarify the professional role of the psychiatrist and generate support from those who are charged with the primary care of the medically ill.

A final factor contributing to the growth of interest in health promotion in personal medical care is also an economic one, but more closely linked to the economic concerns of the medical profession than those of the public. We are experiencing an immense growth in medical manpower. Between 1960 and 2000 there will have been a doubling of the number of physicians per capita, from 13.6 to 27.1 per 10,000, with about half of that growth yet to come (6). This means that physicians will have more time to spend with patients. In the past, one of the constraints on health promotion in personal medical care has been the physician's time, with care, comfort, treatment, and cure generally being seen as having higher priority than health promotion in any given doctor-patient interaction.

In spite of these economic, scientific, and professional factors that have encouraged the development of a preventive and health-promoting focus to personal medical services, there is one very powerful factor that has worked in the opposite direction. Our medical care system has a strong bias toward the value of technologic interventions as opposed to cognitive or psychosocial ones. This is reflected in our undergraduate and residency curricula, in the distribution of our research resources, in professional and public attitudes, and, most important, in our reimbursement system. Medical students are taught, patients expect, scientists study, doctors admire, and insurance companies reimburse technical procedures rather than talk to patients, regardless of scientific data concerning which is more valuable, more cost-effective, or has greater impact on health (7).

PERSONAL PSYCHIATRIC CARE SYSTEM

If this major economic barrier to the practice of behavioral medicine could be overcome, it would seem at first glance to be an attractive opportunity for contemporary psychiatry, continuing the theme of psychosomatic medicine and consultation-liaison psychiatry, facilitating the always popular "remedicalization" of psychiatry, and contributing to health promotion and disease prevention, which are major new emerging goals for the personal medical care system as well as the public health system. However, there are some problems to consider.

First, psychiatry has traditionally focused on patients with psychopathology, on behavior that is deviant, conflicted, maladaptive, symptomatic, or in some framework seen as related to psychiatric distress or disorder. There are many schemes for conceptualizing those relationships; and there is an active dialogue in the profession regarding the boundaries of appropriate concern for psychiatrists. Some would include all psychological functioning that is impaired by psychic conflict; others, all reactions to stress or trauma; others, only definable clinical syndromes that go beyond the pains and miseries of everyday life. However, no one sees the psychiatrist as expert on all behavior, or even on all behavior that might have undesirable consequences. If you invest in the stock market and lose money, you need a new broker, not a psychiatrist. If you decide to spend your vacation in southern California, and it rains every day, that is unfortunate but not psychopathology; similarly, if you like ice cream more than broccoli, prefer reading to jogging, or enjoy a cigar after dinner.

It is true that knowledge of the adverse health consequences of such behavior might produce conflict, but this knowledge is relatively recent and is usually of a slightly increased probability of a distant consequence, not the kind of knowledge that either deters behavior or convinces us that it is psychopathologic when it persists. If an individual ignores imminent danger to his health, such as binge eating by a brittle diabetic or persistent smoking by someone with severe emphysema, our categories of pathologic behavior are relevant. However, we are faced with the apparent paradox that most of the behaviors of interest to health promotion and disease prevention may be associated with far greater morbidity and mortality than is most psychopathology, but, from the point of view of psychiatry, they are not pathologic. Psychodynamic formulations related to the concept of masochism are helpful in understanding and treating maladaptive behavior that is an unconsciously motivated means to pain, disease, suffering, or death. Psychiatry can make an important contribution to the management of patients with this dynamic, but these patients constitute a relatively small proportion of all persons whose behavior has negative consequences for their health. Masochism refers to motivation, not effect, and self-destruction is more often an unintended consequence than an unconscious goal.

One corollary of this is that psychiatrists do not now see most of the persons who could be helped by behavioral medicine interventions unless the patients happen to have some additional psychopathology. These individuals are more likely to enter the general health care system, if they enter the system at all, rather than the mental health care system. Of course, the development of new professional roles for psychiatrists could change this, but only at the cost of shifting psychiatrists away from their current concern with the mentally ill, a move that would be irrational for the next several decades, with most projections suggesting a serious shortage of psychiatrists and an oversupply of most other physicians during this period.

Expertise in behavior in general, rather than psychopathologic behavior in particular, and interest in strategies for influencing non-pathologic behavior are generally associated with psychology rather than psychiatry; it is no accident that psychology as a profession and behaviorist models as conceptual frameworks have been prominent in behavioral medicine. However, there are important contributions that psychiatry can offer.

Psychiatrists are familiar with the problems of translating scientific theories into clinical applications. They have experience with the roles of motivation and compliance, placebo effects, the therapeutic alliance, transference, resistance, and, in general, the many variables other than the particular theory of behavior that must be considered in translating such a theory into a strategy for clinical intervention. Most of the data available suggest that these nonspecific variables are far more powerful than any specific theory in determining outcome; the history of psychotherapy is the history of the repeated rediscovery that understanding of a specific theory, whether it be hypnotism, psychoanalysis, behaviorism, or interpersonal psychiatry, is not as important in developing and applying a clinical method as is an understanding of the general principles of the clinical relationship. One of the potential roles of psychiatrists in health promotion is to participate in conceptualizing and developing clinical strategies for the modification of health-related behaviors in the area of personal rather than public health medicine — strategies that are not only based on what we know about behavioral risk factors and on scientific theories of behavior modification, but also informed by psychiatry's understanding of the clinical situation. In many ways this role is analogous to the role that educational psychology has played and continues to play in the development of public intervention strategies.

In recent years, psychiatry's long-standing interest in clinical treatments has extended to include the testing and evaluation of those treatments. Instruments for measurement, methods for research design and statistical analysis, along with a convergence of those who were primarily interested in the evaluation of drugs and those interested in the process of psychotherapy are opening an era in which psychiatry will be central, not only in transforming models of psychological functioning into strategies of clinical intervention, but also in testing and evaluating those strategies and developing scientific and professional criteria for accepting or rejecting them. The evaluation of preventive interventions in behavioral medicine should in many respects be easier, since the outcome measures are more public and more easily specifiable. Psychiatry will be able to contribute to this process.

Who is going to apply these clinical strategies, actually to treat the individual patients in a disease-preventive health-promotion system? These patients do not have psychopathology, do not come to the attention of psychiatrists, and, as mentioned above, would distract psychiatrists from other vitally needed roles. Furthermore, the kinds of behavior modification strategies that have been most effective in modifying undesirable but non-psychopathologic behavior are seldom very interesting or professionally rewarding to psychiatrists (which means that they are unlikely to do them very well). It is much more likely that this role will become part of primary medical care, with a significant portion of it being delegated to physicians' assistants and other health professionals, who might find it more rewarding. This is similar to the history of the application of behaviorist strategies to the treatment of phobias, where psychiatrists pioneered in developing techniques but then developed programs to train others to apply them.

In summary, the basic research necessary to identify those behaviors that are related to health will come from epidemiology and basic sciences. The psychological theories that provide the framework for individual intervention strategies are likely to come initially from psychology. They will be integrated with the clinical models provided by psychiatry, and the interventions that result will be tested and evaluated by the emerging field of psychiatric treatment evaluation. The interventions themselves will be prescribed by primary care practitioners and delivered by those practitioners or their assistants and other health professionals who work with them. A major question will be the relative value and cost-effectiveness of mass, public health, educational-type interventions as compared to individually prescribed and administered, personal, medical care-type interventions. Several studies have demonstrated both the efficacy and the feasibility of public education programs designed to influence attitudes and behavior relevant to health (8). In spite of the obvious efficiency of these educational strategies, however, concerns such as low compliance, high drop-out rates, and the well-known power of individual transferences, specific prescriptions, and the individual tailoring of intervention programs to the health vulnerabilities, behavior patterns, and psychological characteristics of a specific patient all suggest that the personal care model may have much to offer.

THE FUTURE

A discussion of the psychiatrist's role in health promotion should not stop with consideration of the promotion of physical health. Paradoxically, at present we know more about the links between behavior and physical health than between behavior and mental health. What do psychiatry and psychiatrists have to offer toward the prevention of psychiatric disorders and the promotion of mental health? Here again the distinction between public health and personal medical strategies is appropriate.

Public health activities that are more specifically related to psychiatric issues include educational programs concerning sex, drugs, alcohol, indications for psychiatric consultation, social and family relationships (9), developmental crises, and the management of stress. Such programs are, of course, very popular. However, data regarding their impact on psychiatric disorders are very few, and at this point the profession can contribute more by assessing these programs than be developing new ones.

What of psychiatric health promotion in personal medical care? In one sense, by the time a patient gets to a psychiatrist, it is too late — at least for primary prevention — while secondary and tertiary prevention are what the standard clinical practice of psychiatry is all about. However, this is not always the case. Psychiatrists see patients in stressful, vulnerable, although not psychopathologic, situations such as medical illnesses or recent bereavement. They employ intervention strategies similar to those used in the management of patients with psychopathology, but their goals are largely preventive. In some situations, such as prior to major surgery, there is even evidence that such interventions make a difference (10).

Psychiatrists also see patients who have potential impact on the lives of others, particularly their immediate families. There is a traditional medical responsibility to be concerned about that impact, but, in psychiatric practice, it is often honored in the breach. How often do we consider genetic counseling if the issue is not raised by the patient, although there are a number of psychiatric disorders where relevant data are available, not usually known to patients, and might have an impact on their choices? How often do we see or assist the children of our hospitalized patients? A recent study explored what parents tell children following a parental suicide attempt. Perhaps the most striking finding was that the question had not previously been discussed in the literature (11).

These special opportunities for psychiatric health promotion and disease prevention are little more than extensions of the traditional, clinical psychiatric role. If there are to be major strides in the prevention of psychiatric disorders through the personal health care system, there will have to be an impact on people who do not now have psychiatric disorders and do not see psychiatrists. This means that interventions will be delivered through the primary care system, with psychiatrists designing and evaluating them. At present there are two major barriers to this: one is the prejudice against psychiatric problems that pervades the health care system; the other, more serious one, is our ignorance about which behaviors are critical and which interventions influence them. It is ironic that, at this point, we know more about behavioral factors that contribute to physical disease than those that contribute to psychiatric disorders. However, this knowledge will develop, and an important future role for psychiatry is to ensure that psychiatric problems are included in the revolution of the personal medical care system as it expands to embrace disease prevention and health promotion. It would be prudent, this time, first to accumulate knowledge as to which behaviors are important risk factors and, only after that, to seek public support for preventive efforts that are based on that knowledge.

REFERENCES

1. Caplan, G.: *Principles of Primary Prevention*. New York: Basic Books, 1964.
2. McDermott, W.: Medicine: The public good and one's own. *World Health Forum 1979*, 1: 125–234, 1979.
3. Roemer, M. I.: The value of medical care for health promotion. *Am. J. Pub. Hlth.*, 74:243–248, 1984.
4. U.S. Public Health Service. *Healthy People: The Surgeon-General's Report on Health Promotion and Disease Prevention*. Washington, D.C.: Government Printing Office, 1979.
5. Hamburg, D. A.: Frontiers of research in neurobiology (editorial). *Science*, 222:4627, December 2, 1983.
6. U.S. Department of Health and Human Services, Public Health Service. *Health, United States, 1982*. Table 52. DHHS Publication No. (PHS) 83-1232. Washington, D.C.: U.S. Government Printing Office, 1982.
7. Reimbursement for physicians' cognitive and procedural services: A white paper. American Society of Internal Medicine, January, 1981.
8. Maccoby, N., Farquhar, J. W., Wood, P. D., and Alexander, J.: Reducing the risk of cardiovascular disease: Effects of a community based campaign on knowledge and behavior. *Comm. Hlth.*, 3:100–114, 1977.
9. Taylor, R. L., Lam, D. J., Roppel, C. E., and Barter, J. T.: Friends can be good medicine: An excursion into mental health promotion. *Comm. Ment. Hlth. J.*, in press.
10. Janis, I. L.: *Psychological Stress: Psychoanalytic and Behavioral Studies of Surgical Patients*. New York: Wiley, 1958.
11. Shapiro, T.: Personal communication, 1983.

Index